Viella Historical Research
14

Martin Elbel

Beyond the Wall

Franciscan Friary in Early Modern Olomouc

viella

First edition: October 2019
ISBN 978-88-3313-257-0

The text was supported by the GACR, project Centre for Transdisciplinary Research into Cultural Phenomena in Central European History: Image, Communication, Behaviour, reg. No. 14-36521G, and by the 2015 UP FoA, Excellence Programme project Additional Funding for the Centre for Transdisciplinary Research into Cultural Phenomena in Central European History: Image, Communication, Behaviour.

The book was published thanks to financial support granted in 2019 by the Ministry of Education, Youth and Sports of the Czech Republic as part of the Institutional Development Plan of the Faculty of Arts, Palacký University Olomouc.

Translated by: Eva Černínová with Elizabeth Allyn Woock

Cover illustration: Francis Lawrence Korompay-circle, *The community of the Olomouc Franciscans paying homage to Cardinal Troyer, Bishop of Olomouc, during his inauguration entry in 1747*, 1783 (?). Archbishopric of Olomouc, AMK, KE 2988, O 410, today in the exhibition of the Archdiocesan Museum in Olomouc. Photo: Zdeněk Sodoma.

viella
libreria editrice
via delle Alpi, 32
I-00198 ROMA
tel. 06 84 17 758
fax 06 85 35 39 60
www.viella.it

Contents

Acknowledgements

This book was inspired, supported and shaped by many of my teachers, colleagues, and students – both at Palacký University Olomouc and elsewhere. I can hardly be just to all of them but I feel I need to mention, at the very least, Ian Christie, Maria Craciun, Ivo Hlobil, Libuše Hrabová, Antonín Kalous, Jarmila Kašpárková, Gábor Klaniczay, Jozef Matula, Jaroslav Miller, Karel Müller, Jana Oppeltová, Judith Pollmann, Radmila Prchal Pavlíčková, Jan Stejskal. I have learned a lot from our conversations throughout the various stages of my research. In particular, I am grateful to Petr Regalát Beneš OFM, Howard Louthan, and Jiří Mikulec, who read the original version of the book and provided me with many valuable comments. I also greatly benefited from my studies and stays at the Central European University in Budapest, the Institute for Advanced Studies in the Humanities in Edinburgh, the Netherlands Institute for Advanced Study in Wassenaar, and in particular, the Warburg Institute in London. Apart from the archives and libraries mentioned in the Bibliography, whose collections I consulted, I am also very much indebted to the British Library in London, whose vast resources and helpful staff enabled me to broaden my horizons and keep me updated with recent literature. I am very much thankful for the institutional support from Palacký University. Eva Černínová translated the text and Eli Woock made revisions – without their help the English version would be published much later, if ever. My appreciation goes also to the staff of Viella, especially to Andrea Settis Frugoni, who made the whole publication process smooth and enjoyable. Finally, my biggest thanks to Adéla Rádková and my son Theodor, whose support, encouragement, and inspiration not only helped me to finish this book, but also made it a thoroughly wonderful experience.

Fig. 1. Franciscan Friary of St Bernardino in Olomouc, from *Tabula Conventuum Almae & Magnae Provinciae Bohemiae S. WENCESLAI D. & M., Ord. Fratrum Min. S. P. FRANCISCI Strict. Obs. Reformatorum complectensis Anno 1737*. Engraving, 433x550 mm, detail. The map was published in Severinus Wrbczansky, *Nucleus Minoriticus, seu vera et sincera relatio originis et progressus Provinciae Bohemiae* (Vetero-Pragae: Typis Joannis Caroli Hrabae, 1746).

Introduction

In 1719, Valentin Bernard Jestřábský, Silesian priest and renowned preacher, published his *Various Visions of a Common Peasant*, a book about an angel and a peasant travelling around the world. They visit a variety of places, where the angel instructs the peasant about the world and the principles of Christian conduct. In one chapter of the book they arrive at a monastery, and as usual the peasant bombards the angel with questions: "Wherefore have the monks built such a high wall around the monastery? Is it to keep thieves and other malefactors away? Or to ensure none of the monks jump out and runs away? Or to hide their actions and behaviour from the laity, to prevent common people from slandering the monks?"[1]

Jestřábský had his peasant ask questions and express views, which he knew (based on his experience of many years) resonated with the common folk. The wall separating the cloister from the surrounding world is the first thing to draw the peasant's attention. As one of the most distinctive features of a monastery, it marks out the community of monks or friars and defines the very essence of a cloister. The wall separates two distinct worlds – the inside and the outside. On the other hand, as the saying went, "the monasteries are within the world and the world within the monastery".[2] This was especially true for mendicant orders. The wall separating the friars from the surrounding community was never completely impenetrable. Those inside interacted with those outside – in churches, in towns and villages, or even in the cloisters. Friaries were swayed by events in the surrounding areas and, vice versa, the urban communities were affected by what went on in the friaries.

It is the permeability of the cloister wall which constitutes the central motif of this book.[3] The interaction of the community of the friars and the community of the local inhabitants took on many forms. All parties involved had their own intentions, expectations and ideas. The course of this interaction was often heated

1. Valentin Bernard Jestřábský, *Vidění rozličné sedláčka sprostného*, ed. by Milan Kopecký, Uherský Brod: Museum of J.A. Comenius, 1973, pp. 119-120.

2. Eduard Winter, *Josefinismus a jeho dějiny*, Prague, Jelínek, 1945, p. 116.

3. The original text was published as *Město a klášter: Františkánský konvent v raně novověké Olomouci*, Praha, Nakladatelství Lidových novin, 2017. This book is an updated and revised version.

and complicated, and its outcome could create a fundamental impact both on the life inside the monastery and on the entire urban community. Megan Armstrong, in her valuable book on the subject, upholds that it was particularly true in times of political and religious upheaval, while another authoritative book by Hillard von Thiessen demonstrated the long-term aspects of the interaction between the mendicants and society.[4] My book aims to follow this debate and analyse this interaction in the "post-Reformation" times, when Catholicism became the only tolerated and openly practiced Christian confession in many countries. I am interested, therefore, not so much in the activities of religious orders across the confessional divide, but rather within the Catholic society itself. In particular, I want to explore how religious orders contributed to the formation of a mono-confessional society, and what role they played in the everyday life of early modern Catholics.

To explore some of the paths suggested in previous research, I decided to analyse these questions at a local level.[5] For my analysis, I eventually chose the Franciscan friary of St Bernardino in Olomouc, one of the thirty houses of the vast Bohemian Franciscan Province of St Wenceslas.[6] There were three major reasons behind this choice. First, early modern Olomouc provided a complex and fascinating setting for such research. The city itself has a very rich history, which reflects the development of the Land of the Bohemian Crown, and the Habsburg Monarchy in general.[7] Since the fifteenth century, Olomouc, as well as the rest of the country, has been seriously afflicted by religious and political turmoil. When the Hussite movement gained a foothold in Bohemia (and in the Czech-speaking Moravian countryside), predominantly German Olomouc quickly joined the ranks of its opponents. It then remained one of the Roman Catholic strongholds in the region. In 1526, Ferdinand I acquired the Lands of the Bohemian Crown for the Habsburgs. At the same time, however, the teachings of Martin Luther started to spread in the monarchy and the religious situation became even more intricate.

4. Megan C. Armstrong, *The Politics of Piety: Franciscan Preachers during the Wars of Religion, 1560-1600*, Rochester, New York, University of Rochester Press, 2004. Hillard von Thiessen, *Die Kapuziner zwischen Konfessionalisierung und Alltagskultur: Vergleichende Fallstudie am Beispiel Freiburgs und Hildesheims 1599-1750*, Freiburg im Breisgau, Rombach, 2002.

5. I am partly building on my preceding book: Martin Elbel, *Bohemia Franciscana: Františkánský řád a jeho působení v českých zemích 17. a 18. Století*, Olomouc, Verbum, 2001.

6. In the eighteenth century, the province comprised thirty friaries, one residence and three female convents (one of Poor Clares and two for Religious Tertiaries). Due to its size, at the general chapter in Milan in 1731 the province was awarded with the honorary title *Alma & Magna*. In 1755, ten Silesian houses were separated and formed the independent Silesian Province of St Hedwig following the annexation of Silesia by Prussia. While the remaining Bohemian province was partly reduced by the state (one-third of the houses were closed down) in the 1780s, the Silesian province was entirely abolished in 1810.

7. Howard Louthan, *Converting Bohemia: Force and Persuasion in the Catholic Reformation*, Cambridge, Cambridge University Press, 2009. See also: Jiří Mikulec, *Náboženský život a barokní zbožnost v českých zemích*, Prague, Grada Publishing, 2013.

While the bishops of Olomouc tried to defend Catholic positions in the country, the (mostly) German-speaking population of the city responded positively to Luther's call. Olomouc itself became divided into several factions, each promoting their own religious and political agendas. The tension escalated during the Thirty Years' War. The Catholic victory at the Battle of the White Mountain, in 1620, enabled the Habsburgs to pursue strict religious policies. As in many other cities, the Olomouc municipal council was purged of non-Catholics and consisted solely of loyal Catholic burghers, while the non-Catholic inhabitants of the city were under constant pressure to convert. Eventually, the number of non-Catholic inhabitants began to diminish, at least nominally. The successful restoration of Catholicism was interrupted by the Swedish occupation in 1642. The withdrawal of the Swedish army in 1650, however, marked the definitive end of religious pluralism. Olomouc became an exclusively Roman Catholic city and remained as such for a century and a half.[8]

Olomouc was a mid-sized city by the standards of the Habsburg monarchy, with a population estimated at around 8,000 inhabitants. It was far behind Vienna, Prague or Breslau; nonetheless, it was still a relatively important political, economic and cultural centre. It was the aspiring capital of Moravia, one of the three major lands (next to Bohemia and Silesia) of the Bohemian Crown. Since the Middle Ages, Olomouc shared this position with the city of Brno (Brünn). However, during the Thirty Years' War all the offices definitively moved to Brno and Olomouc was left with only the honorary title of the capital of Moravia. The citizens of Olomouc tried (in vain) to regain their lost position. To compensate the loss, they adopted several strategies to enhance the prestige of their city; in particular, they sought to exploit the fact that their city remained the religious centre of the country.

The city was indeed a seat of a vast diocese, covering the entirety of Moravia. Its prince-bishops were not only influential ecclesiastics, but also formidable players in Moravian politics. Olomouc was, moreover, a rather affluent see which attracted the attention of many influential families, including the Dietrichsteins, the Lichtensteins, and even the Habsburgs themselves. The latter succeeded in promoting several of their members (most notably the Archduke Leopold William) to the bishopric of Olomouc. While their episcopacy was rather unconvincing, other bishops were notably more active and became major ecclesiastical agents not only in Moravia, but also in the Habsburg monarchy. These bishops were elected by the cathedral chapter comprising fourteen residential and seventeen non-residential canons, who had to be of aristocratic origin and had to study for at least three years at one of the colleges in Rome. They often held canonicates in other chapters simultaneously (usually Salzburg, Breslau, Passau or Prague) and were thus tied with many other religious centres in Central Europe.

Apart from the bishopric and the metropolitan chapter, there were numerous other church institutions in Olomouc and its vicinity. The Premonstratensian

8. For the history of the city, see: *The Transformation of Confessional Cultures in a Central European City: Olomouc, 1400-1750*, ed. by Antonín Kalous, Roma, Viella, 2015.

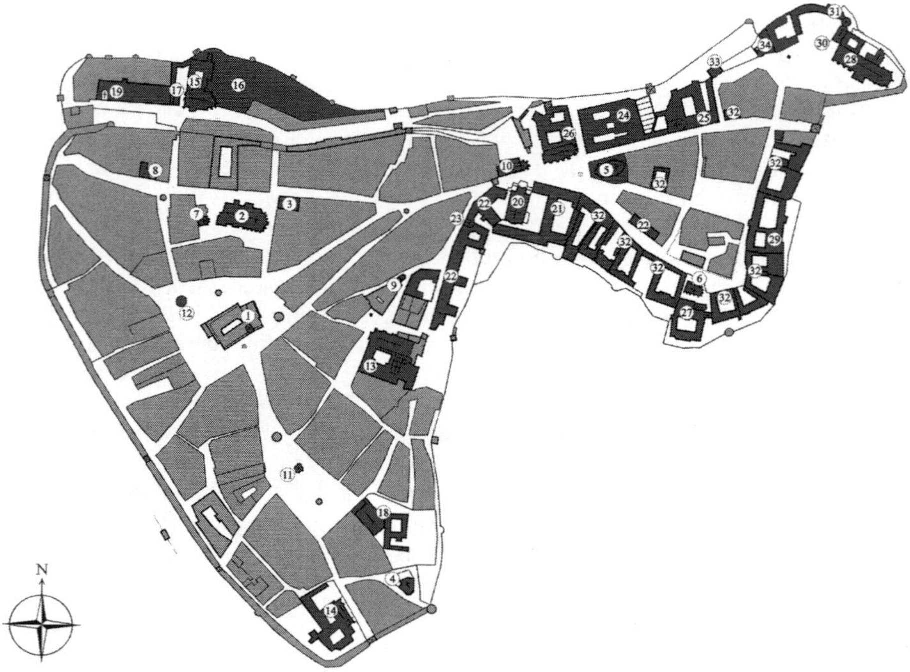

1 City hall with the chapel of St Jerome
2 Parish church of St Maurice
3 Provostry at St Maurice
4 Parish church of St Blaise
5 Parish church of the Virgin Mary in the Suburb
6 Parish church of St Peter
7 Chapel of St Cyril and Methodius
8 Lutheran prayer house (beginning of the seventeenth century)
9 City prison (later All Saints chapel, now the chapel of St John Sarkander)
10 Hospital with the church of the Holy Spirit
11 Plague column of the Virgin Mary
12 Holy Trinity column
13 Dominican priory with the church of St Michael
14 Dominican nunnery with the church of St Catherine
15 Franciscan friary with the church of the Immaculate Conception of the Virgin Mary and St Bernardino
16 Garden of the Franciscan friary (non-Catholic cemetery in the sixteenth century)
17 Sancta Scala chapel
18 Capuchin friary with the church of the Annunciation of the Virgin Mary
19 Ursuline nunnery with the church of St Ursula
20 Jesuit church of the Virgin Mary of the Snows
21 Jesuit residence
22 University
23 Corpus Christi chapel
24 Carthusian monastery with the church of the Virgin Mary
25 Augustinian canonry with the church of All Saints
26 Poor Clares nunnery with the church of St John the Baptist
27 Conventual friary with the church of St James
28 Cathedral
29 Bishop's residence
30 Church of St Anne
31 Residence of the dean of the cathedral chapter with the chapel of St Barbara
32 Residences of the canons of the cathedral chapter
33 Cathedral school
34 Provostry of the cathedral

Fig. 2. Map of Olomouc, from *The Transformation of Confessional Cultures in a Central European City: Olomouc, 1400-1750*, ed. A. Kalous (Roma, Viella, 2015), pp. 18-19. Authors: Bohdan Kaňák and Tomáš Parma.

monastery Hradisko, on the outskirts of Olomouc, was a rival to the bishops' wealth and splendour. The monastery also oversaw the immensely popular pilgrimage shrine overlooking the city from the Svatý Kopeček (Holy Hill), some seven kilometres away. Within the city, the Jesuit college and its university (and the affiliated papal *Collegium Nordicum*) more than matched the bishop's theological and religious authority. Nearby, there were monasteries of several other male religious orders: the Augustinian Canons, the Carthusians (who found refuge within the city walls during the Hussite wars), the Dominicans, and all three major branches (Conventual, Franciscan, and Capuchin) of the Friars Minor. The three female monasteries of the city – the Poor Clares, the Dominican Nuns, and the Ursulines – were also important religious establishments. Although there were practically no other confessions in Olomouc after 1650 (Hussite and Lutheran traditions being obliterated), local religious life was far from homogeneous, and the friary of St Bernardino found itself to be situated amid an intricate network of aims, agendas, and allegiances put forth by many institutions, social groups and individuals.

The second major reason behind selecting the friary of the Olomouc Franciscan was the richness and diversity of surviving sources.[9] St Bernardino was one of the first houses of the Bohemian Franciscan Province to start keeping a chronicle.[10] Its origin dates to 1650, when the superior Modestus Meerstein began writing it as a part of his effort to restore the friary. His first task was to reconstruct the history of the first stage of the friary's existence (1451-1571) and the years of its restoration (1593-1650). Afterwards, Meerstein began recording current events and did so until 1674. Following his death, records were kept by other authors, mostly the superiors of the friary. In the eighteenth century, the province authorities decided to unify the chronicles. All the houses were instructed to start new chronicles (kept in four copies) divided into thematic sections. In 1745 the Olomouc friary followed this order and commenced another chronicle.[11] This chronicle opens with a chapter on the history of Olomouc, including the Swedish occupation, and continues with its own records, which are divided into fourteen sections.[12]

9. For more details on Franciscan sources, see: Josef Svátek, "Organizace řeholních institucí v českých zemích a péče o jejich archívy", in *Sborník archivních prací, zvláštní příloha,* 20, 1970, pp. 548-550.

10. "*ARCHIVUM CONVENTus OLOMUCEnsis AD S: BERNARDinum FF: MIN: REFor: Proviae Boëmiae*". Deposited in the Moravian Land Archive, Brno, fund E 21, Dačice Franciscans, book 9, (mid-seventeenth century-1749). Hereinafter *Archivum.*

11. "*PROTOCOLLUM ARCHIVI Conventus Olomucensis Ordinis Minorum S.P. Francisci Reformatorum in quo Omnia Ejusdem MONUMENTA et DOCUMENTA sub Debitis Titulis Collocata et Consignata sunt*". Today deposited in the Moravian Land Archive, Brno, fund E 21, Dačice Franciscans, book 10. Hereinafter *Protocollum.*

12. A. The beginnings of the friary, B. The origin of the church, C. The construction and repairs of the friary, D. The construction and repairs of the church, E. The list of the vicars and ministers of the Bohemian Province and dignitaries of the friary, F. The benefactors and apostolic syndics of the friary, G. The funds and obligations of the friary, H. Mendicant districts of the friary, I. Notable events, J. Letters of complaint, K. Funerals of friars, L. Third Order funerals, M. Secular funerals, N. Miscellaneous.

Other important sources composed in the friary include the necrology,[13] the register of the members of the Third Order,[14] and the rather paradoxical source (considering this was a mendicant environment), the *Liber Ratiociniorum* – a kind of a "ledger" recording the alms as well as the expenses of the friary.[15] In addition to these five books there is a broad range of other documents.[16] The files of the Moravian Gubernium provide many details about the abolishment of the monastery.[17] Documents written on the provincial level are also very useful, whether the original chronicle of the Bohemian Franciscan Province,[18] the chronicles by Bernard Sannig,[19] or the impressive compendium *Nucleus Minoriticus* by Severinus Wrbczansky.[20] There are, however, two major gaps in the otherwise rich sources. The first concerns visual and material sources. In 1785, St Bernardino was closed and the vacant building was handed over to the Dominicans, who were forced to move here from their monastery at St Michael. They, understandably enough, remodelled both the friary and the church according to their taste, spirituality and traditions, and consequently most of the original furnishing was lost. The other, more serious gap is related to preaching. Not a single text of a sermon delivered in the friary church has survived. The only source we can rely on to get an idea of the nature of these sermons is the popular collection of sermons by Damascenus Marek, which is nonetheless rather exceptional in the environment of the Bohemian Franciscans.[21]

13. Moravian Land Archive, Brno, fund G 10, manuscripts, inv. no. 213, reg. no. 236, *Nekrology of the Franciscan friary in Olomouc and of the Bohemian Province for the years 1404-1783,* (1763-1783).

14. Moravian Land Archive, Brno, fund E 21, Dačice Franciscans, book 11, *Matrica III. Ordinis S. Francisci Olomucii. ErneVertes VerzeIChnVs Deren Wertesten BrVDern VnD SChWestern / eInes preIsWVrDIgsten DrItten so erWehnten BVsser OrDens Vnseres grossen ErzVaters FranCIsCI* (1746-1782). Hereinafter *Matrica.*

15. Moravian Land Archive Brno, fund E 21, Dačice Franciscans, book 10b, *Liber Ratiociniorum Conventus Olomucensis ad Sanctum Bernardinum* (1756-1785). Hereinafter *Liber Ratiociniorum.*

16. Stored partly in the National Archives in Prague (Bohemian Franciscan Archives), the Olomouc office of the Opava Land Archive (Olomouc Archdiocese and the Olomouc Archbishop Consistory) and the State District Archive in Olomouc (specifically the Olomouc Archives – fragments of the registries).

17. Moravian Land Archive, Brno, fund B 2, Moravian Gubernium – Ecclesiastical Department.

18. Library of the National Museum in Prague, Manuscript Collection, sign. VIII F 75, *Chronica Fratrum Minorum de Observantia Provinciae Bohemiae.*

19. National Archives in Prague, fund Bohemian Franciscans, books 17-21.

20. Severinus Wrbczansky, *Nucleus Minoriticus, seu Vera et Sincera Relatio Originis et Progressus Provinciae Bohemiae, Conventuum et Residentiarum, Fratrum et Sororum Sancti-Monialium Ordin. Minor. S. P. Francisci Strict. Observ. Reform. in Provincia sub Patrocinio Sancti Wenceslai Ducis et Martyris, per Bohemiam, Moraviam, et Silesiam Existentium,* Vetero-Pragae, Typis Joannis Caroli Hrabae, 1746.

21. Damascenus Marek, *Trojí chléb nebeský pro lačný lid český,* Prague Old Town, Karel Jan Hraba, 1728. For more on Marek's postil, see: the inspiring study by Daniel Soukup, "Co medle jiného od chudého františkána k očekávání? Postila Trojí chléb nebeský františkána

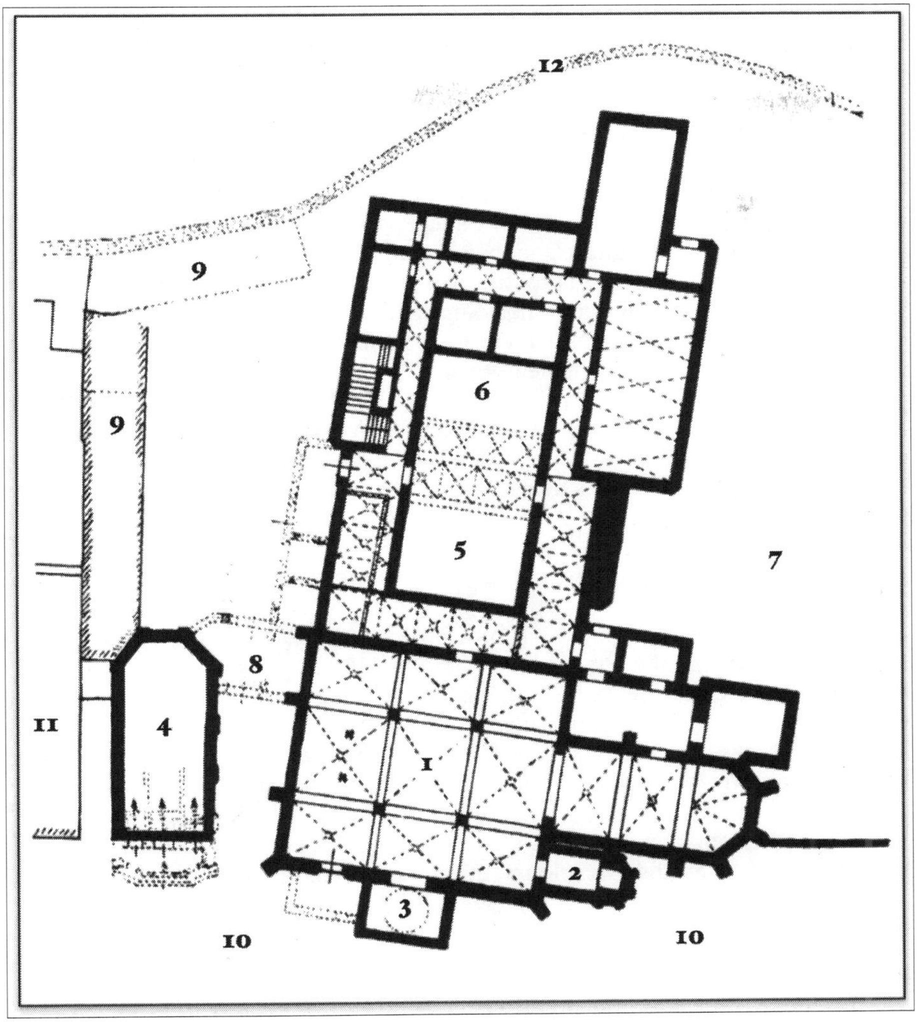

Fig. 3. Ground plan of the friary: 1. church of the Immaculate conception of the Virgin Mary and St Bernardino (1468), 2. Holy Sepulchre (1653), 3. chapel of St Anthony of Padua (1675), 4. Holy Stairs (1726), 5. old friary (1468), 6. new friary (1751), 7. garden, 8. gate, 9. stables, workshops, and stores, 10. Pilten street, 11. convent of the Ursulines, 12. city wall (1526). After: Josef Kšír, "Stavební historie budov Moravské filharmonie v Olomouci," *Zprávy Krajského vlastivědného muzea v Olomouci* 58 (1958): p. 88.

And finally, the third major reason for selecting St Bernardino was the specific character of the Franciscan Order and the way those characteristics were manifested in the particular case of the Olomouc friary. This book aims to point at slightly different trends which depart from the traditional concept of confessionalisation. Instead, it accentuates the plurality and diversity (and sometimes contradictory tendencies) within the Roman Catholic world.[22] Concentrating on the Franciscan Order proved extremely beneficial in studying this issue. Mendicancy affected the role of Franciscans as mediators in many spheres: between the centre and the periphery, high and low culture and the secular and ecclesial environments. It also influenced all the Franciscan activities and motivated the friars to seek effective ways to address the population. The communication strategies of mendicants are, after all, the basic motif, which underlies this monograph. An added value to the choice was the fact that it enabled me to research an institution that flourished in the pre-Reformation period, then was closed, and later revived and needed to renegotiate its position in society. This enabled a discussion on some aspects of the continuity with the Middle Ages. This factor was a significant advantage when compared to the "new" orders usually associated with the Catholic Reform or the Counter-Reformation.[23]

Rather than strictly following chronological order, the book covers several interconnected issues.

The first chapter is something of a prologue to the rest of the book.[24] It is set in the period of the Swedish occupation (1642-1650), the last time early modern Olomouc experienced the coexistence of several confessional groups (the situation was even more complicated by the presence of Swedish soldiers). The local Franciscans, too, became involved in the confessional (and military) clashes, and their activities illustrated some of the dilemmas related to the formation of confessional cultures.

The second chapter discusses the re-establishment of the friary after 1650. It also reflects the preceding developments and the attempts of Franciscans to build

Damascena Marka", in *Františkánský kontext teologického a filozofického myšlení*, ed. by Petr Hlaváček, Prague, Charles University, 2012, pp. 146-178.

22. For the summary of the discussion on the concept of confessionalisation, see: Jörg Deventer, "Confessionalisation – a Useful Theoretical Concept for the Study of Religion, Politics, and Society in Early Modern East-Central Europe?", *European Review of History*, 11, no. 3 (2004), pp. 403-425.

23. John Patrick Donnelly, "New Religious Orders for Men", in *Cambridge History of Christianity, Volume 6: Reform and Expansion 1500-1660*, ed. by R. Po-chia Hsia, Cambridge: Cambridge University Press, 2008, p. 162. See also:,*Communities of Devotion: Religious Orders and Society in East Central Europe, 1450-1800,* ed. by Maria Craciun and Elaine Fulton, Farnham, Ashgate, 2011.

24. An older piece containing parts of this chapter was published as: Martin Elbel, "Dva světy? Konfesijní hranice za švédské okupace Olomouce, 1642-1650", in *Konec švédské okupace a poválečná obnova ve 2. polovině 17. století: Sborník příspěvků ze sympózia*, ed. by Martin Elbel and Milan Togner, Historická Olomouc XIII, Olomouc, Palacky University, 2002, pp. 99-105.

on previous achievements. The reconstruction of the memory of their previous activities was the key – it enabled them to legitimise their position and created a model for their future activities.

The third chapter deals mainly with the original ideal of apostolic poverty and its implementation in the early modern period.[25] Life in strict poverty and the dependence upon alms influenced all activities of the order, both within and outside the friary's walls.

Relationships based on the mendicant character of the order (and shaped by the actual exchange of alms and religious services) are analysed further in the fourth chapter. The alms had a largely reciprocal character, linking the monastery – temporarily or permanently – with a variety of subjects. The important of these were the burghers, with whom the mendicants often entered into alliances that substantially influenced the religious life in the city.

The fifth chapter maps Franciscan strategies to develop the sacred space of their friary and the church. These drew on the international character of the Order (namely its activities in Palestine), which helped the Franciscans introduce and disseminate new types of devotions. The response was not altogether favourable, and some of the changes in the sacred topography of the city required complex negotiations (see the Scala Sancta chapel).

Finally, the sixth chapter explores the circumstances under which St Bernardino was eventually closed. It points to the changing position of the friary in the second half of the eighteenth century. While it continued to perform all its functions and remained highly appreciated at the local level, on the state level many influential individuals came to view the mendicants and other religious orders as useless or even harmful to the society. These voices eventually prevailed, leading to the abolishment of a large number of monasteries during the reign of Joseph II, one of them being the Franciscan Friary of St Bernardino in Olomouc.

To focus on my main research topics and to preserve the integrity of the book, I left many topics unaddressed. For example, I did not deal with internal affairs (unless it was relevant for the interaction of the friars with the outer world), such as the traditionally popular theme of everyday life or the issue of the formation and education of the friars.[26] I also did not discuss, with the exception of a few, the lives of individual friars. After all, there were no *stabilitas loci* in the Franciscan order

25. Parts of Chapters Three and Four were published in: Martin Elbel, "Early Modern Mendicancy: Franciscan Practice in the Bohemian Lands", *Journal of Ecclesiastical History*, 96:1 (2018), pp. 39-56. I am grateful to Cambridge University Press for the permission to re-use those passages.

26. The Czech monasteriologic research is summarized by Jan Zdichynec, "Monasteriologie a klášterní problematika v raném novověku", ed. by Marie Šedivá Koldinská and Ivo Cerman,Prague, Lidové noviny, 2013, pp. 230-267, Ivana Čornejová, *Tovaryšstvo Ježíšovo: Jezuité v Čechách*, Prague, Mladá Fronta, 1995, and Kateřina Bobková-Valentová, *Každodenní život učitele a žáka jezuitského gymnázia*, Prague, Karolinum, 2006. *Locus pietatis et vitae: Sborník příspěvků z konference konané v Hejnicích ve dnech 13. -15. září 2007*, ed. by Ivana Čornejová, Hedvika Kuchařová a Kateřina Valentová, eds., ‚Prague, Charles University, Scriptorium, 2008. *Úloha církevních řádů při pobělohorské rekatolizaci: Sborník příspěvků*

and the friars were transferred from one house to another. Virtually all of them spent their lives in several of the friaries around the province and every community was under constant change. Throughout the text, I, of course, refrained (unless quoting from primary sources) from referring to the Franciscans as "monks" and used the term "friars" instead. In the case of Franciscan dwellings, I adopted a more liberal approach. The term used primarily in the Latin sources is *conventus* or, in compliance with the observance tradition, *domus* (the house). In English, however, the word "convent" strongly evokes a religious house for women. That is why I decided to limit the use of this word and instead use the more traditional term "friary". Apart from that, the term "monastery" is occasionally used as well, as it is more general and better implies the separation of its inhabitants from the rest of the society – the world limited and surrounded by the walls. The walls were though far from being impervious and they constantly provoked and stimulated interaction and communication between the worlds inside and outside.

z pracovního semináře konaného ve Vranově u Brna ve dnech 4.-5. 6. 2003, ed. by Ivana Čornejová, ed., Prague, Charles University, 2003.

1. Divided City

In early August 1649, the Franciscan Modestus Meerstein arrived at the city of Olomouc. He had spent a few tiring days on the road. A few weeks earlier, the provincial definitorium appointed him the superior (*guardianus*) of the Olomouc friary of St Bernardino and he was to take office as soon as possible.[1] It was not safe to travel (for a solitary Franciscan as well as for others) through land which still bore visible marks of the preceding clashes between the Imperial and Swedish armies. Groups of armed men continued to roam the countryside, who could not be expected to show utmost respect to friars. After all, it would not have been the first time ever that a member of his order had been murdered while travelling. Quite recently, in 1631, two Irish Franciscans, Patrick Flemming and Matthias Horg met such a fate. On their way from Prague, escaping the approaching Saxon army, they were held up and brutally murdered.[2] Undoubtedly aware of the danger, Meerstein probably joined a group of other travellers for greater safety.

He had reached his destination now. Close to the city, he could see its medieval walls, reinforced in several places with modern fortification elements. He had a very good view, because the suburbs had been burnt and razed to the ground, the gardens and gazebos – the former pride of wealthy burghers – destroyed, and trees cut down. Behind the walls he could see the ridges of the roofs, partly dilapidated, over which rose the city hall tower and the steeples of several churches.[3] One of these was a tall pyramidal roof with a spire. Unlike most other church roofs, this one was not made of expensive slate, but of roof tiles that gave it a distinctive red colour. Meerstein knew Olomouc very well, and so did not need this clue to realize that this red roof near the walls was the local Franciscan church of the Immaculate Conception of the Virgin Mary and St Bernardino.

1. *Archivum*, p. 38.

2. Their bodies were later deposited and venerated in the Franciscan friary in Votice. Wrbczansky, *Nucleus Minoriticus*, p. 213.

3. For the description of the city at the end of the Swedish occupation and the damages incurred, see: *Relation Von Dem Schwedischen Abzug Auss Denen Inngehabten Posten Im Marggraffthumb Mähren Wie Derselbe Am 8. Julii Zu Ollmütz Seinen Anfang Genommen, Und Noch Ebenselben Tag Glücklichen Vollzogen Worden*, Gedruckt zu Ollmütz, Bey Nicolao Hradetzcky von Brusnaw, 1650.

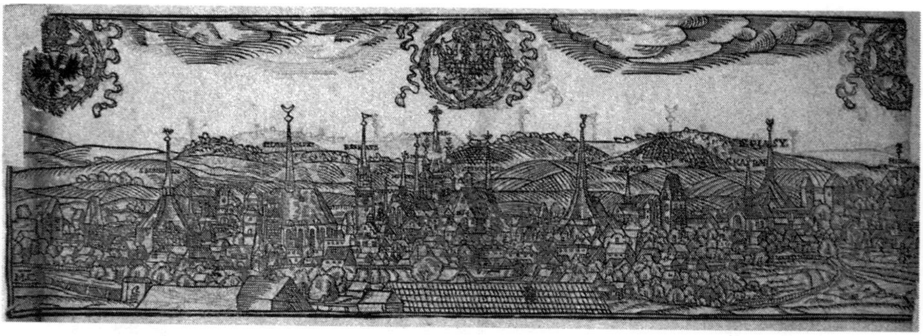

Fig. 4. View of Olomouc in 1597. Monogramist MC, woodcut. Germanisches Nationalmuseum Nürnberg, Graphische Sammlung. Reprinted from *The Transformation of Confessional Cultures in a Central European City: Olomouc, 1400-1750*, ed. A. Kalous (Roma: Viella, 2015), 66-67.

His final destination seemed within reach, but he was soon to find that his troubles were not over yet. Although news of the treaty of Münster and Osnabrück had reached Olomouc over six months prior to his arrival, the Swedish garrison was still stationed in the city, for eight years now. According to the peace arrangements, the Swedish army was to receive military reparations, and until then their garrisons were to remain in the occupied cities in Bohemia and Moravia. Many of the soldiers and their families had no reason to hurry back home. War was often the only life experience they gained and military skills the only competence they had. For some of them, military service also increased their social status, and it is no wonder that for these and other reasons they did not feel like going home. Never mind the fact that many of them did not even have a home at all.

Meerstein arrived in the city on Monday, 2 August. This date was highly symbolic, because this is the day the Franciscans celebrate the Feast of the Portiuncula, one of their most important feasts, as it is connected with the life of St Francis and the very beginnings of the order itself.[4] The new superior perhaps did not think this was mere coincidence and saw it as the promise of new beginnings and a happy renewal of religious life. This Portiuncula was far from being joyful, though. While he was allowed to spend the night in the friary, the very next day he was forced to leave the city. A second attempt was made and also failed – he managed to get in the city through one of the gates, but a Swedish patrol swiftly led him out through another, while mocking and insulting him. The Swedes remembered very well the problems Meerstein's confrere had caused them five years earlier (as described later in the text). Back

4. Porziuncola, or Portiuncula (meaning "a small part") was the popular name for the small chapel of Saint Mary of the Angels in Assisi (nowadays transformed into a large basilica). This chapel is inherently linked to St Francis (who died here) and the beginnings of the Order of Friars Minor. In 1216, Francis had a vision in which he received indulgence from Christ himself. It was later extended to the whole order, and even later to the other believers going to the Franciscan churches. Portiuncula is considered the mother church of Friars Minor. Franciscan churches usually had their own "Portiuncula" altar endowed with indulgences.

Fig. 5. Church of the Immaculate Conception of the Virgin Mary with former chapels of St Anthony of Padua and of Holy Sepulchre. Museum of Art Olomouc, photo: Ivo Přeček.

then, a conspiracy hatched by the Franciscan Michael Jahn very nearly ended the Swedish rule in Olomouc. Although a peace agreement had been signed in the meantime and there was no such danger now, the Swedes were not too pleased about having another suspicious friar in the city. Their attitude changed only after the intercession of the town councillor (and one of the future most prominent benefactors of the Franciscan friary) Tobias Schwonauer, who vouched for the Franciscan with a solemn oath. In all likelihood, the actual decisive factor was the gifts and money with which Schwonauer bribed the garrison commander. Only after his intervention was Meerstein finally allowed to enter the city and settle in the dilapidated friary, which had been occupied for the past five years by only a lay brother, Didacus Hohenleiter.[5]

1. *Swedish invasion*

Returning to Olomouc was important for Meerstein also for personal reasons. It was this very friary where he entered the noviciate on 3 May 1640, at the age of

5. Meerstein described his misfortunes in *Archivum*, p. 38.

thirty. He was quite old for a novice; the other five candidates to enter the noviciate that year were aged seventeen to twenty-three years. And yet, he was expected to become a priest, as he was listed as a cleric in the register. This indicates that he must have received some education before.[6] At that time, the Olomouc friary was thriving under Fr Ludovicus Gessner. The monastery was undergoing renovations (in 1635 the main altar was newly consecrated) and enjoying a period of peace and partial bloom, backed by the Habsburg religious policy following their victory in the battle at White Mountain. The image Meerstein preserved in his memory must have differed substantially from what he saw upon his return. The friary bore the marks of the Swedish looting and of having been uninhabited for five years. The city itself was in no better state. Allegedly, less than a quarter of the original seven hundred burgher houses were habitable, the suburbs razed to the ground, and the nearby Premonstratensian monastery Hradisko burned. Imperial Commander Raimondo Montecuccoli, whose task it was to record the condition of fortified cities, even reported that it would be better to tear Olomouc city's walls down. This would, of course, have meant substantial degradation and the culmination of the misfortunes the city was suffering. Montecuccoli's grim report was corroborated by another report by royal vice-chamberlain (*subcamerarius*) Jan Jakardovský of Sudice who claimed that of the original (vastly exaggerated) number of 30,000 inhabitants, counted in 1640, had dropped to a mere 1,675 by 1650.[7] These lamentations, however, might be slightly inflated. After all, the fact that the Franciscan supporter Tobias Schwonauer, after all these troubles, was able to raise enough money just to bribe the Swedish commander, shows that the hardships of war did not affect everyone in the same way.[8] Still, the Swedish occupation left the city marred, severely impacting life in the city and marking a watershed moment in its history.

Havoc in the city had begun eight years earlier, in 1642. "That was a turbulent year", Meerstein sighed later while writing his chronicle.[9] Even though the country had been troubled for a long time, Olomouc had been spared the worst horrors of war. So far, it "only" had had to provide lodging for the Imperial troops. That

6. He was probably educated at the Jesuit Grammar School in Chomutov, the town where he came from. His name and basic information can be found in the list at the end of the friary chronicle (*Archivum*, unpaged). The list forms Section B and is titled "*Novitiorvm nomina Ad Sacrum Habitum, & Professionem Susceptorum*". It was also suggested that originally he had been a member of the Jesuit Order. See: Vigilius Greiderer, *Germania Franciscana, Seu Chronicon Geographo-Historicum Ordinis S. P. Francisci in Germania, Tomus I. Germania Franciscana Orientali-Australis*, Oeniponte, Typis Joannis Thomae Nobilis de Trattnern, 1777, p. 777.

7. The report by Montecuccoli and Jakardovský is noted in: Václav Nešpor, *Dějiny Olomouce,* Olomouc, Votobia, 1998, pp. 166-167. More sober estimates place the drop as being from 10,000 inhabitants to 2,000 or 2,500. See: Jaroslav Miller, *Uzavřená společnost a její nepřátelé: Město středovýchodní Evropy (1500-1700)*, Prague, Nakladatelství Lidové noviny, 2006, p. 38.

8. Jaroslav Miller, "Zchudlé město bohatých měšťanů?", in *Olomoucké baroko: Proměny ambicí jednoho města (1. Úvodní svazek)*, ed. by Martin Elbel and Ondřej Jakubec, Olomouc, Muzeum umění Olomouc, 2010, pp. 71-77.

9. *Archivum*, p. 33.

year, though the war was moving dangerously close. Fr Paulinus Zaczkowicz, superior of the local friary of Friars Minor Conventuals, was in the city for most of the Swedish occupation and wrote one of the most impressive, though often inaccurate, accounts of this history. He claimed that the forthcoming troubles had been presaged by ominous portents:

> For two years in a row prior to the Swedish invasion of Moravia, a sea of mice emerged around Olomouc, ravaging and devouring the surrounding fields to such a degree that travellers, seized with fear, could hardly walk across the fields, particularly in the evening. The mice were of different colours: white, black, purple, red; their furs wore the following signs: swords, crosses, gauntlets; and they were all frightening. The year the Swedes arrived in Moravia, they disappeared. They were the harbingers of what was to come.[10]

In the spring of 1642, those vague concerns began to take shape. More and more refugees were coming into Olomouc from Silesian towns, bringing alarming news of the advancing Swedish army. Dorstenson – as Meerstein refers to the Swedish Commander, Lennart Torstenson, in his chronicle – invaded Silesia, where he seized Głogów (Groß-Glogau) on 14 May, and six days later defeated the main Imperial army at Świdnica (Schweidnitz). The retreat of the Imperial army opened a path to Moravia for him. It was clear that this time the war would come to Olomouc, too. Panic broke out in the city. The prelates, the nobles, the wives of wealthy burghers, and other people all began to leave in a hurry, trying to save the most important valuables. It was not only the personal property of burghers that needed saving. The treasures of the cathedral and other churches, as well as the most important documents, such as the archive of the metropolitan chapter, had to be taken away as well. The inhabitants of the Franciscan monastery, where Modestus Meerstein and thirteen other confreres were living then, also tried to secure their liturgical vessels and reliquaries.[11]

Being quick was crucial for salvation, as any delay could prove fatal. Only those who set out early had a chance to save themselves. One group left the city as late as the Sunday of Pentecost (8 June), and yet managed to reach safety. The very same day, however, the first Swedish troops appeared near the city. Despite this, many of the leading citizens of Olomouc attempted to escape on Monday. A large group with several top-loaded wagons, accompanied by four hundred infantrymen and a smaller cavalry detachment, headed for Brno. They were, however, unable to breach the closing circle, and the next day they were ambushed by the Swedish soldiers. The Imperial mercenaries fled, leaving the refugees at the mercy of the enemy; later they reportedly returned to the place of the encounter and stole the remaining loot which the Swedes had left behind. The Swedes snatched a bountiful booty, including the treasure of the cathedral church. The soldiers thus also seized valuable reliquaries. They immediately took

10. Paulinus Zaczkovic, *Chronik des Minoriten-Guardians des St. Jacobs-Klosters in Olmütz, P. Paulinus Zaczkovic, Über die Schwedenherrschaft in Olmütz von 1642 bis 1650*, ed. by Beda Dudík, Wien, Gerold, 1881, p. 457.

11. In addition, it also housed similar objects of the Franciscan friary in Nysa, from where they had been saved a few days earlier. *Archivum*, p. 33.

the relics of the saints out and scattered them around the field, where the relics were trampled by horses, much to the understandable outrage of the Catholics. In addition to the prized spoils, the Swedes also captured a number of people, including wives and children of several prominent burghers. The hostages were likely an important Swedish pawn in the subsequent negotiations on the surrender of the city. However, the Franciscan sent away with the church valuables of the Olomouc friary was not among the attacked. Unlike the others, he chose "*ex Dei providentia*" to travel to Kroměříž (Cremsier) instead of Brno.[12] Despite some difficulties, he eventually managed to get through Hungary to Styria.

On Pentecost Tuesday, the same day that the convoy was raided, the vanguard of Torstenston's army approached the city. For a few days preceding, when the first Swedish troops had appeared near the city, the defenders thought it was the vanguard of the Imperial army, whose commander, John Francis of Fernemont, had promised to help Olomouc. In the meantime, Fernemont had been ordered not to risk another battle and was retreating to Hungary. The defenders soon discovered they were left at the mercy of the Swedish army. Commander Antonio Miniati was faced with a great challenge. The Olomouc city walls were derelict, with some sections collapsed (the Swedes had to repair them immediately after conquering Olomouc). The only other military force the city had, besides its militia and a company of university students, was a small garrison consisting of under-armed and under-trained fresh recruits. The vanguard of the Swedish army at once commenced a siege. Miniati, not to lose face and to show good will, defended the city for four days, until he saw the main body of the Swedish army approach the city, at which point he decided to surrender. The capitulation was signed on 14 June 1642.[13] A day later, the Imperial troops left the city to make space for five Swedish regiments. According to the custom, the defenders marched under flying banners, with loaded guns and lit fuses. They were thus allowed to leave in full glory, but the true state of their morale is reflected in the fact that from the entire group of around six hundred people, eventually only thirty soldiers arrived in Brno.[14] The disgrace Miniati fell into with the court due to his surrender was not justified. Zaczkowicz recorded in his chronicle, shortly after the occupation of the city, that Torstenson inspected the city fortifications and was quite upset to find that a section of the walls was badly damaged and demolished. He allegedly said that if he had known it, he would not have agreed to negotiations and would have taken the city by force.[15]

The inhabitants were thus spared direct violence and looting. Moreover, the capitulation accord contained a number of clauses intended to protect the local population.[16] One of them involved religious beliefs. Roman Catholics were

12. *Archivum*, p. 33.

13. Nešpor, *Dějiny Olomouce*, p. 160.

14. Miroslav Koudela and Zdeněk Kašpar, *Švédové v Olomouci (1642-1650)*, Praha, Danal, 1993, p. 18.

15. Zaczkovic, *Chronik Des Minoriten-Guardians*, p. 463.

16. Friedrich Flade, *Tagebuch des feindlichen Einfalls der Schweden in das Markgrafthum Mähren während ihres Aufenthaltes in der Stadt Olmütz, 1642-1650*, ed. by Beda Dudík, Wien, Gerold, 1884, p. 10.

to maintain all their rights, including the right to perform services. According to the terms of the capitulation, the local monasteries were to be preserved, including all their possessions. This concerned the Jesuit college, the six male (Franciscan, Conventual, Capuchin, Dominican, Augustinian and Carthusian) monasteries, and the two female (Poor Clares and Dominican) convents. Only the Premonstratensian Hradisko Monastery outside the city walls was torn down for fortification reasons.

There were fourteen brethren living at St Bernardino then.[17] Compared with other clergy, they enjoyed – together with the other mendicants – a relatively privileged position. This became evident in the first few months, when the Swedes decided to impose a *contributio* on the local clergy. They summoned the bishop-administrator and ordered him to pay a thousand imperial thalers if he and the other clergy wanted to remain "protected". Shortly after this money was paid, however, the Swedes demanded another two thousand, and later their demands continued to grow even higher. Part of the *contributio* was eventually paid with the help of the Jesuits, but other fees were beyond their capacity. To satisfy the Swedish demands, bishop-administrator Stredele had to ask other friars, including the mendicants. The latter paid a visit to the commander to request a remission of the fees, referring to their poverty. The commander allegedly told them that he was well aware of their poverty as well as the fact that they lived on alms only. He stated that he had never asked the mendicants for any money and that they were exempt from any fees. With this he indirectly confirmed that he was mainly interested in the property of the bishop, the chapter, and the Jesuit college. This Swedish benevolence towards the mendicant monasteries was also welcomed by local residents, especially those who had decided to leave the city. The inviolability of the monasteries, duly observed in the first two years of the occupation, made them a perfect place to store valuables. And not only small objects. The buildings of the monasteries, now mostly empty, could also accommodate various goods and workshop equipment. Although much of this property succumbed to decay or looting during later years, the mendicant houses did provide a relatively safe hideaway.[18] Interestingly enough, the monasteries were used also by Swedish officers as a place to hide their loot and valuables.

The city monasteries were hence under the commander's protection and at least initially spared looting. On the other hand, the Swedes were aware that such institutions could eventually become centres of resistance. Their main concern was that, due to their organisation and involvement in a wider network, monasteries could become efficient informants for the Imperial army. Suspicion fell primarily on the Jesuits, who ended up being expelled (all but one) from the city on 9 October 1643. Safeguards were installed in the other monasteries, and friars' contacts outside the city were monitored. The situation improved with time, and many of the measures were considerably mitigated – the mendicants were even allowed to leave the city to collect alms in the surrounding villages.

17. *Archivum*, p. 34.
18. Miller, "Zchudlé město bohatých měšťanů?", p. 74.

The Swedes themselves had reasons to support a peaceful coexistence between the local population and the Swedish garrison. In the first few months it was unclear how long the Swedes would stay. Olomouc was deep in the interior and all depended on the luck of the Swedish army operating in the Bohemian Lands to determine whether the city would be held or relinquished. It also had a strategic position in case the Swedes wanted to advance on Imperial Vienna. It was therefore expected that Imperial soldiers would try to quickly win back this important post. The Swedish commanders were acutely aware of the fact that there were many people in the city who, partly due to their religious convictions, would never reconcile themselves to the presence of Protestant soldiers, and would do everything to assist Imperial attempts to regain the city. Any denominational disputes could become a dangerous trigger. Therefore, the commanders did their best, at least at the beginning, to not provoke the local Catholic citizens and to prevent any clashes. They repeatedly issued a decree requesting that people of all faiths should live in peace, avoiding arguments. The decree proved insufficient. Several times, they personally intervened to subdue an emerging conflict. And yet, the atmosphere remained tense. For months, and ultimately years, the space enclosed in the city walls had to accommodate people whose relationships were largely influenced by, aside from economic and personal interests, different and often clashing types of "loyalties": with the Emperor, Swedish crown, Catholic faith or evangelical beliefs. Given the circumstances it was clear that conflicts would soon arise.

Following an agreement with the city council, the Swedes were given the church of St Blaise for their Protestant services, which was a rather bizarre Gothic structure with an irregular heptagon-shaped ground plan. However, they soon found the church inadequate, due to its size, condition, and location on the edges of the city; especially since there were many other churches in the city, including the cathedral, three other parish churches, and several monastic churches. After several months, they requested a partial surrender of the parish church of St Maurice; the Protestants would alternate here with the Catholics. The latter refused the suggestion as the idea of sharing the shrine with heretics was not an option for them. They tried to elude the Swedish request by saying that the request was subject to the bishop's approval, while the bishop himself (the notorious pluralist Archduke Leopold William of Austria) did not live in the city and was difficult to get in touch with. The Swedes insisted and Jesuit Melchior Pollinger, the temporary administrator of the church, realised that he was powerless against such pressure. However, when the Swedes went to hold their first service at St Maurice on the morning of 14 December 1642, they found the gate locked. When a messenger was sent to fetch the keys, Pollinger was nowhere to be found. He only sent word that he no longer had the keys because they were inside the church on the main altar. The Swedes first tried to force the other Catholic priests to open the church, but in the end there was nothing left to do but climb into the church through a broken window and unlock the church from within.

Although at first glance, the story seems like a desperate attempt of an individual to face greater odds, in fact, Pollinger may have had a slightly more sophisticated goal in mind. The key to understanding this is provided by a brief note in the

Fig. 6. Parable of the false shepherd from the Gospel According to John. Monogramist MS, woodcut. Germanisches Nationalmuseum Nürnberg. From Robert W. Scribner, *For the Sake of Simple Folk: Popular Propaganda for the German Reformation*, (Oxford; New York: Oxford University Press, 1994), 54.

Franciscan chronicle, which says that the Lutheran pastor entered the church as a thief and robber, as is written in the Gospel.[19] Meerstein is referring to the Gospel of John, Chapter 10, where Jesus says of himself that he is a good shepherd. The first verse of the chapter says: "Verily, verily, I say unto you, He that entereth not by the door into the sheepfold, but climbeth up some other way, the same is a thief and a robber". The theme is developed even further, speaking of a false shepherd who does not care about his sheep, who works only for the money, and runs away when the wolf approaches. This is the image that Pollinger managed to manipulate the Lutheran pastor-shepherd into. After all, using this theme in denominational controversies was nothing new, having been introduced a hundred years earlier by Luther's followers, paradoxically, who spread it through woodcuts.[20]

The following day the Swedes wanted to return the keys to Pollinger, who refused. Instead of the parish temple, the Rorate devotions were demonstratively held at the St Cyril and Methodius chapel in the cemetery of St Maurice Church. The Catholics made sure that their church services were well-attended, and

19. *Archivum*, p. 34.

20. Robert W. Scribner, *For the Sake of Simple Folk: Popular Propaganda for the German Reformation*, Oxford, Oxford University Press, 1994, pp. 52-54.

their loud singing drowned out the much more modest evangelical services.[21] The confrontation did not last long, and the Catholics had to move to the Dominican church of St Michael. They found some consolation in the fact that the advantageous location of the church on one of the Olomouc hills again helped the singing and the organ to sound sufficiently around the city. Perhaps it was a sort of compensation for the Swedes' limitation of the use of church bells and chimes in the astronomical clock to prevent sending signals to the Imperial forces. Finally, however, in 1646, Catholic services were moved to the Franciscan church of St Bernardino. Meerstein's chronicle says, rather pompously, that the local Catholics chose this church to be their main shrine "*ex pristina devotione*", due to the previous esteem for the friars.[22] By this time, however, there was not a single Franciscan priest left in Olomouc. The last of them – Priest Michael, who will be discussed later in the text – had to leave the city in 1644.

2. *Confessional disputes*

This conflict proved that the coexistence of various confessions, complicated further by the war, would be quite a challenge. The city, seemingly homogeneous prior to the occupation, was to be divided for several years. There were local burghers and Swedish soldiers (including Germans and members of other nations besides the Swedes), and there were both Catholics and Protestants. The preserved narrative sources (written mostly by the Olomouc Catholics) tend to argue that the two spheres overlapped. On one side, there were foreign, heretical mercenaries and on the other were the local citizens, loyal to the emperor and the Catholic Church. This division was in fact much more complicated. There were undoubtedly many individuals among both the Swedish soldiers and the local bourgeoisie whose political and religious commitments could be defined as conflicting or unequal. Moreover, the boundaries were far from rigid.

In terms of the burghers, their attitudes were largely influenced by preceding developments. In the early seventeenth century, Olomouc was largely evangelical, but winning the Battle of White Mountain opened the way for the emperor to enforce the monopoly of the Catholic Church. At the beginning of 1625, a charter was issued that ordered Moravian burghers to either become Catholic or sell their property and leave the country. In June of the same year, the non-Catholic citizens of Olomouc were summoned to the city hall (not all inhabitants of the city but only the heads of families or households) and asked about their decision. A total of 117 insisted on maintaining their faith. After having been "urged" by the city council, this number was reduced to fifty-three after a few days, then to twelve, and eventually to merely four burghers.[23] Now, with the arrival of the Swedes, many of them had the opportunity to restore their old faith. Meerstein, however, claimed that with the exception of one renegade, the Olomouc residents had stood

21. Zaczkovic, *Chronik Des Minoriten-Guardians*, p. 19.
22. *Archivum*, p. 34.
23. Nešpor, *Dějiny Olomouce*, p. 155.

firm in their faith, a fact that surprised even the Swedes; they allegedly had never met such strong and relentless people.[24] This view was indeed rather idealised. Zaczkowicz, who was better informed about life in the occupied city, complained of apostate burghers on several occasions.[25] And yet no massive return to the "faith of the fathers" took place. Firstly, reconversion was quite risky. It was not clear how long the Swedes would occupy Olomouc, and post-war restoration would present the issue of repression and perhaps exile for these individuals. Another contributing factor was the fact that the social structure of the burghers changed during the occupation. The population size gradually diminished during the eight years of occupation and the people who stayed in the city were those with some property they needed to watch over. Many of them (Mayor Tobias Schwonauer included) were loyal Catholics who profited from the post-1620 changes and who were interested in maintaining the status quo. Typically, they enjoyed a high status within the city and thus appeared quite often on the pages of the chronicles, helping to generate the image of a loyal Catholic city. This image, however, hides a reality that was much more intricate.

The Swedes found themselves in a similarly complicated situation. Among their soldiers and officers there were Christians of all denominations. Although the vast majority of soldiers serving in the Swedish army professed the Augsburg faith, there were also many Roman Catholics or Calvinists. The attitude of the Swedish garrison towards the Catholic confession, and to the local monasteries, was often unclear and much more complex than it may have seemed. First of all, the Swedes and the monasteries maintained surprisingly active communication; in particular, the Swedish soldiers were very interested in the Franciscan friary. There was a well in the monastery which was said to have been blessed by John of Capistrano himself. According to legend, its water cured fever and other diseases. The soldiers would often come to collect the water from the monastery. Not only that – they would also request *Schedae B. Salvatoris*, slips of paper with a healing prayer for fever.[26] Puzzled, the Franciscan priest always provided them with the holy inscriptions. He wondered why, despite being Protestant, they desired for something they were supposed to consider "papist superstition".[27] The Swedish

24. *Archivum*, p. 37.

25. Zaczkovic, *Chronik Des Minoriten-Guardians*, pp. 98-104.

26. *Archivum*, p. 4. The origin of this devotional object was attributed to the Franciscan lay brother and healer, St Salvador of Horta. See: Bernardus Sannig, *Rituale Franciscanum, continens varias Absolutiones, Benedictiones, Conjurationes, Exorcismos, Ritus, ac alias Caeremonias Ecclesiasticas, ad utilitatem Christi fidelium et praxim Sacerdotum, maxime Ordinis S. Francisci ex variis Ritualibus coordinatum*, Neo-Pragae, Typis Joan Nicolai Hampelii, 1685, pp. 290-291.

27. In Dalmatia, Muslims would also come to Catholic priests to ask for a similar slip, called a '*zapis*'. Peter Burke, *Popular Culture in Early Modern Europe*, revised reprint, Aldershot, Scolar Press, 1994, p. 55. The Jesuits also used similar means in their missionary activities. See: Trevor Johnson, "Blood, Tears, and Xavier-Water: Jesuit Missionaries and Popular Religion in the Eighteenth-Century Upper Palatinate", in *Popular Religion in Germany and Central Europe, 1400-1800*, ed. by Robert W Scribner and Trevor Johnson, London, Macmillan, 1996, p. 195.

officers displayed a similar interest. Not only were the mendicant friaries exempted from the contribution obligation, often they even received food and other gifts from the commander or some of the officers. These were not only professed or closet Catholics, as evident from Meerstein's record in the Franciscan chronicle. When describing these gifts, Modestus noted that the noble donors "would not refer to what they were donating as the alms but as a gift of reverence [honorarium donatum, Eine Verehrung], like heretics".[28] In general, they also had fairly good knowledge of the Catholic world, partly acquired during military campaigns. This proved unfortunate for Fr Raphael, an Italian Conventual Friar Minor, who did not want to stay in the city any longer after two years of Swedish presence and decided to return home. He made thorough preparations for the journey, equipping himself with a new horse, a red jacket, and handsome riding boots with spurs. All dressed up, he was walking down the street shortly before leaving when he had the misfortune of running into the Swedish commander and several officers. The commander stopped the poor Italian and said: "Father! Surely this isn't what St Francis would wear?" And turning to his officers: "A Franciscan, I say!" He made him swap his new spurred boots with a soldier who had boots without spurs. The Conventual likewise lost his new jacket.[29] Although referring to the poverty of St Francis only served as a pretext, it is interesting that even the Swedish officer had a good idea of what a follower of the "pauper of Assisi" should look like.

The incident illustrates the importance attached to external markers. They could often identify which faith the person was considered to belong to. When the attempt to re-conquer Olomouc in 1644 left dozens of dead in the streets, some thought that Catholics and Protestants should be buried separately. It was a problem, however, to determine who had been of which faith in life, as belonging to an army was not a concrete indicator. In the end, soldiers who wore a cross, rosary or *Agnus Dei*, were buried as Catholics and the rest as Protestants.[30] However, these external features were hardly credible considering the partiality of the Swedish soldiers for devotional objects described above, as well as the fact that many of the dead had been robbed in the meantime.

These and similar reports show that "religious identity" of early modern Europeans could often be rather elusive. Instead of clearly defined categories with strict boundaries, it might be useful to see it as a "pole" – a perfect ideal to which individual participants (some more, some less) are attracted. There were many similar "identity" poles to which individuals were exposed, thus, adherence to a particular confession could agree or, on the contrary, collide with obligations to the ruler and other secular authorities, neighbours and community, traditions and customs.[31] The system of interlinking connections and loyalties was furthermore complicated by local relationships. While one neighbour could be "a cursed papist

28. *Archivum*, p. 34.

29. Zaczkovic, *Chronik Des Minoriten-Guardians*, p. 62.

30. *Ibid.*, p. 51.

31. Simone Laqua-O'Donnell, "Catholic Piety and Community", in *The Ashgate Research Companion to the Counter-Reformation*, ed. by Alexandra Bamji, Geert H Janssen, and Mary Laven, Farnham: Ashgate, 2013, p. 288.

or heretic", another neighbour of a different faith could be a close friend and godparent of one's children. Religious affiliation was, to a large extent, a fluid identity which changed with the situation, was repeatedly negotiated, and often intensified only at moments of confrontation. The affiliation manifested differently on different levels and in different situations, and these manifestations were not necessarily consistent and could contradict each other. The portraits of "Saint" Luther with a halo, Protestants seeking Catholic sacramentals, and Catholics blaspheming the Virgin Mary were not only anomalies or marginal curiosities, but an integral part of religious life.

Believers were, naturally, aware of the differences between the faiths. Religious boundaries were a recognised fact in the mid-seventeenth century. Problems occurred only when the believers themselves were asked to define the boundary and describe the differences between "us" and "them". External signs and an emphasis on the tradition of "the faith of our fathers" played a major role. Negative self-definition was also important, as well as the (often *ad hoc*) development of the image of the "other". Expectations of what a member of a different faith behaved like were often a more important factor than what a member of one's own faith did. Any such biases in relation to other confessions, and confusion regarding one's own belief, naturally did not mitigate confrontations.

3. *Conspiracy*

The interdependence of various identities and loyalties can be illustrated in the case of Franciscan priest Michael Jahn. By all accounts, he was a very interesting and controversial man. In 1635, he was removed from office as Provincial Definitor and Superior of the Prague Friary of Our Lady of the Snows, due to a serious accusation, the essence of which remains unknown. Jahn, however, appealed to Rome and managed to fully vindicate his reputation. On 20 February 1636, he was triumphantly restored to his office during the provincial chapter in Brno. The friar in charge of the chapter records wrote a note about malicious individuals wronging the innocent and bemoaned that this was nothing new in religious communities.[32] In 1641, Jahn became one of the lecturers of the newly opened philosophical studies at the Olomouc friary. His appointment once again led to a disagreement. This time, Jahn was brought back to the province from his studies in Italy by the Commissioner-General himself. He installed Jahn as a lecturer and ordered the province authorities to punish any brothers who would make objections after Jahn was re-admitted "to the bosom of the province".[33]

32. NA Prague, Bohemian Franciscan Archives, book 68, *Acta praecipua & notabilia conclusae in Capitulis Provincialibus et Diffinitoriis celebratis, Ab Anno 1614 ex Provinciae Protocollo excerpta – Statuta praecipua in Capitulis Provincialibus et Diffinitoriis facta ab Anno*, 1614-1759, p. 1.

33. *Archivum*, p. 31. This note suggests that Jahn may have gone to Italy to study without the permission of the superiors, and could have therefore been temporarily considered a renegade friar.

Whatever the truth about his Italian stay and return to the province, after the arrival of the Swedes, Jahn soon became the most important person in the Olomouc friary. Although the provincial chapter held in Znojmo in January 1643 appointed Fr Francisco Leo as the superior of St Bernardino, neither he nor the other appointed aids were able to take office due to the danger caused by the war. Jahn became the unofficial superior of the remaining friars.[34] By then, Olomouc was suffering from a lack of Catholic clergy, and some of the churches needed to be taken over. Jahn was charged with the cathedral, and so he and the rest of the monastic community moved to the abandoned building of the capitular deaconry. The main reason for Jahn's growing influence was, however, the fact that he had managed to befriend the commander of the Swedish garrison, George Paikul of Pomerania.[35] Frequently invited by Paikul to his residence, Jahn gradually won the favour and, over time, the confidence of Paikul, and, even some of his officers. He was so well-liked that he was even told some secret information and, in addition, many entrusted him with the valuables they had acquired during the campaign. The locals, namely the clergy, were not always appreciative of his close ties with the Swedes. Even Meerstein's chronicle is somewhat embarrassed to report that Paikul was "too intimate" with Jahn at festivities, sharing food with the friar. The Conventual Zaczkovic went even further as to accuse Jahn of setting the Swedes against the other friars, who then had to work on the fortifications. One reason for his hostility was the historic animosity between the Franciscans and the Conventuals, accompanied by competency disputes. Around this time, Jahn established contacts with the mother superior of the local monastery of Poor Clares, which had until then been overseen by Conventual superiors. Jahn tried to persuade the abbess to move the convent to the Franciscan province. Such attempts were common and typical for the coexistence of both the branches of the Order of Friars Minor from the very beginning of their division. From the Franciscan point of view, it was an attempt to spread reform to other institutions and to help revive the original Franciscan ideal. From the Conventual perspective, it was a mere appropriation and violation of an ancient system.[36]

Jahn's good relations with the commander annoyed not only other friars in the city, but also some of the Swedish officers, particularly the Lutheran pastor who ministered to the soldiers. Although he remains anonymous, the friary chronicle

34. *Archivum*, p. 36.

35. Modestus Meerstein believed that the good relations with the Swedish commander were due to the fact that Jahn allegedly came from Pomerania, which made him a compatriot of Paikul (*Commendantis conterraneus*) – *Archivum*, p. 36. Other sources of the order indeed sometimes refer to him as Father Michael Jahn Pomeranus. Yet other sources (specifically those reporting on him secondhand) distort his name to Pater Pomeranus or Pater Pommer. Zaczkovic refers to him as Michael Pomer. Zaczkovic, *Chronik Des Minoriten-Guardians*, p. 496. The Olomouc summary chronicle even speaks of Jahn as Petr Pumer. See: Josef Prucek, "Olomoucká souhrnná kronika z let 1432-1656 sestavená B. Dudíkem", in *Ročenka Okresního Archívu v Olomouci*, 1983, p. 176. In reality though, Jahn was from Pěná near Jindřichův Hradec in Bohemia (lat. Pomerium – hence "Pomeranus"). I am indebted to Petr Regalát Beneš OFM for this information.

36. Zaczkovic, *Chronik Des Minoriten-Guardians*, p. 508.

comments on the activities and conflicts he had with Michael Jahn. The first entry briefly describes how the pastor, out of contempt or ignorance, wore the decorated chasuble from St Maurice Church inside out when preaching. The other entry gives more detail. It tells the story of the pastor losing a host on his way to see a dying person. He dropped the host, without noticing, and hurried on. A devout woman – clearly a Catholic, the wife of a local cobbler – saw it and called out to him to return for the host. The pastor snapped at her, telling her it was none of her business and that he could easily have a new one made. And yet, he told his aid to hand it to him and then went on. Shocked, the woman ran to tell Father Michael. He wasted no time and saw the commander the very same day, vividly describing (*exaggeravit*) what had happened. Such a lack of respect for the Eucharist (and in particular the fact that Catholics had witnessed the whole action) sent the commander into such a fury that, in an outburst of anger, he ordered the pastor to sit astride a wooden ass as his punishment. It was only thanks to the intervention of the other officers, who eventually managed to calm the commander, that the pastor was spared the punishment and public humiliation. The incident turned Jahn and the pastor into irreconcilable enemies. Their disputes continued and before long, they shifted from the verbal level to the physical level. One day, Jahn was talking to an Imperial trumpeter at the commander's residence, who had arrived in the city to negotiate. Suddenly the pastor came in and allegedly began to berate Jahn for being a damned idolater until he physically attacked and punched Father Michael. The Franciscan was, nonetheless, stronger. He grabbed the pastor by his hair and pushed him to the ground. Fortunately, the nearby officers managed to pacify the two priests and prevented further violence. The commander had no doubts that the pastor was the only culprit in the brawl and threatened him with severe punishment should he ever enter his home again.[37]

Jahn's position seemed unassailable. Many people sought his help, which only strengthened his position as an intermediary between the burghers and the Swedes. Nothing changed even after 1644, the year the Emperor's army under the command of Ladislav of Waldstein drew near to win the city back. The Swedes trusted Jahn so much that they even let him collect alms in the Imperial camp, which had better supplies. The besieged city was starving, and it was extremely difficult to obtain any kind of alms. The Swedish officers in all likelihood also reckoned that the Franciscan would mention – whether deliberately or unintentionally – what he had seen in the Imperial camp upon his return and thus unwittingly become their spy. After one of his trips, Jahn indeed told the Swedes about the Imperial plan to launch a massive attack near the Church of St Blaise. The Swedes concentrated most of their forces there, and after a fierce battle, the attack was thwarted. They would soon see, though, that they were wrong about Father Michael, having underestimated his abilities and overestimated his loyalty. While the Swedes were focused on the St Blaise attack, Jahn managed to smuggle 1,100 Imperial soldiers into the city on the night of 19 October 1644, behind the backs of the unsuspecting Swedes: 600 to the capitular dean's palace, 200 to

37. *Archivum*, p. 35-36.

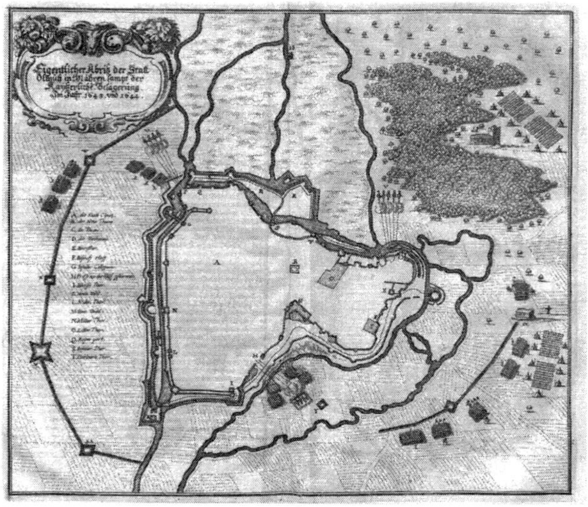

Fig. 7.Olomouc besieged by the Imperial Army (1643-44) in Merian's *Theatrum Europaeum.* Regional Museum in Olomouc, M. Merian 1650, inv. no. V 396.

the bishop's residence, and 300 to a mill belonging to one of the local hospitals. The detachment in the bishop's residence played the key role, as it was supposed to secure advanced points in the city (especially the New Gate separating the castle district from the city centre), thus covering the other detachments who were to occupy the Castle Gate and let the rest of the army into the city. This detailed, sophisticated plan unexpectedly failed, however. The commander of the detachment in the bishop's residence was apparently to blame, hesitating so long to attack that his soldiers lost their cover.[38]

The Swedes immediately attacked the residence and forced the Imperial army to retreat. The remaining units tried to conquer the Castle Gate, but the element of surprise had been wasted. The Swedish Reiters gradually sent the isolated groups of soldiers fleeing. In the end the Swedes also conquered the deaconry. A large number of soldiers were decimated, and the rest fled for their lives. Michael Jahn and several burghers involved in the conspiracy joined the fleeing crowd, for obvious reasons. Furious, the Swedes plundered St Bernardino in retaliation, taking away all the mattresses and blankets from the cells, among other things. The church and the sacristy were spared, although this is where the Swedes could have done the greatest damage and gained valuable loot. Meerstein wrote in his chronicle that the Swedish soldiers explained that they had had bad experiences with looting sacred sites, which, as a rule, would bring bad luck. Apart from the fear of God's punishment, Gustavus Adolphus' ban on sanctuary looting, widely observed, appears to have played a role.[39] This "inspection" of the Franciscan

38. Prucek, "Olomoucká souhrnná kronika", p. 176.

39. The prohibition of looting Catholic churches is discussed by Peter Englund, *Nepokojná Léta: Historie Třicetileté Války*, trans. by Dagmar Hartlová and Luděk Mandaus, Prague, Lidové noviny, 2000, p. 172.

monastery only increased the fury of the Swedish commanders, as they failed to find out what happened to the valuables the officers had entrusted Jahn with. The only remaining Franciscan, lay brother Didacus, was sent to the Imperial camp to tell Jahn that the friary would be razed to the ground unless he returned the treasures. Jahn had no choice but to submit, and Brother Didacus returned with the eagerly anticipated answer that the valuables were hidden in the church under a tombstone.

The conspiracy planned by Michael Jahn drew a great deal of attention. The whole event is described by a number of sources, including the monumental work *Theatrum Evropaeum*.[40] No wonder, as this was the most important attempt to recapture the city. The Imperial troops tried several more times to conquer the city by frontal assault. On 11 November, after seven o'clock in the evening, in the dark, a few soldiers managed to get over the city walls (near the Franciscan monastery, incidentally) and enter the city, where they were all killed. Ladislav of Waldstein gave up and decided to starve the city instead. This tactic eventually failed as well, because after more than seven months of siege he was ordered to quickly march off to help besieged Brno on 9 March 1645. The Swedes thus kept Olomouc until the end of the war.

The siege, and the unsuccessful conspiracy in particular, transformed the *modus vivendi* of those in the city. The status of the remaining friars suffered a sharp decline. They understandably adopted a very reserved attitude to what Michael Jahn had done; Zaczkowicz and his chronicle even accused Jahn of being irresponsible.[41] He had his reasons. The monasteries were searched and he himself was physically attacked. All the friars were pressured to take an oath of loyalty, and after they refused, they were charged with a high *contributio*: altogether two thousand thalers a month.[42] They were, however, unable to pay such a high amount. The inability to meet this requirement was a welcome excuse for property seizures in monastic buildings, followed by the expulsion of friars, which took place on 15 October 1645.[43] Although the measure was never diligently observed, and some friars were allowed to return, the conditions of the first phase of the occupation were never restored. The only friars to remain in the city on a permanent basis were the Franciscan lay brother Didacus and Paulinus Zaczkowicz, mentioned above. There was an overall decline in public manifestations of religious life, and the city's population continued to drop, the buildings began to dilapidate, and both the sides suffered from exhaustion.

This status quo lasted another four long years until the end of the Thirty Years' War. Then one evening, a large flock of storks arrived in the city, settling on

40. Mattheum Merian, *Theatri Evropaei, Fünffter Theil. Das Ist Außführliche Beschreibung Aller Denckwürdigen Geschichten Die Sich in Europa ... Vom Jahr 1643. Biß in Gegenwärtiges 1647. Jahr Allerseits Begeben Und Verlauffen*, Franckfurt am Mayn, 1651, pp. 533-535.

41. Zaczkovic, *Chronik Des Minoriten-Guardians*, p. 50.

42. The Jesuits and the friary had to pay a total of 800 thalers, the Dominicans and the Franciscans 300 each, the Capuchins and the Conventuals 110 each, and the Dominicans and the Poor Clares 200 thalers each. Zaczkovic, *Chronik Des Minoriten-Guardians*, pp. 54-57.

43. Prucek, "Olomoucká souhrnná kronika", p. 177.

the rooftops of the canon residences. They took off the next morning to continue their journey up north.[44] The storks allegedly announced the departure of the Swedes, just as, years before, the mice had been harbingers of their arrival. News of peace agreements reached Olomouc on 24 November 1648. The city once again resounded with the ringing of bells. Bell ringing had been forbidden, as the Swedes feared that the burghers would use it to give signs to the Imperial army. Both the Catholic and the Protestant churches celebrated thanksgiving masses on 11 January. The tension in the city abated somewhat, and the Swedish commander tried to adopt a friendlier attitude to the rest of the population. He even expressed the wish to see a proper "papist" Corpus Christi procession prior to his departure. The Conventual superior Zaczkowicz was happy to grant him his wish. Together with another priest, two Capuchins, and the Franciscan lay brother Didacus, they prepared everything with great care and enthusiasm. The city council called for all the guilds to attend and bring their guild flags, hitherto hidden in churches and cellars. Four altars were erected on the Upper Square and the city was decorated with branches. The beginning of the celebration, however, was marred by a sudden change in weather. Just as the procession was formed, the sky clouded over, the first flashes of lightning appeared, and it began to rain. When the procession arrived at the first altar and the priest began to read the gospel, the rain ceased. As soon as the procession moved again, it started to rain again, but when it reached the second altar it cleared up. The same happened with the third altar. At a time when such phenomena were perceived as manifestations of God's will and supernatural interference, the course of this procession must have provoked high expectations and hopes in many participants – the miracle and triumph of true faith seemed to be near. At the fourth altar, however, the storm reached its full vigour. Participants in the procession and the audience scattered. Running away, some threw down the guild flags, seriously damaging them. Drenched, the priests had to exert great efforts to complete the worship. Once the devotions were over, the storm ceased, and the sky became clear. The Swedes watched the scene from the windows, and their laughter was supposedly louder than the accompanying music. Even Zaczkowicz, the organiser of the procession, referred in his chronicle to this event as a comedy.[45]

Modestus Meerstein arrived at the city a few weeks after the storm. It took almost another year for the Swedish soldiers to leave, though. The reparations took a long time to pay, and so the Swedes left for good as late as early July 1650. The occupation symbolically concluded with the reconsecration of the cathedral and later the other churches. On 24 July, a thanksgiving procession was held leading from St Maurice to the newly consecrated cathedral, where a *Te Deum* was celebrated.[46] The weather was fair, unlike the case of the preceding procession. The whole ceremony, however, was more than just a gesture of gratitude for being finally delivered from the Swedish yoke. It was also a public ritual held to purge the local sanctuaries and public space from the previous desecration by heretics,

44. Zaczkovic, *Chronik Des Minoriten-Guardians*, pp. 597-598.
45. *Ibid.*, pp. 152-153.
46. *Ibid.*, pp. 160-161.

and to manifest that the city was once again purified, united, and thoroughly Catholic.[47] The Franciscan friary of St Bernardino and its missionary work thus entered a new stage. The local Franciscans would now work in an environment that was, at least officially, homogeneous in faith for the first time since their arrival in Olomouc (and would do so almost until the abolition of the friary).

47. For more on processions and the collective identity of confessionalized towns, see: Heinz Schilling, "Urban Architecture and Ritual in Confessional Europe", in *Religion and Cultural Exchange in Europe, 1400-1700*, ed. by Heinz Schilling and István György Tóth, Cambridge, Cambridge University Press, 2006, pp. 131-132.

2. Renewal

Two months after the Olomouc thanksgiving procession, the first post-war chapter of the Bohemian Franciscan Province assembled in Znojmo, presided by Maxentius ab Arco, Commissioner-General for Germania. The main agenda was an overall restoration of the province, and, in particular, the appointment of reliable friars as superiors of the individual friaries so as to guarantee the success of the whole process. The former Olomouc conspirator Michael Jahn was appointed the Minister Provincial.[1] Modestus Meerstein was confirmed as the superior of the St Bernardino.[2] With seventeen Franciscans already living in Olomouc, Meerstein faced the difficult task of repairing the friary, securing a livelihood for his confreres, and above all, integrating them into the city organism. This was not the first time the Franciscans had returned to Olomouc and started from scratch. St Bernardino had witnessed various turns of events since it was established in 1453. The most challenging period was the 1570s. The Franciscan province was experiencing a profound crisis; the numbers of friars were dropping, and Franciscans were abandoning one house after another. Eventually, the crisis also afflicted Olomouc, even though it was one of the oldest and most important houses in the province. In 1571, the friary was vacated and handed over to the Olomouc bishop. It would not be restored until 1593, when the new friars had to start afresh under strikingly different conditions. This twenty-two-year-long gap closes the medieval history of the friary and opens a new phase.[3]

1. *Capistrano's legacy*

The devastating crisis that hit the Bohemian Province was caused mostly by the Reformation seeping into Bohemian Lands. Another significant reason for the

1. In 1656, Jahn was ordained a bishop by Cardinal Adalbert von Harrach. He became the last bishop in Duvno (Bosnia-Herzegovina). Jahn visited this war-ravaged diocese, but was soon forced to leave. He died in Bosnia in 1663. I am indebted to Petr Regalát Beneš OFM for this information.

2. *Archivum*, p. 38.

3. For more on the province in the sixteenth century, see: Klemens Minařík, "Provinciálové františkánské české provincie v letech 1517-1600", *Sborník Historického Kroužku*, 17 (1916): passim.

crisis was the structure and the character of the Bohemian Franciscan Province. The foundation for the province was laid in the mid-fifteenth century, during the mission of John of Capistrano.[4] Accompanied by twelve brethren and an armed suite, Capistrano travelled through Vienna to Moravia, touring Brno, Olomouc, and Znojmo on the way. From there he continued to Bohemia, where he only visited the peripheral parts ruled by Catholic lords, and later to the nearby imperial cities and to Silesia. In July 1454, he returned briefly to Olomouc, and from there he continued his journey to Hungary, which culminated with his death (23 October 1456), after the successful defence of Belgrade. The aim of his Bohemian mission was primarily to drive the Utraquist (i.e. Hussite) Bohemians back to the Roman Church. In addition to negotiations with local Catholic leaders and polemics with Utraquist clergy, Capistrano relied heavily on his own spectacular sermons to trigger a wave of conversions.[5]

And yet, despite reports sent by Capistrano himself and accounts given by his legendists, the outcome of the mission was somewhat ambiguous.[6] The introduction of the Franciscan Observance to the Bohemian Lands, however, proved much more promising. By then, the Observant movement had met with great success in Italy. Thanks to charismatic figures such as Bernardino of Siena and John of Capistrano, the reform movement within the Order of Friars Minor quickly spread and gained popularity, as evident also from the almost instant canonisation of Bernardino of Siena in 1450, a mere six years after his death. The Observants were drawing attention even outside Italy and Capistrano, as the Vicar General was commissioned to promote the movement beyond the Alps. Friaries advocating strict observance (often led by Capistrano's disciples) became missionary centres that would continue to fight Utraquism even after Capistrano's departure, as Capistrano himself had allegedly prophesied.[7]

At that time, the original network of monasteries of the Order of Friars Minor, built gradually since the thirteenth century, still existed. Although most of the houses had survived the Hussite wars, they belonged to an unreformed branch of the order and were thus deemed unacceptable by Capistrano. There were, in short, two ways to implement the Observant reform. The first was to use the network of monasteries of the Order of Friars Minor to introduce reform into the existing houses. This would require the local communities to adopt stricter statutes,

4. Giovanni Hofer, *Giovanni da Capestrano: Una vita spesa nella lotta per la riforma della Chiesa*, l'Aquila, Provincia dei Frati Minori d'Abruzzo, 1955, pp. 383-459. More recently, Petr Regalát Beneš, "San Giovanni da Capestrano e gli inizi dell'oservanza francescana in Boemia e Moravia", in *Cultura, società e vita religiosa ai tempi di S. Giovanni da Capestrano: Atti del V convegno storico internazionale: Capestrano, 21-22 ottobre 2002*, ed. by Edith Pasztor, Capestrano, Centro studi S. Giovanni da Capestrano, 2003, pp. 109-141.

5. František Šmahel, "*Spectaculum fidei* českomoravské mise Jana Kapistrána", *Z kralické tvrze*, 14, 1987, pp. 15-19.

6. Jan Stejskal, "A Catholic City in the Hussite Era, 1400-1450s", in *The Transformation of Confessional Cultures in a Central European City: Olomouc, 1400-1750*, ed. by Antonín Kalous, Roma, Viella, 2015, p. 36.

7. Amandus Hermann, *Capistranus Triumphans: Seu Historia Fundamentalis de Sancto Joanne Capistrano*, Coloniae, apud Balthasarum Joachimum Endterum, 1700, p. 296.

submit to the authority of Observant superiors and, last but not least, relinquish their privileges and give up any earthly possessions. While some friars might have been tempted by the idea, it was very unlikely that the entire community would accept it.[8] Such attempts met with fierce resistance and often failed. This was the experience, for example, of Olivier Maillard, the Vicar General of the Ultramontane branch (covering the western part of Europe), who tried to introduce the reform in the Conventual Franciscan monastery in Paris in 1502. The local community rebelled against him, and Maillard was forced to ask two local bishops for help. This must have been embarrassing, as the plea clearly showed that Maillard was powerless. Moreover, he was dragging an external authority into internal decision-making, which had always been considered a dangerous limitation of the sovereignty of the order. On top of this, it soon transpired that even the bishops' help would not suffice. When the bishops visited the monastery after sending prior notice, the local friars welcomed them by singing antiphons and litanies. However, whenever the bishops stood up to read the reform decree, the friars burst into singing another piece and thus successfully prevented the bishops from speaking. After four hours of musical production, the bishops finally gave up. They succeeded only the next day, when escorted by a company of royal archers.[9]

The other option to introduce the Observant reform was to establish new Observant houses that would counterbalance the "fallen" monasteries. This was the preferred strategy, even at the risk of threatening the unity of the order. On 14 October 1449, Pope Nicholas V authorised Capistrano to found twenty friaries in the transalpine regions and incorporate them into the Cismontane (Eastern) congregation of the Observants.[10] The Capistrano's friars were a new and attractive religious community that soon gained a number of supporters, often at the expense of other orders. Yet the foundation of a new monastery was always a complicated task. The superiors of the order had to make sure that there would be enough benefactors not only to sponsor the construction of the monastery, but also – and above all – to guarantee the sustainability of the religious community. In general, there were two ways to achieve this. The first was to secure funds from an aristocratic patron. Such a patron would build a monastery in town on one of his estates and also set up a foundation to support at least some friars: typically nine

8. Observance was not the only reform movement to find its way beyond the Alps. The Saxon province, for example, saw the rise of a moderate movement advocating for the constitutions of Martin V (*Constitutiones Martinianae*, partly written, ironically enough, by Capistrano). The two movements clashed in particular in Lusatia and Silesia. See: Ludovic Viallet, *Les sens de l'observance: Enquete sur les reformes franciscaines entre l'Elbe et l'Oder, de Capistran a Luther (vers 1450-vers 1520),* Berlin, LIT Verlag, 2014.

9. This motif was used by François Rabelais, himself a former Franciscan, in his novel *Gargantua and Pantagruel* (Garg. XXVII). See: Alban John Krailsheimer, *Rabelais and the Franciscans*, Oxford, Clarendon Press, 1963, pp. 13-14.

10. Petr Hlaváček, *Čeští františkáni na přelomu středověku a novověku,* Prague, Academia, 2005, p. 29. For general information on the Franciscan Observance, see: *A Companion to Observant Reform in the Late Middle Ages and Beyond*, ed. by James Mixson and Bert Roest, Leiden, Brill, 2015.

priests and three lay brothers. In exchange, the friars were obligated to provide pastoral care and regularly say Masses for the sponsor and his family.

The other option to secure a friary was to negotiate its foundation in one of the royal cities. This was always a very appealing prospect for mendicants, as large cities were their main sphere of activity. In such cases, the city gave the order a plot of land (typically outside of the city walls in the suburbs) and the construction of the house was financed from donations by local citizens and institutions. The friars who came to live in the monastery had to make a living by begging in the city and the nearby area. This method of foundation, however, required favourably inclined citizens in both the city and its surroundings, which was not always the case in Utraquist Bohemia. Therefore, in Bohemia the friars had to rely on the former scenario; most of the friaries in the fifteenth century were founded with the help of the aristocracy (Kadaň, Tachov, Jindřichův Hradec).[11] The latter scenario was adopted in Moravia and Silesia, where the local population mostly spoke German and hence were unaffected by the Hussite movement. It was in these regions that the Franciscan Observants found the most enthusiastic support and where they established their major strongholds (with the Breslau friary being the central house of the province for a long time). This pattern, however, had fatal consequences. First, the German background of the province greatly complicated and weakened the missionary activities countering the Czech Utraquists. For example, Olomouc had the first Czech preacher appointed as late as 1495, more than forty years after the friary had been founded.[12] Second, the focus on the German-speaking inhabitants of Moravian and Silesian towns led to a sudden decline of the province in the second quarter of the sixteenth century. It was this section of the population that was captivated by Luther's ideas, and the Observants suddenly lost their most influential patrons. In addition, the new reform movement met with a positive response even among the friars themselves, and their network of friaries significantly contributed to spreading the reform.[13]

The Olomouc friary was no exception and its history closely followed the fate of the province as a whole. John of Capistrano arrived in Olomouc on 18 August 1451, having visited Vienna and Brno. He preached first in front of the cathedral, then in the square, and eventually – allegedly the square was not able to accommodate all the spectators – on a plain outside the city walls, in a place called

11. The friary in Pilsen was an exception due to the fact that the city was prevalently Catholic and that the Observants had merely taken over the local Conventual friary. On the other hand, the attempt to establish a house in Prague came to nothing, although the "heretic king" George of Poděbrady himself helped to establish it. See: "O trojím těžkém začínání františkánů observantů v Praze (1460-68, 1482-83 a 1604-11)", in *Historia Franciscana II.*, ed. by Petr Regalát Beneš and Petr Hlaváček, Kostelní Vydří, Karmelitánské nakladatelství, 2005, pp. 66-104.

12. Klemens Minařík, "Vikáři české františkánské provincie od r. 1451 do r. 1517", *Sborník Historického kroužku*, 16 (1915), p. 2.

13. For the history of the Franciscan Observance in Central Europe, see: Beneš, "San Giovanni da Capestrano", pp. 109-141; Hlaváček, *Čeští františkáni*, and later *Die Böhmischen Franziskaner im ausgehenden Mittelalter: Studien zur Kirchen- und Kulturgeschichte Ostmitteleuropas*, Stuttgart, F. Steiner, 2011; and Viallet, *Les sens de l'observance*, passim.

Fig. 8. John of Capistrano as the defender of Belgrade, 1456. Fresco in the choir of the church of the Immaculate Conception of the Virgin Mary. Museum of Fine Arts, photo: Zdeněk Sodoma.

Pilten (in Czech Bělidla – literally the Bleaching spot). He preached as usual against usury, extravagance, luxury and games, but above all, against Utraquism, specifically against the Compacts of Basel and communion under both kinds. Although he preached in Latin, and the speech needed to be subsequently translated into German and Czech, his performance was so spellbinding that he supposedly moved much of the audience to tears. It is possible that this is not merely a traditional legend stereotype spread by his supporters. The combination of personal charisma, lively gesticulation, and a variety of visual aids (especially the trigram **yhs**, the name of Jesus) made Capistrano's preaching a truly extraordinary experience. The power of this *ars praedicandi* was further nourished by the rumour of Capistrano's sanctity and the expectations of potential miracles. Capistrano would not disappoint his audience in this area either. People around him claimed that he had miraculously healed (using the biretta or blood of Bernardino of Siena) almost a hundred people in Olomouc. It was said that about three thousand people returned to the Catholic Church, moved by his preaching and the miracles he performed.[14]

14. Štěpán Kohout, "Pobyt Jana Kapistrana v Olomouci", in *Ročenka Státního Okresního Archívu v Olomouci*, Olomouc, SOA Olomouc, 1995, 117-140.

Capistrano spent less than three weeks in Olomouc before returning to Brno. Before he left, however, he tried to negotiate support for establishing one of his friaries, which is quite obvious from the filiation charter he granted to Olomouc burghers.[15] Capistrano administered several such filiations on his travels to selected individuals, monastic communities, and cities.[16] It was an effective tool serving to promote the settling of Observants and create strong links with the local society.[17] The recipients of the filiation charter gained a share in all the devotions and spiritual benefits (all masses, fasts, pilgrimages, prayers, etc.) of the Observant friars of the emerging Transalpine province; provided, of course, that the city and its residents materially supported the Franciscan community.

The immediate response to the filiation and the details of negotiations concerning the foundation of a friary are unknown. The provincial chronicle implies that the first friars sent to build a local community arrived at the city on Candlemas of 1453. Three months later, on 13 May 1453, the abbot of the Hradisko monastery Nicolas Rus, on behalf of Bishop John Ház, consecrated the foundation stone of the new monastery. He did so outside the city walls, at the place of Capistrano's last and greatest sermon. This area between the city walls and one of the branches of the Morava River was alternately settled and abandoned in the past depending on the changing water regime of the river. As the city was being founded, this area was deemed unsuitable for permanent settlement and remained outside the city walls. In the fifteenth century, this area was still abandoned, but probably less swampy, and so it was possible to begin construction.[18] The allocated piece of land was of considerable symbolic value to the friars. Not only was it a place sanctified by Capistrano's sermon, but with its *extra muros* status it fulfilled the ideal of an Observant house. It was located on the periphery, as opposed to the old monasteries of unreformed orders within the city walls. The Observant monastery was, in all likelihood, the first building in this area, and soon inspired the construction of several burgher houses in its vicinity. In 1526, in fear of the Ottoman Turks, the entire suburb was walled in and fully incorporated in the city proper. Nonetheless, later on there were doubts as to whether the site was suitable at all, and the friary's inhabitants repeatedly complained of the unbearable humidity threatening their health.

Three years later, on 25 July 1454, John of Capistrano returned for a short visit to Olomouc, and he was able to see for himself the latest developments in the city. Construction work had only just begun and completion was nowhere in sight, yet his followers in the city had managed to secure a fairly decent status. Although they were still living in temporary accommodations, sufficient alms and generous support from secular and church authorities guaranteed that Olomouc would become an important Observant centre. Its significance was also recog-

15. The text is in *Archivum*, p. 198.

16. Jaroslav Dřímal, "K brněnskému pobytu a filiačním listům Jana Kapistrána", *Časopis Matice moravské*, 63, 4 (1939-1940), pp. 374-391.

17. Viallet, *Les sens de l'observance*, pp. 159-201.

18. The church itself was built on the top of a natural dune formed by alluvium – I owe this information to Dr Josef Bláha.

Fig. 9. Trigram yhs on the façade of the civic house in Ostružnická street 22. Olomouc, Museum of Fine Arts, photo: Zdeněk Sodoma.

nised by the fact that Olomouc was chosen as the venue for the next chapter of the Transalpine Province in 1455. Moreover, while visiting the premises, Capistrano supposedly sanctified the monastery well, whose water was then considered to possess healing power.[19] The well was then of great importance for the Olomouc friary, because – unlike the original Brno friary (demolished in 1644) – this house could not boast a cell where Capistrano had stayed.

Similarly, the Christograms, made up of a minuscule trigram of the letters **yhs** (or eventually **ihs**), and usually surrounded by twelve or twenty-four rays, were important. These trigrams were actively promoted by Bernardino of Siena and John of Capistrano and soon became the "logo" of the Franciscan Observance.[20] Although it was a rather complex symbol with many possible interpretations (including the somewhat naive attempts to link this symbol to the Jewish Kabbalah), it quickly became popular among lay people thanks to its visual simplicity and appeal. The trigram soon became a popular apotropaic symbol, put on houses and various objects or drawn on a piece of paper and worn as a personal talisman. Following Capistrano's visit, several of these signs appeared in Olomouc, installed on objects, buildings, and in the public space. Four of them are documented as existing until as late as the eighteenth century: three on houses and one on the gate to Pilten – the latter allegedly made by Capistrano himself.[21] There must have

19. *Archivum*, p. 4.

20. This trigram is also typical for the iconography of Bernardino of Siena and John of Capistrano. Engelbert Kirschbaum and Wolfgang Braunfels, *Lexikon Der Christlichen Ikonographie*, 8 Bde, Rom, Freiburg, Basel, Wien, Herder, 1994, passim. See also: Lina Bolzoni, *The Web of Images: Vernacular Preaching From Its Origins to St Bernardino Da Siena*, trans. by Carole Preston and Lisa Chien, Aldershot, Ashgate, 2003, pp 3-4.

21. Hermann, *Capistranus Triumphans*, pp. 804-805.

been many more originally. A restoration survey of the friary's church discovered another sign, carved into the plaster right next to the triumphal arch.[22]

The survey of the church also uncovered another artefact pointing to Capistrano's much darker side. After one of the great stones paving the area in front of the main altar was lifted, it was found that its underside was covered with Hebrew inscriptions, and that the stone had been actually retrieved from the abolished Jewish cemetery in Olomouc. Capistrano's mission had significantly revived anti-Judaism and led to open hostilities towards Jews, which culminated in the burning of forty people in Breslau. In Moravia, Capistrano's sermons had not resulted in similar bloodshed; nonetheless King Ladislaus banished Jews from the royal cities by royal decree, issued on 22 July 1454 (three days before Capistrano returned to Olomouc). While, for example, the city of Uherské Hradiště defied the decree, Olomouc drove out the Jewish community and closed down its ghetto. It was probably then that one of the tombstones was symbolically set as a witness of the "victory over the synagogue" in the floor of the emerging Franciscan church, so that the priest saying the mass stood directly on it.[23]

It is not known whether the friary profited directly from the expulsion of the Jewish community, but the mere fact that all the debts of the burghers to Jewish creditors were subsequently waived could have been a significant incentive for donations to the friars. In any case, support from the burghers did not drop and construction continued, slowly but surely.[24] The continued interest of the city's inhabitants in the Franciscan Observance is also evident in the fact that in 1462, Olomouc was one of the proponents of Capistrano's beatification. Papal Legate Laurentius Rovarella eventually consecrated the monastery church on 28 August 1468. The celebration had considerable political significance as King Matthias Corvinus attended it.[25] The new church was dedicated to the Immaculate Conception of the Virgin Mary (probably the first *patrocinium* of this type in the Bohemian Lands) and to Bernardino of Siena. This church was built in the Luxembourg Gothic style – its historicising and simple architecture was probably meant to reflect the order's ideals of poverty. The Observant church, however, soon became a centre of artistic activity, clearly devout and propagandistic. The most prominent of these works is a large fresco on the northern, gospel side of the presbytery. A Hungarian artist probably made it in haste during one of the visits of Matthias

22. Ivo Hlobil, "Bernardinské symboly Jména Ježíš v Českých zemích šířené Janem Kapistránem", *Umění*, 44 (1996), pp. 223-234.

23. Marcin Wodziński, "Středověké židovské náhrobky na Moravě", in *Židé a Morava: Sborník příspěvků přednesených na konferenci konané 10. listopadu 1999 v Muzeu Kroměřížska*, Kroměříž, Muzeum Kroměřížska, 1999, pp. 8-17. Cf. J. M. Minty, "*Judengasse* to Christian Quarter: The Phenomenon of the Converted Synagogue in the Late Medieval and Early Modern Holy Roman Empire", in *Popular Religion in Germany and Central Europe, 1400-1800*, ed. by Robert W Scribner and Trevor Johnson, London, Macmillan, 1996, p. 85.

24. Kohout, "Pobyt Jana Kapistrana v Olomouci", p. 130.

25. Antonín Kalous, *Matyáš Korvín (1443-1490). Uherský a český král*, České Budějovice, Veduta, 2009, p. 214.

Corvinus to Olomouc.[26] It is a monumental black line drawing on a white background, capturing the successful defence of Belgrade in 1456 along with its main protagonists: John of Capistrano and John Hunyadi, the father of Matthias Corvinus.[27] During the next half-century, several other frescoes reflecting the order's spirituality were made. They portrayed St Francis and other saints (including a large fresco of St Christopher dated 1520) and, above all, the highly skilled Passion of Jesus (Carrying of the Cross and the Deposition from the Cross) and the rosary image of the Virgin Mary.[28] The monastery also produced a number of illuminated manuscripts for its own purposes and for other church institutions.

2. *Returns*

In the 1490s, Jan Filipec, bishop of Oradea, supporter and later a member of the order, had the friary rebuilt so that it became one of the largest houses in the province. Provincial chapters were held here several times, and in 1526 Olomouc became the centre of the Moravian *custodia* (Pilsen was the centre of the Bohemian *custodia* and Nysa of the Silesian one).[29] Soon, however, the friary faced the first signs of a crisis. One of the first preachers of the Reformation in Olomouc emerged from their very own ranks. Brother Rafael of Breslau began to preach Luther's ideas and allegedly defamed his religious community by meeting with women and his followers.[30] Sometime in early 1525, the superior decided to take action against the renegade brother. Not only did they bar him from preaching, but they also imprisoned him in a monastic cell. These measures did not stay a secret for very long. The disappearance of the preacher only further escalated tensions and the radicalisation of his followers. On Shrove Tuesday, a crowd of about two hundred armed guild members and journeymen tore into the friary, and demanded the release of their beloved preacher, threatening to use force. The hastily summoned councillors managed to pacify the crowd, but only with great difficulty.[31] The friars were thus spared the fate that, in 1611 (also during Carnival,

26. Milan Togner, "Gotická kresba na Moravě", in *Od gotiky k renesanci: Výtvarná kultura Moravy a Slezska 1400-1550*, ed. by Ivo Hlobil a Marek Perůtka, vol. 3, Olomouc, Muzeum umění Olomouc, 1999, pp. 490-496 dates the fresco to 1479.

27. Antonín Kalous, "Between Hussitism and Reformation, 1450s-1520s", in *The Transformation of Confessional Cultures*, pp. 55-59.

28. Ivo Hlobil, "K ikonologii, symbolice a významu růžencového obrazu v kostele Neposkvrněného Početí Panny Marie v Olomouci-Bělidlech", *Sborník Památkové péče Severomoravského kraje*,1 (1971): pp. 9-16. More recently Antonín Kalous, "Declaratio Brevis Corone Immaculate Virginis: a Source for the Late Medieval Popular Piety", *Umění*, 55 (2007), pp. 40-44.

29. Minařík, "Provinciálové františkánské české provincie v letech 1517-1600", p. 9.

30. For similar cases, see: Robert W Scribner, *Popular Culture and Popular Movements in Reformation Germany*, London, The Hambeldon Press, 1987, p. 157.

31. Later, Rafael left the order for his hometown of Breslau (where he probably became a preacher). National Museum Library, Manuscript Collection, sign. VIII F 75, *Chronica Fratrum Minorum de Observantia Provinciae Bohemiae*, 15th-18th century, p. 310. The commotion

although under much more dramatic circumstances caused by the invasion of the Passau troops) hit the community of the Prague friary of the Virgin Mary of the Snows: all fourteen friars present in the house were slaughtered.[32] Yet this event was a breaking point in the developments of the friary. Together with other Moravian and Silesian cities, Olomouc had for a long time been a significant stronghold against Utraquism and one of the most important footholds of the Observant province. Now, the German-speaking population was increasingly championing Reformed teachings, the goals of which were even more radical than those of the Utraquism.

This naturally affected the life of the Olomouc Bernardines (the term favoured by the German-speaking population, in contrast to the Czech *bosáci* or 'barefoots'). As mentioned earlier, the Olomouc friary, like other Moravian houses, could not rely on funds from the nobility and depended mainly on the immediate support of the local community. Any crises and fluctuations in public opinion could have a significant impact on the subsistence of the religious community. Although almsgiving and mass stipends persisted for a while, the situation gradually began to worsen until it forced the Franciscans to make serious concessions. The most distinct of these was an agreement concluded with the city council on 29 September 1541. Based on the contract, the friars transferred part of the monastic garden to the city, with the condition that the city waived their taxes. The agreement included a clause that the Franciscans would be given the land back if they demand it in the future. It therefore imposed no restriction or threat to the existence of the monastery. The extensive garden was a luxury the friars could not afford in the given circumstances, and not having to pay the taxes must have been a welcome relief.

At first glance, it was an advantageous transaction – if it were not for one circumstance that was rather unpleasant and humiliating for the Franciscans. By this time, a considerable part of the citizens had leaned toward the Reformation, which led to increasingly frequent conflicts between burghers and the bishop of Olomouc. Because Olomouc was a royal city, the bishop had limited powers to intervene in the city. One of the few pressure tactics he could use in conflicts with the ever-growing Lutheran community was the refusal of funerals on the holy ground of parish churches and adjacent cemeteries. The city council tried to respond to this pressure by establishing a new cemetery beyond the city walls. The acquisition of the Franciscan garden, however, allowed for funerals to take place directly in the city, which was a great success in the confessional clashes. Non-Catholics

triggered by the arrest of the preacher is also described in one of the Olomouc chronicles, see: SOA Olomouc, Olomouc Archives – books, inv. no. 5701, sign. 1738, *Memorabilia Metropolis Moraviae Olomucensis. Extract aus einen uralten Manuscripto (1432-1614). - Denckwürdige Sachen, welche von einen gewissen Burger in Olmütz (lutherischer Religion) (nehmlich Valentin Ecker, ein Schlosser) beschrieben worden (1618-1715)*, unpaged.

32. See: the studies in *Čtrnáct mučedníků pražských: Vpád Pasovských a závěr vlády Rudolfa II*, ed. by Petr Regalát Beneš, Petr Hlaváček, and Tomáš Sterneck, Prague, Charles University, 2014. For the Carnival violence, see: Burke, *Popular Culture in Early Modern Europe*, p. 204.

could now be buried (much to the displeasure of the bishops, understandably) virtually under the windows of the friary, which once aimed to become a bastion of Catholic orthodoxy. Over the next thirty years (until 9 September 1571) about 220 non-Catholics were buried at this site, renamed *Gottesacker*.[33]

The expansion of Lutheranism in Moravian and Silesian towns had another, equally grave, consequence for the Franciscans, besides the loss of the benefactors. A large share of the friars came from these cities, and now, with a change in the religious situation, the influx of novices into the order began to slowly but steadily diminish.[34] In addition, many friars followed Luther's example and left the Order. The communities that remained often struggled with discipline.[35] Soon, the situation began to seem unbearable. Normally each house would consist of at least twelve friars. Most friaries, however, had a much larger capacity – after reconstruction in the 1490s, the Olomouc house could accommodate up to forty people. As of 1517, the twenty-seven friaries of the Bohemian province housed over six hundred brothers – more than twenty people lived in one house. Fifty years later the situation was completely different. By 1571, there were only seventeen friars living in the entire province, struggling to manage the remaining six friaries. In the end they decided to abandon the large and maintenance-intensive St Bernardino friary in Olomouc – at that time inhabited by two friars only. The province then included a mere five houses. Besides the oldest and most respected friary of the province, Brno, there were houses in Znojmo, Jindřichův Hradec, Bechyně and Pilsen.[36]

However, the Olomouc house was not to be abandoned permanently. It was arranged with Bishop William Prusinovský that the Franciscans could have their house back at any time. By the time the friary was abolished, paradoxically, the first signs of Catholic restoration began to emerge in both the country and the city. The Jesuit Order was especially active, and their Olomouc college was soon promoted to university status. A part of it was the Papal *Collegium Nordicum*, which trained the clergy for the northern and north-eastern regions of Europe.[37] However, the renovation of the Franciscan province was delayed, and so Prusinovsky, fearing the vacant object would start to dilapidate or fall in the hands of the Protestant city council, offered the house to the Jesuits as accommodation for the alumni of the seminary for noblemen. It took another twelve years for the Franciscans to gather strength to eventually reclaim their friary. In 1593, around the Epiphany, Bishop Stanislaus Pavlovsky solemnly returned the place to Pro-

33. Ondřej Jakubec, "The Divided City, 1520s-1600", in *The Transformation of Confessional Cultures*, pp. 82 and 84.

34. Later Franciscan authors blamed the decline in numbers on riots and plague.

35. This was also the case of the Olomouc friary, where master Daniel Cordatus complained to the city council about the new superior and the disputes and scandals he caused. Olomouc, Olomouc Archives – fragments of the registries (1426-1786), inv. no. 4415, carton 160.

36. Minařík, "Provinciálové františkánské české provincie v letech 1517-1600", p. 85.

37. Jakubec, "The Divided City, 1520s-1600", pp. 87-93. See also: Zdeněk Hojda, "Collegia Nordica v Olomouci a Branievě 1578-1619", in *Acta Universitatis Carolinae – Historia Universitatis Carolinae Pragensis*, 30, 1 (1990), pp. 49-95.

vincial Maximilian Nolet of Styria. Despite a plague that killed two friars that very same year, the order managed to maintain its position. In 1597 or 1598, the Franciscans even regained part of the garden they had once ceded for the burials of non-Catholics.[38]

The re-settlement of the Olomouc house ushered in the restoration of the whole province. Shortly after, the friary in Tachov was reopened too, followed by others. In 1603, the Minister General Francesco de Sosa himself set out for the Bohemian Province and visited Prague. If the Franciscans wanted to take their role in the Bohemian Lands and Central Europe seriously, they needed to be close to the Emperor's court. Thanks to influential supporters, they managed to obtain the abandoned Carmelite monastery with the Church of the Virgin Mary of the Snows; Rudolph II confirmed the handover of the monastery in 1606.[39] The authorities of the order focused both on the material and the spiritual renewal of the province. All the Transalpine provinces were to renounce the Observant statutes and instead join a more rigid Reformed branch of the order. For this purpose, a group of Italian *Riformati* were sent to the Bohemian Province. The provincial chapter in Jindřichův Hradec in 1608 welcomed the friars and decided that they would be given the Olomouc monastery of St Bernardino – provided that the friary remained a part of the province and reported directly to the Minister Provincial.[40]

The new friars were solemnly introduced to Olomouc on 27 July of the same year. A year later, St Bernardino was empty again. The Italian friars were allegedly in constant disagreement with each other and eventually fled from Olomouc. Consequently, in 1609, St Bernardino was settled once again by local friars. Within a year, however, Italian and Polish Reformed friars were back again. They tried to gain independence from the jurisdiction of the Bohemian Franciscan Province, which provoked a sharp response from the provincial authorities as well as the Bishop of Olomouc, Cardinal Dietrichstein. The conflicts went on until the Reformed brothers left Olomouc in 1617. According to the sources of the Bohemian Province, their behaviour was criticised even by the lay people. Moreover, as none of the Reformed spoke German, their contribution to the religious life in Olomouc was minimal. The chronicle is silent about this episode, mentioning only the reconsecration of the main altar in 1615, and the death of two Italian brothers.[41]

This period of controversy ended, and so did the first attempts to implement the Reform, when Moravia joined the rebellion of the Bohemian Estates in 1619. The position of the Catholic believers, and the religious orders in particular, deteriorated drastically. After refusing to pray for the new King Frederick V, the Olomouc Franciscans reportedly became a target of hatred by the new city officials. One day, an armed group invaded the monastery, dragging the friars (with insults

38. The burials would briefly take place again between 1619 and 1620, during the Rebellion of the Estates, after the Franciscans had been expelled from the city.

39. Beneš, "O trojím těžkém začínání", pp. 90-96.

40. Klemens Minařík, "Provinciálové františkánské české provincie v letech 1600-1750", *Sborník Historického kroužku*, 18 (1917), p. 55.

41. *Archivum*, pp. 19-20.

and mockery, as the chronicle emphasised) to the Upper Square under the pillory, where they were threatened with execution. The brothers survived, thanks to the intervention of some influential citizens, but had to leave the city immediately. They travelled to Nysa, Silesia, where they remained until the uprising was defeated. In 1621, they came back and reportedly reclaimed all the liturgical objects and books they had wisely stored at the city hall before being driven out.[42]

Although only a few brief notes have been preserved in the chronicle, these suggest that the subsequent period brought successful and general restoration of the friary – particularly in the thirties under Ludovicus Gessner as superior. In 1636, two bedrooms were added. The next year, the refectory was remodelled and two more bedrooms were built. The following year the dormitory was renovated, and the damp walls of the church treated. This bustle indicates that the friary population kept growing – especially since the province's philosophy studies were established here.[43] The increase in numbers was also reported as the reason for moving the main altar towards the church nave in 1635, in order to make more room for the choir of the friars.[44] The growing number of vocations is probably the most telling sign of the successful renewal, but it also testifies to the ongoing consolidation of the Catholic faith in the city.[45] The new inhabitants of the friary also needed to be fed and clothed, which, given the mendicant character of the order, depended mainly on the support of the local community. The fact that the house could accommodate a growing number of friars on a long-term basis testifies to the existence of a functional network of relations with the local population. It seems that the Franciscans were on exceptionally good terms with the new city officials: the bailiff (*Reichsvogt*) Magnus Brandel of Brandenfels (d. 1635), the councillor Johann Mandelius (d. 1640) and his son-in-law Tobias Schwonauer (d. 1659). That these were no isolated supporters of the order is evident from the decision to build three new crypts in 1635: one for the friars themselves, a small one for bailiff Brandel and a large one for other benefactors.[46]

3. *Moulding the tradition*

It was at the end of this promising and apparently successful decade that Modestus Meerstein joined the Franciscan Order in Olomouc (1640). His return ten

42. *Archivum*, p. 20.

43. *Archivum*, p. 30.

44. The altar was newly consecrated to honor the Immaculate Conception of the Virgin Mary, St Bernardino, St Louis, and also the recently beatified John of Capistrano. In addition, two side altars were sanctified: one to honour St Catherine, St Clara, and St Elizabeth, and the other, "Portiuncula", to honour St Francis, John the Ev., and St Barbara. *Archivum*, p. 25.

45. Tomáš Parma, "The Stormy Path to a Single Religion, 1600-1650", in *The Transformation of Confessional Cultures*, pp. 112-115.

46. It is quite telling that the first person to be buried in the friar crypt in front of the main altar was not one of the friars, but one of the benefactors – Adam Bess, Baron of Wirckles. Also, Mandelius would be buried in the same crypt, while Schwonauer would later build his own crypt under the chapel of the Holy Sepulchre. *Archivum*, p. 26.

years later and his role as superior were marked by efforts to restore the friary to its pristine glory. Repairing the damaged roof, glazing windows, and furnishing the monastery were but a few of the tasks that awaited the new superior.[47] The church also needed to be cleaned, whitewashed and newly paved. In 1653, a new high altar was purchased, and in the same year, the chapel of the Holy Sepulchre was built by Mayor Tobias Schwonauer. Moreover, the provincial philosophical studies were restored to the friary, with one of the most learned theologians of the province, Anthony Bruodin of Ireland, briefly teaching there. Remodelling the house and providing for all its inhabitants was one thing. An even more important task was to become part of the city's life again.[48] This was probably one of the main reasons why Meerstein took on another task in the midst of all his activities.[49] He started gathering all surviving pieces of information about the history of the friary and began to write the friary's chronicle. His efforts to build on the previous history were an integral part of the strenuous renewal.[50] Perhaps in some ways it was even more important than the actual reconstruction of the friary, the church and its altars. Preserved sources were, however, scarce. When describing the history of the monastery before 1571, all Meerstein could rely on were a few written documents and oral tradition. The origi-

47. *Archivum*, pp. 39-40. It is not known whether any of the medieval frescoes were still visible then. No mention of them has been found in the period documents. The restoration survey suggests that most of the church was replastered in the seventeenth century and decorated with architectural trompe-l'œil. It seems only the Passion paintings along the sides of the triumphal arch and the fresco of St Christopher remained exposed. Milan Togner and František Sysel, "Restaurátorský a uměleckohistorický průzkum interiérových stěn kostela Neposkvrněného početí P. Marie v Olomouci", *Ročenka Okresního archívu v Olomouci*, Olomouc, SOA Olomouc, 1984, pp. 78-83.

48. Equally important was defending the position of the friary in the Province, which now counted fifteen friaries with almost three hundred friars. House number one was the Virgin Mary of the Snows Friary in New Town, Prague, the seat of the minister provincial. The prestige of the other friaries depended on how old they were. Olomouc managed to maintain its formal status as the fifth friary in the hierarchy of the Bohemian province, after Tachov, Kadaň and Głogów (Glogau). St Bernardino holds this position in all the registers and overviews of the Franciscan province, both domestic and foreign. Brno, in contrast, originally the oldest and hence the most respected house (moreover, guarding Capistrano's habit as a valuable relic) of the entire province, was one of the friaries to lose its position. The old friary outside the city walls was torn down for defensive reasons during the Thirty Years' War. The city promptly helped the Franciscans build a new monastery inside the city at the church of Mary Magdalene. Due to the different location and the changed dedication, the new Brno friary had to settle for fifteenth place in the provincial hierarchy. Although this seems to be trivial, the hierarchy played a crucial role in the life of early modern friaries. The ranking of the houses – as well as the ranking of provinces in the structure of the order, and the ranking of friars at the provincial chapters or within the friary – was closely monitored and often led to disputes. Wrbczansky, *Nucleus Minoriticus*, passim.

49. Meerstein is also known as the author of a musical guide for Franciscan worship. See: Modestus Meerstein, *Hymni Cum Antiphonis, Qui Secundum Ritum Sanctae Romanae Ecclesiae, & Seraphicae Religionis S. Francisci in Publicis Processionibus Cantari Solent Ad Uniformem Normam Relati. Ut Sic, in Psalmis, & Hymnis, & Canticis Spiritualibus Canentes & Psallentes in Cordibus Vestris*, Olomucii, Vitus Henricus Ettelius, 1666.

50. Cf. Louthan, *Converting Bohemia*, p. 133.

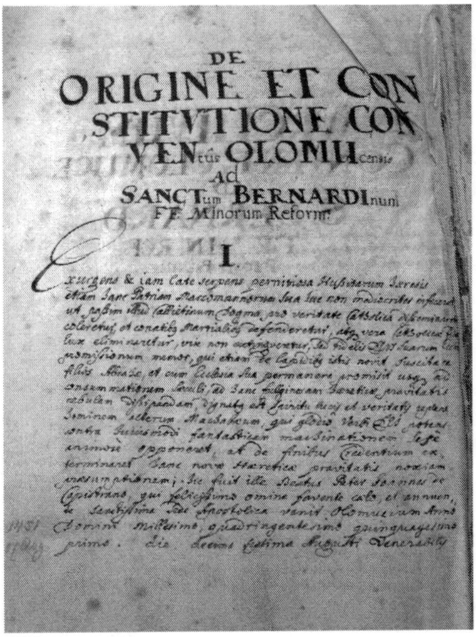

Fig. 10. First page of the Meerstein's chronicle. Moravian Land Archive in Brno, E 21 Franciscans of Dačice, book no. 9.

nal archive of St Bernardino was reduced to ashes in the fire of the Jindřichův Hradec friary, where it had been relocated at the outbreak of the Thirty Years' War. In addition to Piccolomini's Bohemian chronicle, Meerstein could draw on only a few sources from the provincial archive, specifically the provincial chronicle entitled *Chronica Fratrum Minorum de Observantia Provinciae Bohemiae* and Gonzaga's printed chronicle *De Origine Seraphicae Religionis Franciscanae*, supplemented by other writings. With these sources he was able to briefly describe the beginnings of the friary associated with the visit of John of Capistrano and to draft the basic outlines of the later developments.[51] The final picture he put together was, though, quite fragmented.

The most important source for the chronicler was the necrology, located directly in the church, and thus spared the fate of the other archival documents. As Meerstein noted in his chronicle regarding the year 1474: "All that the old records disclosed for the sake of the memory of the descendants, concerning the following years, were the names of the dead and those buried in the friary".[52] The first

51. It was from Gonzaga that Meerstein mistakenly learned that there had been two Franciscan friaries in Olomouc, one inside and the other outside the city walls. He admitted though that he had not been able to find any other data on the existence of the other friary. *Archivum*, p. 3. Cf. Franciscus Gonzaga, *De Origine Seraphicae Religionis Fra[n]ciscanae eiusqu[e] progressibus, de Regularis Obserua[n]ciae institutione,* Romae, ex typographia Dominici Basae, 1587, pp. 456-457.

52. *Archivum*, p. 4. The necrology was in the friary hallway as late as 1936. See: František Bolek, *Katolické Kostely a Kaple v Olomouci*, Olomouc, Lidové závody tiskařské a

of many is superior Francis de Kossel, who died in the friary in 1473. There then follows a list of more than three hundred names; the last entry dates back to 1550. Most of the records are terse. They include only the name of the friar, given in accordance with the previous practices of the order (i.e. the religious name and place of origin; in the early modern period friars kept their surnames) and whether it was a priest, a cleric or a layman – for example, Christopher of Jawor, priest; Martin of Genoa, cleric. Rarely is there additional information about the position in the house (e.g. cook, gardener, sacristan or preacher), advanced age (e.g. old man aged sixty), social origin (e.g. a noble title associated with a total of seven people) or the circumstances of death (for example the thirty-five brothers who died in 1483, during six days of helping those stricken by the plague). For some of the deceased, there are also details about their virtuous life.

However, much more interesting is the wider context of the whole source. The first two centuries of the friary's history – as told on the first seventeen pages of Meerstein's chronicle – consist mainly of the names of the deceased friars. Thus, the history of St Bernardino becomes more so the history of the people who died there than the people who lived within its walls. This detail is extremely important. The necrology incorporated into the chronicle expressed not only the community's commitment to praying for their deceased confreres. It was also an important source of continuity and legitimacy. The necrology illustrates the important fact that intercessions for the dead and the cult of the saints are two closely interconnected and complementary phenomena.[53] The friars would thus hold masses for the benefit of their deceased confreres, while those who died in a state of grace would pray in heaven for the existing community of friars and eventually for the whole city. A closer look, indeed, reveals clear hagiographic elements in the necrology. Several names on the list are paid greater attention and are also graphically highlighted. One of them is, for example, Bernardinus Bavarus (died 1476), referred to as "a companion of the blessed John of Capistrano".[54] Eight other names on the list are marked with a red asterisk or written in red. The first is the minister provincial John of Meissen, who died in 1492 during the provincial chapter held in the Olomouc friary. Next to his name there is a note stating his merit in the formation of the independent Bohemian province, but also that he "raised one dead boy and made many other miracles".[55] The others include three friars from Olomouc: the lay brother Jodocus, who supposedly glowed with celestial light day and night and whom the locals nicknamed the "Angelic light that illuminates our dwellings with the grace of God" (died 1506); the priest Barnabas (died in 1550 as the last person before the friary was temporarily closed down in 1571); and the lay brother Felicianus (died 1505) renowned for posthumous

nakladatelské, 1936, p. 46.

53. The relationship between the living and the dead was subject to a complex and clearly defined reciprocity of gifts in the Catholic world. Natalie Zemon Davis, *The Gift in Sixteenth-Century France*, Oxford, Oxford University Press, 2000, pp. 167-168.

54. *Archivum,* p. 5.

55. *Archivum*, p. 9.

miracles.[56] Meerstein recounts one of these miracles and claims that it was widely remembered by Olomouc citizens:

> In the small hours of one morning, before Matins, both the church bells began to ring. Awoken, the superior thought that some of the brethren had started chiming the bells outside the required hours. He went angrily down the stairs to reprimand the brothers at fault. When he entered the church, however, he saw candles lit on all altars and the whole church filled with light. Awed by the sight he ran to gather the rest of the brothers to come see the wonder. Upon entering the church, they saw a great number of unknown friars in the choir, who seemed to be preparing to sing psalms. The whole scene soon disappeared, though, and the candles went out; only the altar of St. Ursula [under which Felicianus had been allegedly buried] remained flooded by a great glow of merciful light.[57]

The memory of these friars' holy lives – together with the relics associated with the visit of John of Capistrano (the well, the filiation granted to Olomouc burghers, and several trigrams of **yhs**) – constituted sacred capital which could be used by the friars to legitimise and promote their position in the city. As early as the 1630s, the superior Ludovicus Gessner took steps that testified to the conscious effort to cultivate this memory and to export it outside the friary walls. He attempted to localise the graves and dig where the remains of Brother Felicianus were thought to be. Although the digging went quite deep, the remains were never found. Ironically enough, this failure only reinforced Gessner's belief that his judgment had been correct and that soon after Felicianus had died, his grave became the centre of the emerging cult.[58] He ventured to claim that one of his predecessors had the remains collected and transferred to another, safer place – perhaps to another province – once the Reformation began to spread in the city. The assertion need not have been as absurd as it may sound. Similar "rescue operations" had happened in the past. Only a few years earlier, the transfer of the remains of Norbert of Xanten from Magdeburg to Prague received wide publicity. Celebrations accompanying the transfer illustrated the ambitions of the Emperor and of the Bohemian clergy to portray Prague as the safe bastion of true faith, as opposed to the heretical Magdeburg.[59] The festivities created an impressive and comprehensible counterpart for the Renewed Land Ordinance, which banned all non-Catholic confessions from the country, and which was issued on the very day after the end of the celebrations.

In any case, the efforts of the Olomouc Franciscans to promote the cult of their confreres continued, and as evidence shows, they were not completely unsuccessful. The mention of the Olomouc friars and the revelation at the St Ursula altar appeared, for example, in the *Menologium,* a monumental catalogue of the order's saints by the Bavarian Franciscan Fortunatus Hueber.[60] Thanks to

56. *Archivum*, p. 13 (Felicianus), p. 14 (Jodocus) and p. 17 (Barnabas).
57. *Archivum*, pp. 13-14.
58. *Archivum*, p. 13.
59. Louthan, *Converting Bohemia*, pp. 34-45.
60. Fortunatus Hueber, *Menologium, Seu, Brevis, & Compendiosa Illuminatio, Relucens in Splendoribus Sanctorum, Beatorum, Miraculosorum, Incorruptorum, Extaticorum, Beneficorum, Et Quocumque Sanctimoniae, Vel Virtutis Fulgore, Illustrium, Singularium, Aut Prae-*

Franciscan author Heinrich Labe, the same piece of information was entered into Balbín's *Bohemia Sancta*, where the Olomouc friars – together with Agnes of Bohemia, John of Capistrano, James of the Marches, and fourteen Prague martyrs – represent the Franciscan tradition in the Bohemian Lands.[61]

The chronicle, however, was not limited to the adoration of selected friars. Its ambitions went much further as it extended the notion of holiness not only to those exemplary individuals but also to the community as a whole. Two of the longer narrative passages in the older part of the chronicle are descriptions of the storms that hit the city in the late fifteenth century. The shorter account relates to 26 July 1497, a day when Olomouc was hit by "a storm so ghastly that the entire city trembled in fear of flooding".[62] At one point a flash of lightning struck the Franciscan church, but fortunately did not kill anyone or cause any major damage. It was St Anne's Day, and thus the friary's salvation was considered a miracle caused by her intercession. To thank the saint, an altar of St Anne was installed in the church, adorned with an appropriate "old school" painting. Another, longer passage gives an account of a similar event that allegedly had taken place two years earlier:

> That year, in 1495, a dreadful storm broke out before Easter, along with a great earthquake that set the whole of Olomouc trembling. A voice was heard in the air, shouting thrice: "Hit! Strike!" And another voice answered: "I cannot, because the clog-monks [*Monachi lignipedes, die Klotzmönich* – a derogatory term referring to the Observants] are preventing me from doing so!" Meanwhile the frightened burghers noticed that the entire friary seemed to be on fire and blazing with flames. A big crowd of people quickly gathered to save the friary from the fire. But when they ran inside the friary and the church, all they found were the friars lying humbly on the ground face down with their arms outstretched, incessantly calling God to save people and avert the destruction of the city – which is also what happened.[63]

Meerstein claims that, in memory of this miracle and in gratitude to the Observant community, the city commissioned statues of all the friars depicting the fateful prayer. One of these sculptures allegedly existed as late as 1634, stored in the city hall. When the Superior Ludovicus Gessner found out, he decided to visit Mayor Johann Mandelius, coincidentally a Franciscan benefactor and apostolic syndic. Gessner asked for permission to see the statue and possibly borrow it. His wish was granted; the superior borrowed the statue and returned it two days later. The following morning, before dawn, there was a pounding on the gate of the friary. When the gate-keeping brother opened the door, he saw only the statue in front of the gate. He went to wake the superior, and the two then carried the statue

cellentium Famulorum Famularumque Dei, Martyrum, Confessorum, Virginum, Viduarum, Poenitentium, Monachii, Typis Ioannis Lucae Straubii, 1698, col. 1213 (9. Jun.).

61. Bohuslaus Balbinus, *Miscellanea Historica Regni Bohemiae Decadis I. Liber IV. Hagiographicus, Seu Bohemia Sancta, Continens Sanctos Et Beatos Bohemiæ, Moraviæ, Silesiæ, Lusatiæ*, Pragae, Typis Georgii Czernoch, 1682, *Pars prima*, pp. 64-65 (Agnes), pp. 179-180 (John of Capistrano), pp. 180-181 (James of the Marches), pp. 187-188 (Jan of Meissen), *Pars secunda*, pp. 90-91 (Felicianus, Jodocus and Barnabas).

62. *Archivum*, pp. 11-12.

63. *Archivum*, p. 10.

Fig. 11. Franciscan Heaven, from Fortunatus Hueber, *Menologium, seu, Brevis, & compendiosa Illuminatio, relucens in Splendoribus Sanctorum, Beatorum, Miraculosorum, Incorruptorum, Extaticorum, Beneficorum, et quocumque Sanctimoniae, vel Virtutis Fulgore, Illustrium, Singularium, aut Praecellentium Famulorum Famularumque Dei, Martyrum, Confessorum, Virginum, Viduarum, Poenitentium* (Monachii: Typis Ioannis Lucae Straubii, 1698), frontispiece.

inside. The superior ordered the gate-keeper not to tell anyone about the incident. Several days later, Ludovicus Gessner went to see the mayor again and asked for the statue once more, pretending he planned to have a copy made for the friary. The servant was sent for the statue, but returned empty-handed as the sculpture had disappeared. It was not until the mayor began to scold the poor servant that the superior interrupted him and excitedly told of finding the statue before the friary gate. Ostensibly moved by the miracle, the mayor donated the statue to the friary.[64]

In addition to the sculptures, a thanksgiving procession was introduced in memory of the miracle. It was held every Easter Tuesday, leading from the parish church of St Maurice to the Franciscans, where service took place. Afterwards the Franciscans walked the procession back to the St Maurice church. The procession was held until the 1630s, although attended only by the St Maurice chaplain, four singers, and a handful of believers. In 1640, the Franciscan preacher Ludovicus Sartorell tried to restore the tradition. He reminded the faithful of this event in his sermon. The following day so many people joined the procession (including the city councillors) that they could hardly fit in the church.[65]

These events, in which the Franciscans were the protectors of the city community, were an extremely valuable argument the Franciscans could use to build their position and reintegrate into the city's organism:

> Afterwards the people treated our friary and church with a greater respect compared to other local monasteries, of which there are seven for men and two for women. This was partly due to the effort spent in hearing confessions, preaching, services, comforting the sick, and in other pious acts, and partly due to the persistence with which the brethren engaged themselves (for the city was drunk on Hussite corruption) to bring the souls led astray from Christ back into the womb of the Church, which is what had obviously been going on for many years since the blessed John of Capistrano left for Hungary. This is why even today, on major feasts people assemble in the local church (continuing the former respect for the brethren) in greater quantities than in other churches in the city.[66]

This self-assertion of their mission and significance in the life of the city was not limited to the past only. While the processions, statues, and relics were indeed what Judith Pollmann called "Catholic mnemonic tools", for the friars they were also a challenge for the future and eventually also a reminder of model scenarios.[67]

Looking closely at the chronicle, we can find indeed distinct parallels between the records from the older "medieval" stage of the friary's history and the more modern events, which are portrayed as echoes of ancient legends. For example, the reminiscence of John of Meissen, who was supposed to have miraculously

64. *Archivum*, pp. 10-11.

65. The Swedish occupation, however, interrupted this tradition again, and Meerstein admits that when this record was written, the procession had become largely ignored. *Archivum*, p. 11.

66. *Archivum*, p. 12.

67. Judith Pollmann, *Memory in Early Modern Europe, 1500-1800*, Oxford, Oxford University Press, 2017, p. 101.

resurrected a dead boy, resonates in 1627 with a "strange and dumbfounding incident, glorious for our order". It involved a serious traffic accident. A wagon (incidentally belonging to the local Jesuits) was transporting a heavy load when children, busy playing, got in the way. A boy was hit and rendered unconscious. The mother, immediately summoned up, gathered the poor boy in her arms and, not knowing what to do, she ran to ask the local hangman for help. He, however, told her that it was too late and returned the lifeless body to the woman. Wailing, the desperate mother was carrying the child home when:

> just at that moment, the Vesper bells started ringing on the feast of St Francis; and filled with hope and trust she hastened to our church. In tears she made a promise and prayed earnestly with growing intensity, up to the Magnificat; and lo and behold, the boy on the mother's lap began to recover consciousness, to breathe, to open his eyes, to laugh, and before the Magnificat was over, he stood up healed and walked away with his mother home, watched in astonishment and admiration by all those present.[68]

To commemorate this miracle, every year on the feast of St Francis the boy, "crowned with a beautiful wreath, walked around the main altar with a lighted wax candle, which he sacrificed to God and St Francis to thank them". Unfortunately, Meerstein leaves us in the dark about what happened to the boy later, or whether the ritual was maintained after 1650. There would have been a mention, however, if he had joined the order.

Both the dangerous storms of the 1490s have their parallel in the chronicle in the descriptions of contemporary storms that hit the place in the seventeenth and eighteenth centuries. One of them was the storm that broke out the night before the Epiphany of 1639. A mass was being held by two priests in the church when a big storm burst out. A flash of lightning flew into the church, filling it with a "thick sulphuric smoke", and flew out again through the window. Outside, it knocked over a Polish wagoner, who was right at that moment pulling on a bell at the friary gates. The flash sent him to the ground, burning him from "neck to heel, without touching his clothes". No one in the church was hurt. Neither was there any record of damage – with one minor yet important exception. There was a small hole in the altar of St Ursula – the same altar that was linked to Brother Felicianus' grave and the miraculous light – as if it had been pierced with a thin needle.[69]

A more tragic storm, though equally symbolic, took place on Saturday, 13 August 1700. The chronicle gives the following expressive account:

> Shortly before the brothers began to pray Compline, the sky above our friary suddenly grew menacingly dark, and many people ran inside our church, driven by fear, to ask for blessing. As Salve Regina was being sung, an enormous, unparalleled, and certainly supernatural storm broke out, bringing along a whirlwind that tore a part of the roof and knocked it off the top of the church down onto the Chapel of Saint Anthony of Padua, destroying its vault with one stroke.[70]

68. *Archivum*, p. 22.
69. *Archivum*, p. 30.
70. *Archivum*, p. 126.

A female member of the Third Order and a small child were killed instantly. The mother of the child was found alive in the debris but succumbed to her injuries the following day, after receiving extreme unction. The other three women that were in the chapel at the time of the disaster managed to save themselves at the last moment. A great commotion was set in the church in the meanwhile:

> There was confusion, horror, turmoil, and people screaming all around, as the church was completely full. Some thought and claimed that the church had been struck by lightning; some believed that the whole church was collapsing; some were searching for their wives, and others were running into the cloister to save themselves. Everyone was scared and confused. Nobody knew what had happened, what to do, and what was to come. The entire church was full of dust, and as the storm left the sky overcast and pitch dark, no one could see anything and it seemed as if the church was all shrouded in smoke. The brothers in the choir, however, did not cease singing litany, and eventually gave the benediction of the Blessed Sacrament.[71]

The next day, the dead Tertiary was buried in the crypt under St Anthony's chapel, while the mother and the child were buried a day later in a little cemetery behind the friary church. It was discovered that the storm had seriously damaged not only the friary but also the city. The roofs of the Franciscan church were, nonetheless, hit the hardest and the recently built chapel of St Anthony of Padua was in ruins. Clearing away the debris, the friars made a stunning discovery. Under the rubble, they found two intact pictures of the Virgin Mary. Although the rest of the chapel was completely destroyed, these two paintings escaped allegedly unscathed, including the glass they were covered with.[72]

Similar to the story of the miraculously healed boy, these descriptions – the accentuated motif of an unexpected storm concentrating on the monastery, the miraculous survival of selected paintings, and friars persisting in their prayers despite the terrible storm – create impressive parallels between the "golden age" of the local Franciscan community and early modern times.[73] The living inhabitants of the friary created the sacred community together with their dead confreres, thus becoming their heirs and followers.[74] The chronicle carefully crafted a story of continuity of Franciscan charisma and its capacity to produce miracles – the miracles that had happened once might happen again. Sermons, processions and other commemorative rituals then communicated this message to the

71. *Archivum*, p. 127.

72. *Archivum*, p. 127.

73. For a similar use of memory and tradition in the Second Order, see: Jarmila Kašpárková, "Gedächtnis und Observanz: Die Chronik des Bernard Sannig für das Znaimer Klarissenkloster", in *Ordenshistoriographie in Mitteleuropa Gestaltung und Wandlung des institutionalen und persönlicshen Gedächtnisses in der Frühen Neuzeit. Referate der gleichnamigen Tagung in St. Pölten von 22. bis 23. September 2014*, St. Pölten, Diözesanarchiv, 2015, pp. 138-166 and Petr Zemek, *Reformace, protireformace a rozvinutí poreformačního katolictví v Uherském Brodě - křesťanská víra v proměnách času*, Uherský Brod, Muzeum J. A. Komenského v Uherském Brodě, 2006, pp. 367-384. See also: *Layered Landscapes: Early Modern Religious Space Across Faiths and Cultures*, ed. by Eric Nelson and Jonathan Wright, London, Routledge, 2017.

74. Cf. Pollmann, *Memory in Early Modern Europe*, pp. 96-102. See also: Anthony P. Cohen, *The Symbolic Construction of Community*, London, Routledge, 1985, p. 99.

Fig. 12. Fire of the New Gate in 1676. The Franciscan friary is depicted in the background, to the right. Bachelor thesis of Matyáš Schmidt after Anthony Lublinský (?). Engraving, Land Archive Opava, branch Olomouc, collection University of Olomouci, thesis, vol. 1, f. 13.

public. They presented the Franciscans as a holy community mediating with the supernatural to help the city and its inhabitants.[75] And this claim implied that the deeds of the friary and fates of the city are intrinsically intertwined.

75. Cf. Clare Copeland, "Sanctity", in *The Ashgate Research Companion to the Counter-Reformation*, ed. by Alexandra Bamji, Geert H Janssen, and Mary Laven, Farnham, Ashgate, 2013, p. 231.

3. Poverty

Although the restoration of St Bernardino and its integration into the city's organism was successful, the times were marked by tension and new challenges. This became evident as early as 1640, in the case of a seemingly petty dispute that broke out between the Olomouc mendicants and the Sodality of St Anne, managed by the Jesuits.[1] The Franciscans, the Conventuals and the Dominicans complained that the sodality assumed the right to carry the cross and candles before the hearse at funerals of their members. This was traditionally reserved for friars and local priests, and the sodality was accused of violating the custom. Although the consistory decided in favour of the mendicants, the conflict highlighted an important circumstance. While Franciscans, like many other religious communities, returned in the seventeenth century to the same friary, their old home was now surrounded by a quite different social and religious environment. Franciscans were confronted with brand new institutions, new circumstances and problems, and their position needed to be renegotiated.

The whole city was, to begin with, Catholic for the first time since the Observants arrived.[2] If there were any non-Catholics at all, they did not constitute a major missionary challenge. The chronicle does not mention any Catholic conversion assisted by the Franciscans in the second half of the seventeenth century. The Holy Trinity altar in the cloister, where the conversion ceremony usually took place, began to be used for this purpose again only in the eighteenth century, when a garrison with a number of Protestant soldiers was permanently placed in the city.[3] The Franciscans needed to adapt to this transformation, and find new missionary priorities and ways to appeal to the city inhabitants if they wanted to secure their existence. As a mendicant order, the Friars Minor were dependent on acceptance and support from the local population or other church institutions.

1. Opava Land Archive, Olomouc office, Olomouc Archbishop Consistory (1452-1949), sign. C9, carton 2213, *Průvody a poutě v Olomouci a na sv. Kopeček* (1617-1897), fol. 10-16. Cf. Zdeněk Orlita, "Pohřební průvod mezi pietou a reprezentací", in *Církev a smrt. Institucionalizace smrti v raném novověku*, ed. by Martin Holý and Jiří Mikulec, Prague, Institute of History, 2007, pp. 187-208.

2. Radmila Prchal Pavlíčková, "The Evolution of Catholic Identity, 1650-1700", in *The Transformation of Confessional Cultures*, pp. 121-39.

3. See: Chapter 6.

These efforts were hampered, paradoxically, by the very success of the Catholic renewal, which resulted in a society of homogeneous faith, and by the restoration and flourishing of ecclesiastical institutions.[4] Most local monasteries underwent internal reforms over time, which helped improve the standards of religious life and the picture that the (at least formally Catholic) burghers had of the friars. The Franciscans themselves, however, lost a significant part of their former exceptionality, where they had been perceived as the "true" friars upholding the original ideals as opposed to the "fallen" friars. To make matters worse for the Franciscans, two new orders had appeared in the city alongside the traditional religious communities: the Jesuits and the Capuchins.[5] These dynamically evolving orders aroused similar interest from the population as the Observants two centuries earlier. The orders were, moreover, quite closely connected. The Capuchins had by then established themselves as a separate branch of the Friars Minor, seeking to restore the most rigorous observance of the Franciscan Rule, specifically in terms of poverty. They thus questioned the demands of the Franciscans claiming that they, and only they (as opposed to the "fallen" Conventuals), were the true heirs and followers of St Francis's legacy. The Franciscans and the Capuchins coexisted in latent tension, which from time to time led to open conflict.[6]

The story of the Jesuits was similar. Although the Jesuits had their own separate spirituality, they shared a great deal of similarity with the Franciscans in how they defined their mission and formed a relationship with the local community.[7] Moreover, it was a spiritually related order, which often promoted similar forms of piety as the Franciscans. On the other hand, it was clearly Jesuits who took the initiative and were more successful in spreading these cults, while the Franciscans were pushed into the background. A good example is the custom of building a nativity scene in the church. This practice, so reminiscent of the legendary celebration of Christmas by St Francis in Greccio, is mainly associated with the Jesuits, at least in Central Europe. While a nativity scene at the Jesuit church in Prague was reported as early as 1560, it found its way on a large scale to the Franciscan churches only at the end of the seventeenth century.[8] Considering the interest this display aroused and the devotional potential it offered, the absence of nativity

4. R.J.W. Evans, *The Making of the Habsburg Monarchy 1550-1700: An Interpretation*, Oxford, Clarendon Press, 1979, pp. 123-133.

5. The Franciscans (and the Jesuits) allegedly attempted to prevent the Capuchins from coming to Olomouc. Opava Land Archive, Olomouc office, Olomouc Capuchins, book 5, *Liber memorabilium notatu dignorum quae contingerunt a prima Nostri Olomucensis Fundatione*, 1685, pp. 1-2.

6. Martin Elbel, "The Making of a Perfect Friar: Habit and Reform in the Franciscan Tradition", in *Friars, Nobles and Burghers – Sermons, Images and Prints: Studies of Culture and Society in Early-Modern Europe*, ed. by Jaroslav Miller and Laszlo Kontler, Budapest, Central European University Press, 2010, pp. 149-155.

7. John W. O'Malley, *The First Jesuits*,Cambridge, Mass., Harvard University Press, 1993, p. 94.

8. For more on the nativity scene and the Jesuits, see: Vladimír Vaclík, *Chrámové betlémy v Čechách a na Moravě*, Prague, Vyšehrad, 1990, p. 15. For more on the Franciscan nativity scene, see: Alfred Karasek and Josef Lenz, *Krippenkunst in Böhmen und Mähren vom*

scenes in Franciscan churches is striking. The Franciscans were pushed into the background in yet another case – a particularly sensitive one for the Franciscans. The lowercase trigram **yhs**, associated with the fifteenth century Franciscan observance and its prominent representatives Bernardino of Siena and John of Capistrano, began to be connected in its capital letter form **IHS** mainly with the Jesuits.

The Jesuits, to a large extent, took over the Observants' place in society. They were considered to be the "vanguard" of the Catholic Church, the religious elite and the potential source of a renaissance in the Church. The non-Catholics, on the other hand, considered them insidiously dangerous and the quintessence of what was condemnable in the Catholic Church. They provoked, in short, as extreme emotions as the Observant friars in the fifteenth century: spanning from uncritical admiration to fundamental hate. In addition, the Jesuits came at a time when the Bohemian Franciscan province was in its deepest crisis. By the time the Franciscans overcame this crisis in the seventeenth century and undertook rudimentary reforms, the Jesuits had firmly established themselves and the Franciscans were left to cope with it. It is no wonder that the relationship between the Franciscans and the Jesuits was often constrained, even though, unlike the Capuchins (or other mendicant orders), the Society of Jesus was not competition for the mendicants due to its organisation and property. It always depended on the local situation, how the relationships between the communities developed and what turn of events they undertook in various periods of time. Yet, the problem was too general to be reduced to local relations.

The religious transformation within the population and the loss of their former privileged status were a major challenge, both in general and for each friary. The Franciscans had to focus on three interconnected areas in order to respond adequately. The first and foremost were the previous achievements and the rich tradition of the order. Past success and popularity, also reflected in the cult of the saints of the order, were valuable symbolic capital, particularly compared to the new orders.[9] The second area was the public image of the order and the friars, which was constantly threatened by traditional anti-fraternalism, supported largely by Utraquists and Evangelicals, but also partly by Catholics.[10] Lastly, they had to continually highlight the points that set them apart from other orders. The key to success in each of these three areas was the same. It was necessary to focus on the fundamental principle of the tradition and spirituality of the order – the idea of absolute poverty as a path to evangelical perfection.

Frühbarock bis zur Gegenwart, Marburg, N.G. Elwert Verlag, 1974, p. 96, p. 132, p. 139 and p. 309.

9. This primarily involved the cult of Francis of Assisi. See: André Vauchez, *Francis of Assisi: The Life and Afterlife of a Medieval Saint*, trans. by Michael F. Cusato, New Haven, Yale University Press, 2012, p. 230.

10. For more on the traditional antifraternalists, see: e.g. Geoffrey Dipple, "'Si sind all glichsner': Antifraternalism in Medieval and Renaissance German Literature", in *Defenders and Critics of Franciscan Life: Essays in Honor of John V. Fleming*, ed. by Michael F. Cusato and Guy Geltner, Leiden-Boston, Brill, 2009, pp. 177-192.

Fig. 13. Map of the Bohemian Franciscan Province in 1737, from *Tabula Conventuum Almae & Magnae Provinciae Bohemiae S. WENCESLAI D. & M., Ord. Fratrum Min. S. P. FRANCISCI Strict. Obs. Reformatorum complectensis Anno 1737*. Engraving, 433x550 mm. The map was originally published in Severinus Wrbczansky, *Nucleus Minoriticus, seu vera et sincera relatio originis et progressus Provinciae Bohemiae...* (Vetero-Pragae: Typis Joannis Caroli Hrabae, 1746).

1. *Marriage to Lady Poverty*

Life in poverty was nothing uncommon in monasteries, and it was one of the traditional commitments of religious life, along with the promise of chastity and obedience. In the case of monastic and other orders, the commitment concerned only those who joined the order. These individuals were expected to surrender any property, but the requirement did not apply to the monastery itself. Shared poverty was naturally also an ideal professed by all the orders. In reality, though, many monasteries – given the role they played in medieval society – gradually acquired substantial liquid and non-liquid assets. Some of the orders or reformist movements tried to work against this and return to what they considered to be the original ideal. A prominent example of this is the Cistercian reform, discussed in the famous polemic between Bernard of Clairvaux and Abbot Suger. Compared to these movements, St Francis went even further by introducing a new, radical element into the religious life.[11] His Rule specified this explicitly, requiring an

11. For more on the broader context of the development of mendicant movements, see:

inexorable attitude: "Let the brothers not make anything their own, neither house, nor place, nor anything at all. As pilgrims and strangers in this world, serving the Lord in poverty and humility, let them go seeking alms with confidence, and they should not be ashamed because, for our sakes, our Lord made Himself poor in this world".[12] Unlike other religious communities, the Friars Minor could not have any property as individuals or as a community: "they must avoid, individually and as a group, property and power over secular things, for their poverty is highest, exceeding the poverty of all friars".[13] They were supposed to live in absolute poverty and rely exclusively on God's mercy and alms. The requirement was all the more important because it was also present, in various forms, in the teachings of a number of heretical movements. In contrast, Friars Minor emphasised the voluntary aspect of such a life and obedience to Church authorities. By offering an "orthodox" alternative to the views of various heretical sects, they helped to counter these movements and – equally important – contribute to the rehabilitation of the ideal of poverty in the eyes of both the church and secular authorities.

This was not only a reaction to social problems. Poverty was not to become a mere exaggerated attribute of religious life. On the contrary, for Francis and his circle, it occupied a central place in spiritual life and became the main virtue contributing to an evangelical life and truly following Christ:

> Among the other outstanding and exceptional virtues which prepare in us an abode and a dwelling for God and which show an excellent and unencumbered path of going to and arriving before Him, holy Poverty shines with a certain prerogative before them all. By a unique grace, it excels the claims of the others. For it is the foundation and guardian of all virtues and enjoys a principal place and name among the gospel virtues. As long as they have been firmly placed on this foundation, the others need not fear the downpour of rains, the rush of floods, and the blast of winds that threaten ruin.[14]

These are the opening lines of *The Sacred Exchange between Saint Francis and Lady Poverty*, a thirteenth-century text. An anonymous Franciscan author describes the journey of St Francis and his retinue to see Lady Poverty and their subsequent conversation. Poverty first laments that, although she faithfully stood by Jesus Christ until he died, people, including many friars, eventually rejected her. Francis praises the wisdom of Poverty and asks her to take him and his followers as her servants. Lady Poverty accompanies them home, and finally, after

The Origin, Development, and Refinement of Medieval Religious Mendicancies, ed. by Donald Prudlo, Leiden, Brill, 2011.

12. "*Regule a kšaft Serafinského Otce S. Františka, s počátkem, rozmnožením a rozdělením téhož Řádu, a s přiloženým některým duchovním cvičením*", New Town of Prague, U Anny Voršily Hamplový, 1708, p. 11. English version quoted from: *Francis of Assisi: Early Documents, Vol. 1, The Saint*, ed. by Regis J. Armstrong, J.A. Wayne Hellmann and William J. Short, Hyde Park, NY and London, New City, 1999, p. 103.

13. Severinus Wrbczansky, *Quodlibetum Regulare Theologicum Canonico-Morale: Complectens Varia Religiosum Statum Concernentia*, Vetero-Pragae, Typis Caroli Joannis Hraba, Regni Bohemiae Statuum Typographi, 1732, pp. 166-167.

14. "The sacred exchange between Saint Francis and Lady Poverty (1237-1239)", in *Francis of Assisi: Early Documents*, vol. 1, p. 529.

realising the purity of their intentions, she accepts them as hers and gives them a blessing:

> You are blessed by the Lord God Who made heaven and earth, my sons. You who have received me into your home with such a fullness of charity that it seems to me that today I am with you as in God's paradise. I am, then, filled with joy. I overflow with consolation, and I ask pardon for having so delayed in coming. Truly the Lord is with you and I did not know it. I see what I have yearned for; what I have desired I now possess, for I am joined on earth to those who bear the image of Him to Whom I am espoused in heaven.[15]

The Friars Minor were to live in this bond with Lady Poverty, fulfilling the legacy of their founder.[16] They were not supposed to have any tangible assets on earth. Francis's Rule, his other writings (specifically *Testament*) and, after all, numerous stories from his legends constantly reminded his confreres of the requirement.[17] They, both as individuals and a community, had to strictly eschew any property. This applied specifically to their dwellings, which were to continue to be owned by a patron or become the property of the Holy See. Francis strongly advised his companions to fight against accepting property rights over the structures entrusted to them at all costs. Sometimes, he did so in quite a demonstrative manner. For example, seeing a new stone building for his confreres in Assisi, he and a few of his circle began to demolish it. He thus forced the city government to unequivocally declare that the building remained the property of the city and not the brethren.[18] The fact that the Franciscans were only guests in their friaries was sometimes manifested in a ritualised form – the religious community returned each year the keys to the monastery to their patron with a humble request that they be allowed to spend another year in the friary.[19] The Franciscan relationship to their friaries was reflected in the terminology they used. Their texts usually avoid "monastery" (*monasterium*), replacing it with

15. *Ibid.*, p. 808.

16. The influence of these thoughts is manifested in the spirituality of other orders. See, for example, the words of St Teresa of Avila: "Poverty is good and contains within itself all the good things in the world" – where there may be influence by her confessor, Franciscan Peter of Alcantara. Terezie od Ježíše, *Cesta k dokonalosti*, trans. by Josef Koláček, Kostelní Vydří, Karmelitánské nakladatelství, 1991, p. 16.

17. Lee Palmer Wandel, "The Poverty of Christ", in *The Reformation of Charity: the Secular and the Religious in Early Modern Poor Relief*, ed. by Thomas Max Saffley, London-Boston, Brill, 2003, pp. 18-19.

18. "A Mirror of Perfection (1276-1300)", in *Francis of Assisi: Early documents, Vol. 3, The Prophet*, ed. by Regis J. Armstrong, J.A. Wayne Hellmann and William J. Short, Hyde Park, NY and London, New City, 2001, p. 260. Cf. Malcolm Lambert, *Franciscan Poverty: The Doctrine of the Absolute Poverty of Christ and the Apostles in the Franciscan Order, 1210-1323*, rev. and expanded ed., St Bonaventure, NY, Franciscan Institute, St Bonaventure University, 1998, p. 45.

19. This ritual was observed in the sixteenth century, for example, by the Spanish Alcantarians, a reformist group around Peter of Alcantara. Heribert Holzapfel, *Handbuch Der Geschichte Des Franziskanerordens*, Freiburg im Breisgau, Herder, 1909, p. 292.

the term *conventus*, while more radical branches of the order went even further with the simple "house" (*domus*) or "place" (*locus*).[20]

The same applied to all the material assets they acquired. Their religious habits, church and monastery furnishings, and even food – Friars Minor were to use all these things without any legal entitlement. Shortly before he died, St Francis once again demonstrated this by giving his own example. He took off his habit and lay down naked on the earth, waiting for "Sister Death". According to Bonaventure, he only let himself be clothed again when his superior (Francis had never accepted any office in the order) ordered him to do so, saying: "I am **lending** [my emphasis] these to you as to a poor man, and you are to accept them with the command of holy obedience".[21] With Francis dead, it was necessary to legally codify and, possibly, theologically explain the ideals. The reason being that soon after objections challenging the Franciscan claims began to emerge – indeed, was it possible for the Friars Minor to avoid owning anything, even the habit they wore or the bread they ate? The answer to these objections was to emphasise the distinction between two legal concepts: the use (*usus*) and the ownership of things (*dominium, possessio, proprietas*).[22] Use was limited to things that are necessary for life, such as food, clothing and shelter. This is the natural right of every human being given by God, which no one (including Friars Minor) can renounce. The brothers, however, did not have the "political" right (*ius utendi*) to these things – they were only allowed to use them (*simplex usus facti*).

These explanations had been offered by Gregory IX's Bull *Quo elongati* (1230), which, however, did not discuss the question of who actually owned the things Friars Minor used in detail. The answer was provided in Innocent IV's *Ordinem vestrum* (1245), which stipulated that things used by Friars Minor were the property of the Holy See, the Roman Church. Although sanctified by the pope, the views incited disapproval among some theologians. In a conflict between the secular professors of the University of Paris and their new mendicant colleagues, William of Saint-Amour and his colleagues focused their attack on the mendicant teaching of poverty. They called it hypocritical, going as far as to condemn it as heresy.[23] The Franciscan position was defended by Bonaventure, whose arguments were eventually acknowledged and confirmed in *Exiit qui seminat* (1279), a Bull by Nicholas III.[24] Franciscan poverty remained a sensitive and explosive issue, which even brought Friars Minor into open conflict with Pope John XXII. Between 1317 and 1318, he took action against radical groups within the Order

20. Viallet, *Les sens de l'observance*, pp. 117-122.

21. Bonaventura of Bagnoregio, "The Life of Blessed Francis (Legenda maior, 1260-62)", in *Francis of Assisi: Early Documents, Vol. 2, The Founder*, ed. by Regis J. Armstrong, J.A. Wayne Hellmann and William J. Short, Hyde Park, NY and London, New City, 2002, p. 642. The reference to the "Sister Death" is, of course, from Francis's renowned "The Canticle of the Sun".

22. Virpi Mäkinen, *Property Rights in the Late Medieval Discussion on Franciscan Poverty*, Leuven, Peeters, 2001, pp. 57-62.

23. Penn R Szittya, *The Antifraternal Tradition in Medieval Literature*, Princeton, Princeton University Press, 1986, pp. 4-14, p. 55.

24. Mäkinen, *Property Rights*, summary pp. 193-206.

– the Spirituals – accusing them of heresy. Later, in 1323, he also questioned the conclusions of Nicholas III's Bull, which stated that the Friars Minor merely used things without owning them. He also saw heresy in the Franciscan teachings regarding the absolute poverty of Jesus Christ and the apostles.[25]

Poverty remained the key theme of Franciscan spirituality, although Friars Minor now used more cautious language and maintained a status quo in this matter. The issue which proved to be far more serious than the conflict with the Papal Curia was the problem of disunity regarding poverty within the order itself. The first signs of tension appeared while Francis was still alive, escalating shortly after his death. The generalate of Elias of Cortona and his ambitious project to build a magnificent shrine in Assisi created an irreconcilable split between the friars. While some approved of the plan to build an imposing shrine for the recently canonised Francis and supported Elias, others regarded it as a crime against the order and betrayal of the saint's ideals.

It became apparent that the followers of Francis of Assisi were confronted with a big issue which would eventually develop into a serious crisis. Francis himself, after all, had seemed to consider the transformation of Lesser Brothers into a firmly organised order rather a necessary concession more than the ultimate goal of his efforts. After his death, the brothers were faced with a difficult dilemma as to how to institutionalise the legacy of their charismatic teacher. There were two opposing views. The first emphasised the necessity of development and the need to respond to the transforming challenges of the times. The order became more closely involved in ecclesiastical structures – for example, the brothers began to accept the bishops' offices. This, however, had a profound impact on the structure of the order. While Francis was still alive, there were mostly lay brothers (Francis himself never accepted priestly ordination either), but later the number of priests began to increase sharply.[26] They soon became the majority (up to three quarters in early modern times) and the order began to hierarchise. Lay brothers gradually lost power and were pushed into the background.[27] At the same time, the attitude towards education was changing. The initial attempts to keep the simplicity of missionary work were abandoned, and studying began to be considered a prerequisite for further work. The Franciscan priests, like the Dominicans, began to enter universities in the middle of the thirteenth century, where they (for instance, Bonaventure, William of Ockham and Duns Scotus) contributed greatly to the development of scholastic learning. Bonaventure viewed it as a parallel to the history of the church – while the early church was led by ordinary fishermen, later it required learned doctors.[28] All these changes demanded concessions, as

25. Lambert, *Franciscan Poverty*, pp. 208-246.

26. Duncan Nimmo, *Reform and Division in the Medieval Franciscan Order: From Saint Francis to the Foundations of the Capuchins*, Rome, Capuchin Historical Institute, 1987, p. 16.

27. Precise information on the composition of the Olomouc friary is available only from the second half of the eighteenth century. For example, in 1772 there lived 38 priests and 13 lay brothers. See: NA Prague, Bohemian Franciscan Province Archives, reg. no. 2982, book 175.

28. Nimmo, *Reform and Division*, p. 9.

the brothers found themselves in circumstances the founder of the order had not envisioned. This was also why the pope granted the Friars Minor several dispensations during the fifteenth century, and relaxed and modified the auspicious nature of the order.

This was exactly what the opposite camp saw as a problem. For them, this was a clear decay and deviation from the original mission. Their objections also sometimes included doubts that the pope should interfere with the Rule of Saint Francis, given that it had been, as these brothers firmly believed, revealed or even prescribed to Francis by Jesus Christ. Just as part of the Church demanded a return to the Gospel, the Franciscans repeatedly attempted to return to their Rule and adhere to it strictly (*sine glossa*). Their complaints concerning the state of the order were often justified because religious discipline was deteriorating, and many friars were abusing the papal dispensations. On the other hand, some of these brothers tended to believe that they were the chosen ones, encouraged by the texts of Joachim of Fiore. This notion brought them dangerously close to sects.[29]

The clash with John XXII and the suppression of the Spirituals strengthened the moderate wing of the order. At the same time, it triggered further attempts at reform. While the administration of the order and most of the houses were in the hands of the moderate friars, there were new communities emerging, aimed at the literal fulfilment of Francis's Rule in line with their own ideas. They mostly depended on the benevolence of their superiors and their influence never went beyond their province. One of these groups was a community of brothers that formed in central Italy in the 1330s. It later came to be known as the Observants due to their efforts at adhering to the rule. Like others, the group initially struggled with mistrust and bans. As its influence grew over time, Observance was acknowledged at the Council of Constance as a legitimate reformist attempt to revive the order of Friars Minor. It owed its success mainly to prominent figures such as Bernardino of Siena and John of Capistrano. The Observants were granted permission in 1446 by Pope Eugene IV to establish their own administration within the order. Their houses were now semi-independent of the main body of the order and they could create their own custodies and provinces. These were subject to two vicar generals (one for the Cismontane region and one for the Ultramontane region) who were largely independent of the order's minister.[30]

By then, Observance had spread successfully from Italy to other countries. Ultimately, however, the idea of Observance starting a revival of the whole order never materialised. Many of the old houses remained inhabited by the moderate friars, who were in opposition to the Observants and rejected attempts to adopt radical reform. Additionally, other reform groups began to appear, which deemed

29. Marjorie Reeves, *The Influence of Prophecy in the Later Middle Ages: A Study in Joachimism*, Oxford, Clarendon Press, 1969, pp. 175-177.

30. Lazaro Iriarte, *Franciscan History: The Three Orders of St. Francis of Assisi*, Chicago, Franciscan Herald Press, 1983, pp. 62-70. For more on late medieval Observant movements in general, see: Bert Roest, "Observant Reform in Religious Orders", in *Cambridge History of Christianity, Volume 4: Christianity in Western Europe c. 1100-c. 1500*, ed. by Miri Rubin and Walter Simons, Cambridge, Cambridge University Press, 2011, pp. 446-457.

Observance lenient and inconsistent. The situation in the order was no longer tenable at the beginning of the sixteenth century. Pope Leo X decided to take a radical step. On the eve of the Reformation, in May 1517, he split the Order of Friars Minor into two sections. Moderate friars formed the Order of Friars Minor Conventuals (also known as the Minorites). They retained the spectacular Assisi basilica with the saint's grave and all the papal privileges mitigating Francis's Rule. Their monasteries were thus able to, for example, acquire liquid assets. The radical friars were subordinated to the Observants and created the Order of Friars Minor of the Strict Observance (which assumed the informal name of Franciscans). This group, in contrast, retained the original modest Portiuncula chapel and the order's ancient seal. Their superior was also granted the original title of "minister general", while the Conventual superior acquired a new, and thus less prestigious, title of "magister general".[31]

2. *Reform in the times of the Reformation*

The division of the order did not end their problems. The most radical brothers were concerned that the "purified" order had become, in their opinion, too moderately Observant. They continued to pursue strict adherence to what they considered to be the only true way to live according to St Francis's Rule. A mere eight years after the division, another reform movement emerged. It became independent in the sixteenth century and created the third autonomous Order of Friars Minor – the Capuchins. There were, however, many more similar reform movements – about three dozen in the sixteenth century.[32] While most of them were short-lived and limited to individual provinces, others – above all the Discalced in Spain, the Recollects in Western Europe, and the Reformed in Italy and later in Central Europe – developed in powerful movements that once again threatened the unity of the order. Although they failed to gain full independence, unlike the Capuchins, they at least acquired some autonomy within the Order, similar to what the Observants achieved within the undivided order in the fifteenth century.

By then, however, reform efforts within the order began to interlink with more general processes going on in Christendom. Martin Luther and the other reformers fundamentally challenged the essence of religious life. Their teachings had no room for elite "professional" Christians. As the new ideas spread, so did anti-clericalism and anti-fraternalism, which took aim chiefly at the mendicants. The friars thus had to face pressure from the outside and at the same time deal with the situation within their order. Many brothers eventually converted, sometimes even becoming the first local preachers of the Reformation. Often these were the same brothers who had previously sought to restore strict adherence to the Rule. It was the reluctance of the rest of the order to accept the reform, obstructions from more conservative superiors, or the impossibility of meeting all the demands of

31. Nimmo, *Reform and Division*, pp. 641-642.
32. Holzapfel, *Handbuch der Geschichte*, 323-350.

strict observance that might have made them seek different paths. The decline in membership and the rapid drop in numbers in the Transalpine provinces harmed the order on more than just a personnel level. It also damaged its prestige – especially when converts were joined by renowned friars that until then were involved in reform attempts within the order. This was the case of, for example, Bernardino Ochino, former Vicar General of the Capuchins. Worse still was when these gifted converts devoted their skills and enthusiasm to the Reformation. They then became the most radical and implacable critics of the order. Their intimate knowledge of all internal problems and the need to cope with their past in this institution turned them into feared adversaries.[33]

The Catholic Church was well aware of the danger ensuing from the internal disharmony and crisis of the order. At the same time, they also noted the enormous potential that the order had for the renewal of the Catholic Church and ultimately for the confrontation with non-Catholics. They therefore strove to support and take control of the reform process within the order. Leo X's attempt to resolve the Franciscan "schism" was just one of a series of actions which escalated as the process of the Catholic restoration grew in intensity. Religious orders were subsequently also addressed by the Council of Trent, which paid special attention to the Franciscans and Capuchins. The decree adopted during the twenty-fifth session of the Council explicitly confirmed that, unlike other orders, these two reformist branches of Friars Minor could under no circumstances acquire real estate.[34] The decree thus confirmed the specificity of both the orders and, indirectly, the significance of the Franciscan ideal of poverty in the restoration of the Catholic Church.[35] This was, however, far from the last time the Church authorities intervened in the internal reform process of the Franciscans. The Roman Curia, as well as the leaders of the Franciscan Order, were aware of the strength and popularity of the new reform movements within the order (particularly the Discalced, Recollects and Reformed). Their support to those groups – often at the expense of the Observants – was aimed at stimulating a local religious revival and facilitating better central control of some provinces.[36]

This strategy is apparent especially in the Transalpine countries, which were coping with the consequences of the Reformation. The Bohemian Province witnessed the first unsuccessful attempts to introduce the reform in the first two dec-

33. Geoffrey Dipple, *Antifraternalism and Anticlericalism in the German Reformation: Johann Eberlin von Günzburg and the Campaign against the Friars*, Aldershot, Scolar, 1996; Cf. Diarmaid MacCulloch, *Reformation: Europe's House Divided, 1490-1700*, London, Penguin, 2004, p. 155.

34. *Conciliorum Oecumenicorum Generaliumque Decreta. Editio critica. Tomus III. The Oecumenical Councils of the Roman Catholic Church: From Trent to Vatican II (1545-1965)*, eds. Klaus Ganzer, Giuseppe Alberigo, and Alberto Meloni, Turnhout, Brepols Publishers, 2010, p. 152..

35. The order's tradition always insisted that "the poverty of Friars Minor is no invention or human innovation, but is real, genuine, imposed by Christ himself and suggested to St Francis". Jan Damasus Charvath, *Fractio Panis in Refectionem Fratrum Minorum. to jest: Krátký výklad na Regulu Bratří Menších,*V Uherské Skalici, V Joz. A. Skarnycla, 1765, p. 119.

36. Armstrong, *The Politics of Piety*, pp. 46-47.

Fig. 14. Observant habit, from Philippus Bonanni, *Ordinum Religiosorum In Ecclesia Militanti Catalogus Eorumque indumenta in Iconibus Expressa, & oblata. Pars Prima. Editio Secunda* (Romae: Typis Georgii Plachi, 1714).
Fig. 15. Reformed habit, from Philippus Bonanni, *Ordinum Religiosorum In Ecclesia Militanti Catalogus Eorumque indumenta in Iconibus Expressa, & oblata. Pars Prima. Editio Secunda* (Romae: Typis Georgii Plachi, 1714).

ades of the seventeenth century, when St Bernardino was, as mentioned above, selected as a base for incoming reformed Italian friars. A much more successful attempt took place in Bavaria at that time.[37] Provinces in the Habsburg countries followed the Bavarian example later. In 1628, all the friaries of the Tyrolean province joined the Reformed, with the entire Austrian province following suit four years later. In those provinces, the Franciscans managed to avoid disputes between the Observants and the Reformed, which had long plagued the Italian provinces, thanks to top-down implementation of the Reform and conversion of the entire province at once. This model was also followed by the Carniola province and both of the Hungarian provinces.[38]

37. The Reformed friars spread in Bavaria despite the fact that it was part of the Ultramontane family of the order (covering Western Europe) and as such was supposed to be outside the sphere of influence of the Italian *reformati*. For more on the Reformed in Bavaria, see: Trevor Johnson, *Magistrates, Madonnas and Miracles: The Counter Reformation in the Upper Palatinate*, Farnham, Ashgate, 2009, pp. 126-127.

38. The situation was different in Poland, where the Observant and Reformed houses coexisted side by side. Holzapfel, *Handbuch der Geschichte*, p. 347.

This was no easy process, however. It was often confusing and incomprehensible even to the parties involved. It seems that during this process the aims and ambitions of the original Italian *riforma* had changed. It emerged as a manifestation of dissatisfaction with the Observant way of life. Its primary goal was, besides strict adherence to the Rule, the strengthening of contemplative and penitent elements. In 1532, Pope Paul III met these demands, requiring that one or more "recollection houses" be set up in all the Italian provinces to accommodate the brothers who wanted a stricter life. The houses, however, began to associate and seek independence from the Observant authorities. After many dramatic events, the Reform was recognized in 1639 by Pope Urban VIII as a specific internal branch of the order with its own hierarchy (though subordinate to the minister general).[39]

It appears that some of the reformist principles had weakened in the meantime. In any case, the export of the reform beyond the Alps required further changes. In contrast to the Italian friaries, the houses in Central Europe had to participate in the restoration of the Catholic Church, specifically in cities. This clashed with some of the original Reformed ideals such as life in seclusion and the absence of philosophical and theological studies. Instead it was necessary to focus on the general revival of religious discipline and, in particular, on the restoration of the Franciscan ideal of absolute poverty. This revival also had to be publicly presented – the "new" friars were to wear a more distinct (scruffier and patched) habit with a shorter mantle. For many, this was the most comprehensible part of the reform and the Franciscan historian Severinus Wrbczansky had to remind his readers in the eighteenth century that the reform had involved more than "shaving the beard and shortening the cloak, as some would think". He stressed that the main goal of the reform had been strict adherence to the Rule, constitutions and statutes, "and above all, having the holy poverty shine in the church and refectory".[40]

Poverty remained an essential means of institutionalising and legitimising Franciscan charisma even in early modern times. Wrbczansky's quote outlines yet another characteristic of the whole process – the reform took place on two important and interconnected levels. The first level was to promote poverty within the friary walls. This was the reason for the adoption of the Reformed statutes in 1634 (following the example of the Austrian province), and for a number of additional regulations and prohibitions issued at regular provincial chapters. The other, equally significant level was to manifest poverty outside the friaries. The perception and evaluation of the activities of Friars Minor was tied to stereotypes ranging between two extremes. One was the image of apostolic men living in holiness and utter poverty, and the other a picture of hypocritical gluttons growing happily fat in the wealth generated through alms. These stereotypes were not only held by the lower classes.[41] Many of them dated back to the aforementioned Sorbonne

39. Holzapfel, *Handbuch der Geschichte*, pp. 344-348.

40. Wrbczansky, *Nucleus Minoriticus*, p. 28.

41. Similarly, they were not limited to Utraquists or Protestants only. See: Desiderius Erasmus, *Ptochoploúsioi*, in *The Colloquies of Erasmus*, trans. by Craig R. Thompson, Chicago, University of Chicago Press, 1965, pp. 203-217.

Fig. 16. Abuses of the Roman Catholic Church represented by the Franciscans; in the foreground a friar burdened with alms receives an indulgence bull from the pope. Lucas Cranach the Younger, *True and false preaching*, 1547. From Robert W. Scribner, *For the Sake of Simple Folk: Popular Propaganda for the German Reformation* (Oxford; New York: Oxford University Press, 1994), 203.

disputes between mendicants and secular masters in the 1250s.[42] In the following centuries, the figure of the debauched, chubby Franciscan, luring alms from the trusting flock, became integral to the writings criticising Church abuses – whether the Hussite, Humanistic, Reformation or later Enlightened point of view:

> and they wander door to door, etc., with sacks, bottles over their shoulders; and though their diet is to be scanty, they feast on dinners and drink bountiful, and their pantries were found to be bursting with abundance […] And they won't accept a penny or two, for it is little; but pike, carp, a roast, pig they do put in the sack, along with bottles of wine. [...] Others, ruddy, fat, conceited, stay at home for they are too worthy [...] like a cat, though a fish-lover, will not enter the river to catch fish.[43]

The visual aspects of mendicants played an important role in the development of said stereotypes. It was no coincidence that most of the popular names for Franciscans – both neutral (the discalced, greyfriars) and derogatory (cowlies, tufts and slippers) were derived from their typical look. The use of new media – woodcuts and books – in the Reformation facilitated a wider circulation of these caricatures.[44] The figure of a well-fed Franciscan (often laden with alms begged from peasants) and the figure of the pope (trading indulgences), are some of the most common means used to criticise the ills of the medieval Church.

The existence and impact of these stereotypes forced the Franciscans to pay greater attention to external attributes which could resonate with these stereotypes. They could also refer themselves to St Bonaventure, who argued that Christ wanted his disciples not only to be poor, but also to look poor – and to encourage others to follow by showing the way rather than telling.[45] In any case, appearance and the manifestation of poverty were given a lot of attention at the regular provincial chapters and definitoria. The altars and the friaries were to look plain and modest, along with church services. For example, "figural innovations" during liturgy were banned in 1653 – plainchant was to be the only music heard.[46] Particular attention was paid to the appearance of the friars and their behaviour in public. Brothers were forbidden to ride a horse and wear clothing or objects in public that could contradict self-renunciation and poverty (hats, gloves) or symbolise property and ownership (pouches, keys). Crosses and rosaries were to be

42. Guy Geltner, "William of St. Amour's De Periculis Novissimorum Temporum: a False Start to Medieval Antifraternalism?", in *Defenders and Critics of Franciscan Life: Essays in Honor of John V. Fleming*, ed. by Michael F. Cusato and Guy Geltner, Leiden-Boston, Brill, 2009, pp. 105-118.

43. Václav Koranda, *Manualník M. Vácslava Korandy: Rukopis Bibliotheky klementinské*, ed. by Josef Truhlář, Prague, Král. česká spol. nauk, 1888, pp. 45-48.

44. Scribner, *For the Sake of Simple Folk*, pp. 165-166.

45. Comments concerning the Gospel of Luke in *Doctoris Seraphici S. Bonaventurae ... Opera Omnia, Iussu Et Auctoritate Bernardini a Portu Romatino ... Studio Et Cura PP. Collegii a. S. Bonaventura, Ad Plurimos Codices MSS. Emendata ...*, vol. 12, Quaracchi, ex typographia Collegii S. Bonaventurae, 1882, 7: 255a. Cf. Mäkinen, *Property Rights*, p. 61, note no. 13.

46. NA Prague, Czech Franciscan Archives, book 68, *Acta praecipua & notabilia conclusae in Capitulis Provincialibus et Diffinitoriis celebratis, Ab Anno 1614 ex Provinciae Protocollo excerpta - Statuta praecipua in Capitulis Provincialibus et Diffinitoriis facta ab Anno* (1614-1759). Hereinafter cited as *Acta praecipua* or *Statuta praecipua*.

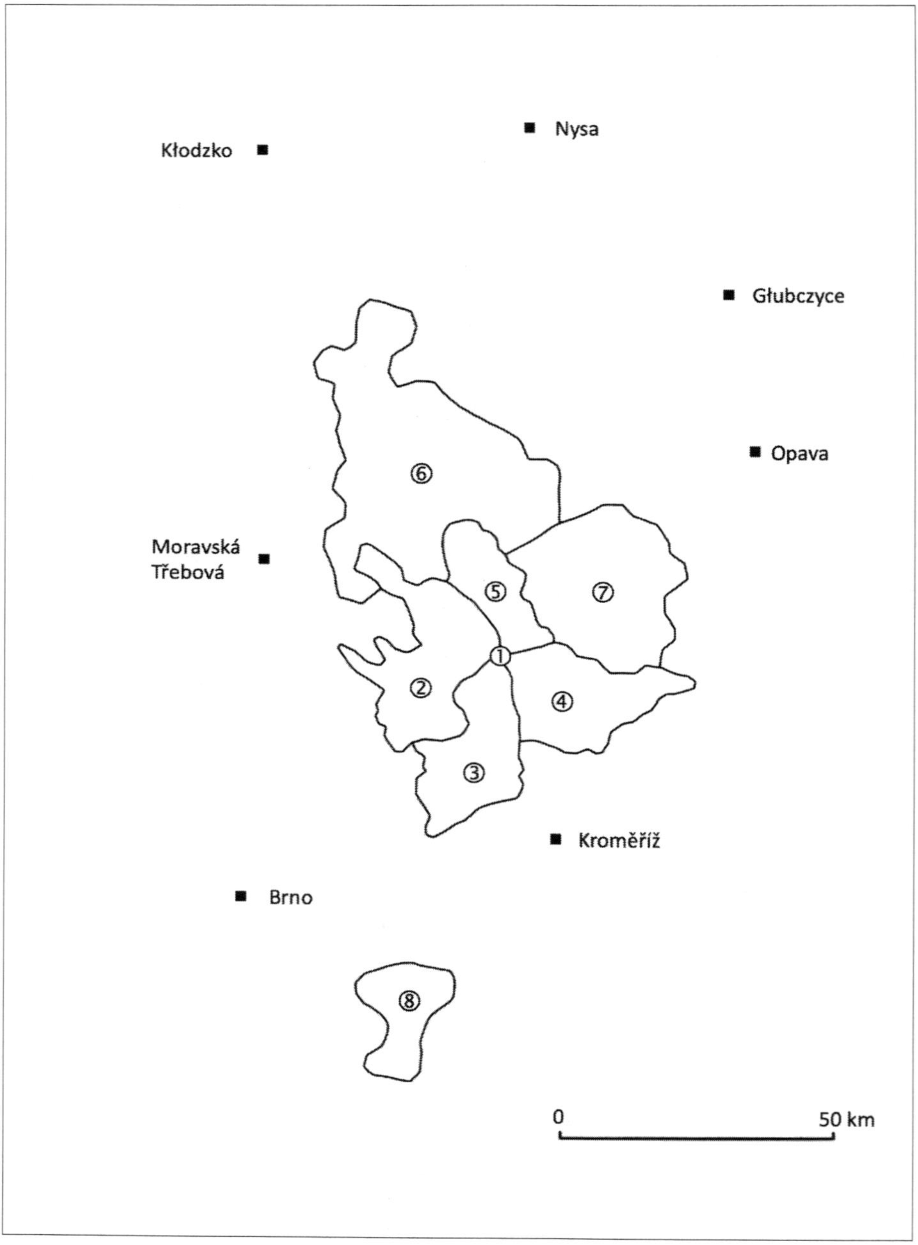

Fig. 17. Mendicant districts of the St Bernardino friary: 1. city (Olomouc), 2. western (Prostějov), 3. southern (Tovačov), 4. eastern (Přerov), 5. northern (Šternberk), 6. montane (major), 7. montane (minor), 8. wine region (Ždánice). Black squares mark nearby Franciscan friaries.

simple, made of wood – anybody who had a sanctified cross (which could be made of, for example, silver) was to wear it hidden in the frock.[47]

The attention paid to external attributes, however, could not only be due to concerns about the restoration or maintenance of the order's reputation. It stems from a much older tradition and is related to the overall concept of the Franciscan mission. Although the mendicant orders are traditionally associated with preaching, the range of means with which they sought to reach their audience was much wider. Imagery was of immense importance, given the low levels of literacy in the population and the limited spatial and temporal impact of sermons.[48] Visual means did not only include frescoes and sacred paintings. The most widespread and most accessible medium were the brothers themselves. The foundations of this tradition were laid by Francis of Assisi himself. *Imitatio Christi* in his concept became an expressive performance depicting the principles of gospel and apostolic poverty in a clear and powerful way.[49] His conversion, the Greccio nativity scene, stigmatisation, death and other dramatic scenes from his life formed only a part. The everyday life of St Francis and his followers had an equally strong visual potential, which the later Franciscan tradition sought to cultivate.[50]

The traditional means of expression of the Franciscans and religious orders in general was their habit. The Franciscan habit consisted of a tunic tied with a hemp cord and a mozzetta with a round hood. In terms of shoes, the transalpine Franciscans initially wore clogs, later replaced by sandals. The directive instructing brothers to wear sandals instead of clogs – a seemingly minor change – was welcomed enthusiastically across the whole province, as clogs worn in rain and snow likely posed a considerable security risk. This is how Father Mauritius Tyrola suffered a fatal injury in Olomouc in 1669 after years of collecting alms in rural areas.[51] Friars could also put a cloak over the tunic (the Observants had a longer cloak and the Reformed a shorter one). But, most important of all, the habit was to be made of a cheap, rough fabric, mostly ashy in colour, and was supposed to be worn and patched:

> This means through mending, repairing the Habit or Tunic, which is done by sewing pieces of old cloth onto those places which are worn out or torn. Holy Father [ie. Francis of Assisi] allows the mending for the three following reasons: Firstly, to preserve the Holy Poverty, so that once a Garment was worn out, a new one was not required, but instead, the old was mended to extend its life. Secondly, for greater humility of the World, and so that Brothers were more disdained and humbled before men, and shaming themselves before the World, they would become dearer and more likeable before the Face of God. Thirdly, for the body needs, so that the mending covered its nakedness and protected the Brother from being cold. Whoever does the mending for the aforementioned reasons is Blessed by God. The mending should not involve work with colourful patches, which

47. *Statuta praecipua*, pp. 1-4.

48. Bolzoni, *The Web of Images*, pp. 122-125.

49. Antonio Attisani, "Franciscan Performance: A Theatre Lost and Found Again", *PAJ: A Journal of Performance and Art* 25, trans. by Jane House, 1 (2003). p. 48-60.

50. Moshe Barasch, *Giotto and the Language of Gesture*, Cambridge (Cambridgeshire), -New York, Cambridge University Press, 1987, see: esp. p. 63.

51. *Archivum*, p. 56.

> would ridicule and degrade our Order; the mending is to match the Habit in colour. The Brothers should never mend for the sake of proud Subservience, or Hypocrisy, in order to be considered and deemed disdained and thus more perfect; they are called to act fully in line with the Orders of their Superiors in this regard.[52]

The excessive attention paid to the order's clothing is one of the traditional nuisances criticised in the Middle Ages. Ironically, however, it is also a manifestation and by-product of the reform processes within the order, as evident from the Franciscan-Capuchin dispute over the "true look" of the habit of St Francis. With the adoption of the reform, poverty once again became the central theme influencing all areas of Franciscan work. Wishing to consolidate their position in society, the Franciscans had to present their reform and the revived ideal of poverty to the local community in a clear and comprehensible way. Patched clothing became an important means of expression in this context.[53]

3. *Alms*

Due to the composition of the order (a majority of priests and minority of lay brethren) and its focus (preaching and pastoral work), manufacturing within the friaries played a relatively minor role. Some houses managed small vegetable gardens or even fish ponds, others produced habits, sandals or medicinal drugs for the friars.[54] But, in general, Franciscan communities were economically fully dependent on local communities.[55] This was, after all, the fundamental essence of the Franciscan ideal of apostolic poverty. The brothers were to live from day to day, without surplus and without reserve, relying on Divine Providence and alms. Physical poverty was not meant to be an end in itself – it was understood as an expression of the dependent position of man before God and absolute trust in God's mercy. Begging thus had, in addition to its economic role, a significant spiritual dimension.[56] Moreover, its social aspects were important, too. Begging brought friars into contact with a much wider range of people – not just those who more or less regularly attended their church. Franciscans travelled beyond the walls of both friaries and cities, which significantly broadened their reach. And, last but not least, begging also clearly demonstrated their poverty and helped to negotiate their position in society.

52. Charvath, *Fractio Panis*, pp. 594-595.

53. Elbel, "The Making of a Perfect Friar", passim.

54. All of these commodities served exclusively for the internal needs of the houses or for other friaries. For example, the Olomouc friary made fabric for habits for the other Moravian friaries. See: *Archivum*, p. 23.

55. Support from the three affiliated women's friaries (Znojmo, Brno and Jawor) was slightly more substantial. As women's religious institutions observed strict confinement, they could not secure a livelihood by begging. Thus they were not only allowed, but directly advised, to acquire real estate – managed by either secular administrators or by the friars themselves. The nuns would then subsidise the nearby friary, usually in return for spiritual services. Wrbczansky, *Nucleus*, p. 176.

56. Nimmo, *Reform and Division*, p. 14.

Mendicancy in early modern times and its various aspects can be very well illustrated using the example of St Bernardino. It was one of the largest houses of the province – over fifty brothers lived there in the eighteenth century. As an urban foundation it did not possess any regular source of income (like smaller friaries founded and sponsored by aristocratic families) and fully depended on the constant support of believers. The city itself would not be capable of maintaining the friary and so alms also needed to be collected from the countryside too – a vast territory surrounding Olomouc and comprising more than 350 towns and villages.[57] This large area was divided into several districts for the purposes of better organized collections. The four largest districts were formed along the main roads leading west, south, east and north, roughly within forty kilometres of the city.[58] Two other districts were located farther to the north (later merged into one). These districts were the largest but their economic significance was rather low – they covered mountainous regions with sparse settlements inhabited mostly by poor people.[59] In 1730, the Olomouc friary was allocated a small district of approximately twenty villages in South Moravia. This was a wine-growing area where the Olomouc friars were allowed to beg solely for the wine (which was not available in the other districts); the other food stuffs here could only be collected by the friars from Brno.[60] The last and by far the most important district was Olomouc itself.

This division of collection districts dates to 1673, when the provincial chapter held in Bechyně tried to precisely define and describe the boundaries of the districts for collections of the friaries. Each house had been allocated an area corresponding to its size.[61] The description of the districts, including a detailed list of all the municipalities, was included in friary chronicles and served as a basis for constructing the itineraries of the collections.[62] The districts were naturally flexible, changing whenever the size of a friary was altered.[63] The collection districts also played a key role in the settling of new houses. It was necessary to carefully

57. Dating to about 1750, the first inventory recorded in the Franciscan chronicle (*Protocollum*) registers 381 municipalities. The second list, drawn up in 1773 in response to the Bishop Consistory circular, records twenty less municipalities. *Protocollum*, pp. 407-410.

58. The districts were the Prostějov district (98 municipalities), the Tovačov district (63 municipalities), the Přerov district (65 municipalities), and the Šternberk district (37 municipalities – this district was later connected to the Přerov district).

59. The large montane district with 63 municipalities covered the Šumperk and Rýmařov regions, while the small montane one with 24 municipalities was the Libavá region.

60. According to the decision of the definitorium as of 28 August 1730, see: *Protocollum*, Section H.

61. Only friars from the Prague friary (the seat of the provincial and provincial studies) could collect alms throughout the province. Prague National Archives, Bohemian Franciscan Archives, book 67, *Tabulae Capitulares Provinciae Bohemiae, & Acta* (1611-1675). The same concession had been made in 1636 for the newly established friary of Irish Franciscans in Prague – which formally did not belong to the Bohemian province. *Archivum*, p. 27. Cf. Jan Pařez and Hedvika Kuchařová, *Hyberni v Praze: Dějiny františkánské koleje Neposkvrněného početí Panny Marie v Praze (1629-1786)*, Prague, Oswald, 2001.

62. Franciscan friary chronicles, in NA Prague, Bohemian Franciscan Archives, and Moravian Land Archive, Brno, Dačice Franciscans, section *Collecturae Conventus*.

63. For example the Zásmuky friary had to be awarded new collection sites in 1754 to

consider whether the begging area of the new house would not disrupt the districts of the surrounding friaries. If the distance between the houses was sufficient and there was enough no man's land, then it was possible to proceed. In some cases, however, this turned out to be an insurmountable problem (specifically in mountainous and less fertile areas) and the idea of a new house had to be abandoned.[64]

Moreover, the Franciscans were not the only friars reliant on alms. Members of other orders, apart from the Capuchins, also made collections.[65] It was therefore absolutely necessary for all these orders (often assisted by church and secular authorities) to reach a compromise and to avoid unsavoury conflicts. This balance was extremely fragile and needed to be repeatedly negotiated. Every attempt at setting up a new religious house upset the equilibrium. The other orders fought the attempts, as the Franciscans could often see for themselves when restoring the original friaries or establishing new ones. On the other hand, they also vehemently intervened against such attempts on several occasions. For example, the Olomouc Franciscans tried to prevent the Capuchins from settling in the city at the beginning of the seventeenth century. Their attempt failed, despite support from the Jesuits. They were much more successful in 1688, when they launched a campaign to prevent the Brothers of Mercy from establishing themselves in Tovačov (Tobitschau). The Franciscans argued that the new monastery would rob their Olomouc friary of a substantial part of the alms and thus endanger its further operations. Their reasoning was found weighty enough to thwart the plans for the new monastery.[66]

The regulations did not stop at the geographical delimitation of the districts. The idea one might get from early Franciscan texts of brothers wandering about the countryside and begging for anything that anyone could offer is misleading. Collecting alms at that time was no longer as spontaneous as it had been in the early days of the mendicant orders. On the contrary, collections were carefully organised and followed a fixed order both in terms of space and time.[67] Each friary had its own itinerary, detailing how many times and in which months each district was supposed to be toured. While the western, northern and eastern districts were toured five times a year, the southern one was visited six times, the montane one three times, and the wine region once a year. In addition, it was clearly specified what would be begged for during each visit. The grain, for example, was begged for in the four main districts in October and November and in the northern moun-

the detriment of the other nearby friaries, as the existing area of the district failed to cover their needs. *Acta praecipua*, p. 30.

64. Klemens Minařík, "Provinciál P. Bernard Sannig, učenec, spisovatel a organisátor františkánské provincie (1637-1704)", *Časopis katolického duchoventsva*, 67 (1926): pp. 216 and 323.

65. For the history of the Capuchins in Bohemia, see: Marek Brčák, *Kapucínský řád a společnost v Čechách a na Moravě v letech 1618-1673*, Prague, MA Thesis, Charles University, 2013.

66. Minařík, "Provinciál P. Bernard Sannig", 66 (1925): p. 458.

67. The timing of the alms was probably set out in the Provincial Authority regulation of 28 July 1749. *Gesetzlexikon im Geistlichen, Religions- und Toleranzfache*, ed. by Peter Karl Jaksch, Erster Band, Von A-D, Prag, Gubernialregistratur, 1828, pp. 65-66.

tain district in December and January. The specifics of every district were naturally taken into account. As the four main districts around Olomouc were the most fertile and rich, the majority of trips headed there and the list of begged victuals was the most varied of all. The montane district was the poorest, with friars collecting primarily flax, in addition to grain and butter.

The complete mendicant itinerary of St Bernardino was as follows. The main collection campaign took place during the summer months – first, the alms collectors set out in June to the southern district for hay. Then in June and July they toured all four adjacent districts begging for butter. In the montane districts, butter was begged for with a slight delay (July and August). In August and September, they begged for poultry in the four districts around Olomouc, and in October and November they returned here to collect grains (in the montane districts it was December and January). In October, the friars also begged for vegetables in the western and southern districts, and visited the South-Moravian district to plead for wine. The begging campaigns countinued even in the winter. In January, they returned to the southern district to collect oil. In February and March, they made the undoubtedly difficult trip up to the montane districts to beg for flax. And finally, twice a year – during Lent and after the Assumption – they begged for eggs in the four main districts.

These basic commodities begged for in the countryside were complemented by daily collections in the city. Even here, some alms had been arranged ahead of time with specific benefactors. For example, the friars were given flour by the bakers on Wednesdays and beef (outside the fasting period) by the butchers on Fridays. Every two weeks they went to beg the wine-sellers. Milk and garden vegetables, in contrast, were begged any day, although the tendency to collect these foods regularly on Saturdays eventually prevailed. Candles were begged for during Advent and Lent, while incense and oil were begged for four times a year at the annual markets. The Franciscans begged for these commodities, and for ink and paper, mostly in vicarages and monasteries – for example, the hosts were donated on a regular basis by the Provost of St Maurice Church.[68] The rich church institutions – the bishop, the chapter and particularly the Premonstratensian Hradisko Monastery – provided the Franciscans with extraordinary donations (bricks, building timber) besides regular alms. The traditional benefactors also included local secular institutions. The city council gifted the Franciscans (as well as other mendicants) with a beer keg every Christmas, Easter, Pentecost and on the feast days of the order.[69] At least once, the friars sent a humble request to the K. K. Tabacks Ober-Directorium, asking for forty pounds of black tobacco at a reduced price.[70]

68. Olomouc State District Archive, Fund St Maurice Vicarage (1510-1952), reg. no. 24, *Účetní kniha* (1727-1751), passim.

69. Olomouc State District Archive, Olomouc Archives – fragments of the registries, reg. no. 3763, carton 132. *Dary klášterům* (1676-98), passim.

70. NA Prague, Bohemian Franciscan Province Archives, reg. no. 2981, carton 175, fol. 6b.

The yield from these collections was usually high enough to provide for all the roughly fifty inhabitants of the Olomouc friary. In 1773, for instance, within the city the brothers received the donations of 46 zentners (2,839 kg) of beef, 4 zentners (247 kg) of candles and 4 pounds (over 2 kg) of incense. The rural districts donated 104 bushels (7,280 litres) of wheat, 220 bushels (15,400 litres) of rye, 80 bushels (5,600 litres) of barley and 14 bushels (980 litres) of legumes.[71] The autumn campaign generated 15 zentners (926 kg) of clarified butter and 3 zentners (185 kg) of salted butter.[72] In terms of poultry, the friars collected 150 geese, 200 ducks and 320 chickens, plus 18,000 eggs. The number of alms and the area of the collection districts placed great demands on the organisation of the collections. Select types of alms – such as poultry, eggs, vegetables or oil – were not begged for across the whole district, but only in nearby locations. The other commodities (unless the donor generously took care of the transport to the friary) had to be temporarily placed in a safe place (usually in a vicarage, manor estate or in the granary of one of the benefactors) and subsequently taken all together to Olomouc. The friary had two horses, a carriage and a sleigh for these purposes. This convenience was largely due to the size of the Olomouc house and of its district. This was by no means the rule; for example, in 1669 the provincial authorities turned down the Kadaň friary's request to purchase horses.[73]

Collecting itself, that is, going around villages and individual houses, was made in each district by a pair of brothers, sometimes assisted by a lay volunteer. The friars were carefully selected. They needed to be incorrupt and thoroughly instructed not only on where to go, but also how to not compromise the order or mendicancy itself. It seems, however, that in the eighteenth century this activity was not particularly popular among friars. The province authorities was forced to address the issue in 1726:

> Experience has shown that many fathers and young brothers, as well as others, agile enough, refuse to collect donations making various fictitious excuses to the great detriment of our friaries. The venerable definitorium hereby requests, in order not to tolerate any such laziness and poor tendencies as have brought us injury, as follows: unless these fathers and brothers publicly prove their infirmity [to collect alms] and promptly agree to collect alms and diligently do so, may these said men be kept inside the friary like the lazy and useless servants they are, may they not be permitted, should they ask, to leave, and furthermore, may they be rid of all the concessions allowed within the friary available to others, namely entertainment and any form of enjoyment.[74]

Alms-collecting indeed placed high demands on the brothers. In the case of one of the four main mendicant districts near the city, the friars collecting donations had to cover (shod in sandals) over two hundred kilometres, and in the case of the montane districts the route was considerably longer. Moreover, travelling

71. Provided one Moravian bushel is approximately 70 litres.

72. The first type of butter was preserved by slowly heating the butter until it melted. The top layer containing the proteins was then removed. The remaining butter was nearly pure fat, which could be stored for considerably longer under certain conditions.

73. *Acta praecipua*, p. 3.

74. *Statuta praecipua*, p. 16 (entry of 1726).

to collect donations could be rough and full of surprises, compared to the clearly structured and regular life in the monastery. The brothers collecting had to communicate with people of varied backgrounds, social status and opinions. Needless to say, they were not always warmly welcomed.

Despite all the difficulties and dangers, it is obvious that the friary could rely on a wide and stable network of benefactors, and that the whole mendicant system operated quite smoothly until it closed down (alms collection was prohibited by Joseph II in 1789). Details about the outcome of the mendicant campaigns are available for the year 1773, when the superior of the Olomouc house was asked by the bishops' consistory to submit a record of how many alms the friary collected per year. At the beginning of his report, the superior cautiously points to the problem of accurately appraising their "income": "Let me, in all honesty, document that the number of our alms humbly gathered, is highly varied as it depends on God's blessings and generosity of our benefactors; if one or even sometimes both is lacking, it happens that many of the alms are not there, sometimes more than half".[75] Based on the emperor's ruling at that time, the friary could house a maximum of 51 friars, of whom 38 were priests. These concerns were shared by the superiors of the province. Between 1768 and 1771, Provincial Lucius Hornisch stipulated that each house should be able to obtain alms the equivalent of 150 guilders a year per priest and 120 guilders per cleric or lay brother. The annual income of alms received for St Bernardino should therefore be 7,260 fl. (guilders) per year. The superior's report stated that while the friary was close to the target amount, it fell

Fig. 18. Two mendicants on the Upper Square in Olomouc. Joseph Freindt, *The city hall of Olomouc from the north-east*, last third of the eighteenth century. State District Archive in Olomouc, Collection of pictorial and photographic materials, inv. no. 770, sig. VII / 154.

75. Opava Land Archive, Olomouc office, Olomouc Archdiocese, sign. Bb 38, carton 241, *Františkáni v Olomouci*, fol. 143.

short, having received 6,934 fl. in alms in total. It was missing about 325 fl. of the above mentioned 7,260 fl. in 1773. The difference was, the superior argued, due to changes in grain prices.[76] He further noted that, given that many friars had been away during the year, there had been no problems providing for all the confreres – despite the fact that the house participated in charitable activities for the local poor.[77]

The superior's data is validated by the friary's book of income and expenditure (*Liber Ratiociniorum*) for the years 1756 through 1785. The economy of the house was fairly well balanced. When the superior and the apostolic syndic counted the commodities remaining in the house every six months, there was a surplus of about 500 fl. on average. The maximum was 1,317 fl. at the end of 1767 and the minimum 95 fl. at the end of 1760.[78] The friary thus had, as a rule, funds to sustain itself for the next two or three weeks. The community would not have survived without regular alms – it clearly relied on regular support from the public. This shows that the ideal of the order's poverty and the associated mendicant way of life was still fully functional in the second half of the eighteenth century – and not just formally so. The friars continued, as the Rule of St Francis prescribed, to live "as pilgrims and strangers", relying on alms. It was this explicit dependence that fundamentally determined the relationship between the friary and the urban community.

76. NA Prague, Bohemian Franciscan Province Archives, reg. no. 2982, carton 175, *Almužny konventu*, unpaged.

77. Florián Josef Loucký, *Popis královského hlavního města Olomouce sepsaný syndikem Floriánem Josefem Louckým roku 1746*, ed. by Vladimír Spáčil and Libuše Spáčilová, Olomouc, Vlastivědná společnost muzejní v Olomouci, sekce historická and Památkový úřad, 1991, p. 56.

78. *Liber Ratiociniorum*, passim.

4. Patrons and Clients

Alms (including mass stipends and other monetary gifts) were a factor which shaped and consolidated the mendicants' ties to their patrons and benefactors. This network of regular or occasional relationships with supporters of the order primarily served to financially secure the friary and its inhabitants. However, it was also a vital and effective tool for the Franciscans to operate in society. It made the mendicants engage with a far wider circle of people, including those who would never have come to their church. This was especially true for the countryside, where the mendicant districts defined spheres of influence of individual orders. The districts overlapped with other networks, connecting the friaries and their environment. A good example of this practice was membership in Third Orders established as part of the friaries, whose members, for the most part, came from areas defined by the mendicants' rounds. Another instance was the export of some of the order's forms of devotion – for example, the consecration of the Stations of the Cross (whether in a parish church or the open landscape) was one of the competencies of the superior in whose mendicant district the site was.

Begging for alms was one of the most important areas of interaction between friars and the local population. Little is known about the communication that took place when mendicants knocked on the door of their potential donors. Likewise, we can only assume what the donors' motivation was; there could have been a plethora of reasons. The donors included both faithful supporters of the given order and believers who saw alms-giving as their Christian duty and as good works which steered them towards salvation. Others felt social pressure or worried that failure to give alms could raise doubts about their Catholic orthodoxy.[1] Whatever the donors' motivation, one thing is absolutely essential: alms-giving was nearly never a unilateral act.[2] On the contrary, reciprocity was a substantial aspect of alms-giving. Donation was associated with the expectation of reciprocal service,

1. The accusation appeared (later, in the sense of enlightened criticism of monastic institutions) in Joseph Richter's *Bildergalerie klösterlicher Misbräuche: Eine nöthige Beylage zur Bildergalerie Katholischer Misbräuche*, Frankfurt-Leipzig, s.n., 1784, p. 251.

2. See: Marcel Mauss, or Lyndal Roper, *Witch Craze: Terror and Fantasy in Baroque Germany*, New Haven and London, Yale University Press, 2004, p. 4. See: also Natalie Zemon Davis, *The Gift in Sixteenth Century France*, Madison, University of Wisconsin Press, 2000.

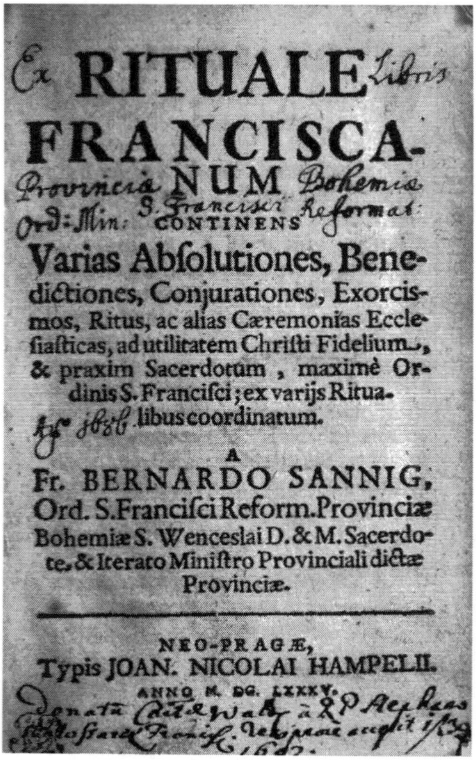

RITUALE
FRANCISCANUM
CONTINENS
Varias Abſolutiones, Benedictiones, Conjurationes, Exorcismos, Ritus, ac alias Cæremonias Eccleſiaſticas, ad utilitatem Chriſti Fidelium, & praxim Sacerdotum, maximè Ordinis S. Franciſci; ex varijs Ritualibus coordinatum.
A
Fr. BERNARDO SANNIG,
Ord. S.Franciſci Reform.Provinciæ Bohemiæ S. Wenceslai D. & M. Sacerdote, & Iterato Miniſtro Provinciali dictæ Provinciæ.
NEO-PRAGÆ,
Typis JOAN. NICOLAI HAMPELII.
ANNO M. DC. LXXXV.

Fig. 19. Front page of Sannig's *Rituale Franciscanum* from 1685. Bernardus Sannig, *Rituale Franciscanum, continens varias Absolutiones, Benedictiones, Conjurationes, Exorcismos, Ritus, ac alias Caeremonias Ecclesiasticas, ad utilitatem Christi Fidelium et praxim Sacerdotum, maxime Ordinis S. Francisci ex variis Ritualibus coordinatum. a Bernardo Sannig. Ord. S. Franc. Reform. Prov. Bohemiae S. Wenceslai D. et M. Sacerdote et iterato Ministro Provinciali dictae Provinciae*, Neo-Pragae, Typis Joan. Nicolai Hampelii, 1685.

whether as blessings, prayers or various sacraments.[3] The relationship between the monastery and the community was thus based on the constant exchange of material gifts from community and spiritual gifts from the mendicants. It was a ritual that embodied the basic elements of the tradition of the order in the given space and time.[4]

1. *Material and spiritual gifts*

The spiritual services rendered by mendicants were in high demand. This was especially true of sacramentals, namely prayers and liturgical acts often associated with sanctified objects that could be subsequently used by believers

3. Some of the donations could also be a sacrifice made to ensure a rich harvest. As much is suggested by a note describing the custom of villagers to donate the first-born calf to the mendicants. See: *Archivum*, p. 119.

4. Edward Muir, *Ritual in Early Modern Europe*, Cambridge, Cambridge University Press, 1997, p. 7.

to protect themselves from misfortune and evil forces.[5] As the sacramentals resembled folk magic in many respects, the Church strove to control their use. *Rituale Romanum,* issued in 1614, substantially contributed to the unification of the devotions in the Catholic Church, but sacramentals were covered only to a limited extent. Moreover, their use was left to the customs of the dioceses.[6] The situation remained ambiguous and incongruous. Sacramentals, extremely popular among the faithful, were ultimately unified and codified largely thanks to the Franciscans – coincidently those from the Bohemian province. In 1685, Bernhard Sannig, the provincial minister and one of the illustrious scholars of the Saint Wenceslas Province, published his *Rituale Franciscanum, continens varias Absolutiones, Benedictiones, Conjurationes, Exorcismos, Ritus, ac alias Caeremonias Ecclesiasticas, ad utilitatem Christi fidelium et praxim Sacerdotum, maxime Ordinis S. Francisci ex variis Ritualibus coordinatum.*[7]

Sannig's handbook became an addendum to *Rituale Romanum* and soon gained great popularity even outside the Franciscan Order. The book soon went through multiple editions, and during the eighteenth century was also published in Cologne, Venice and Rome.[8] One of the reasons behind the popularity of Sannig's book was the fact that it served as a vast catalogue of sacramentals for all sorts of occasions. In addition to various absolutions, conjurations (e.g. protection from storms and lightning) and exorcisms (from diseases, pest birds and, of course, demons), the book contained, in particular, instructions for the sanctification of objects ranging from small devotional items (crosses, candles, rosaries), buildings (houses, breweries) and boats to food and drinks.[9] Many of the sacramentals were used on a daily basis, and it is clear that Franciscans may have been offering them while touring the rural districts.[10] The fact that the sacramentals indeed were an important "currency" used in the interaction between mendicants and society

5. David Gentilcore, *From bishop to witch: The system of the sacred in early modern Terra d'Otranto*, Manchester, Manchester University Press, 1992, pp. 100-101.

6. Moshe Sluhovsky, *Believe Not Every Spirit: Possession, Mysticism, & Discernment in Early Modern Catholicism*, Chicago, University of Chicago Press, 2007, p. 88.

7. Bernardus Sannig, *Rituale Franciscanum, Continens Varias Absolutiones, Benedictiones, Conjurationes, Exorcismos, Ritus, ac alias Caeremonias Ecclesiasticas, ad Utilitatem Christi Fidelium et Praxim Sacerdotum, Maxime Ordinis S. Francisci Ex Variis Ritualibus Coordinatum. a Bernardo Sannig. Ord. S. Franc. Reform. Prov. Bohemiae S. Wenceslai D. et M. Sacerdote et Iterato Ministro Provinciali Dictae Provinciae*, Neo-Pragae, Typis Joan. Nicolai Hampelii, 1685.

8. The editions published abroad in the eighteenth century were usually titled *Rituale Ecclesiasticum*.

9. Jurgen Jensen, *Kirchliche Rituale als Waffen gegen Dämonenwirken und Zauberei: Ein Beitrag zu einem Komplex von Schutz- und Abwehrritualen der Katholischen Kirche des 17. und 18. Jahrhunderts in Italien unter besonderer Berücksichtigung systematisch-ethnologischer Gesichtspunkte*, Münster, LIT, 2007.

10. For similar practices of other mendicant orders, see: von Thiessen, *Die Kapuziner*, pp. 428-449 and Veronika Čapská, "Vytváření prostoru pro působení servitů v českých zemích 17. a 18. století", in *Úloha církevních řádů při pobělohorské rekatolizaci: Sborník příspěvků z pracovního semináře konaného ve Vranově u Brna ve dnech 4. 5. 6. 2003*, ed. by Ivana Čornejová, Praha, Univerzita Karlova, 2003, p. 164.

is also confirmed by Ignaz von Born in his satirical *Monachologia*, where he specifies the Franciscan "animal subspecies" as follows: "He turns small pictures, triangular pieces of paper, amulets and other similar trinkets miraculously into wine and food".[11]

Another significant arena where the exchange of material goods for spiritual favours is evident is in mass stipends. These, according to established practice, were offerings made to the priest for saying mass for a given intention.[12] The donation had to be voluntary, never demanded. The Franciscans themselves emphasized that these were just alms donated for the mass they had said.[13] Yet, it seems that the charge for mass intentions was nearly automatic in the eighteenth century. The amount became stabilized at a uniform charge of 30 kreutzers (1/2 fl.) per mass. The stipends were probably mostly arranged in the church, but there were also stipends brought "to the gate" or acquired through third parties. Quite a few of the stipends were apparently bargained while the brothers collected alms, both in the city and in the countryside. The majority of the stipends covered one or several masses and, excepting the important individuals who paid for multiple masses, remain anonymous. Franciscan sources refer to them jointly as *ex sacristia*. The mass stipends can be grouped with bequests serving to pay for requiem masses. There were, however, generally only a few bequests a year (an average of about ten), typically worth dozens, or exceptionally hundreds, of guilders.[14]

The significance of mass stipends for Franciscan activities is evident from the 1773 statement.[15] Of all the alms earned (6,934 fl), regular collections "yielded" less than half of that number. The Franciscans collected victuals worth 2,107 fl. in the countryside, while in Olomouc alone the victuals amounted to 966 fl.; in addition, the Franciscans received occasional donations from various benefactors worth 961 fl. The remaining income of the friary was made up of alms fees for mass intentions. The sum was considerable – 2,900 fl., which made up two-fifths of the total revenue. Since canon law prohibited grouping several intentions into one mass, the Franciscans at St Bernardino had the resulting duty to say nearly six thousand masses a year for the donors' intentions – a number that could be even higher in some years.[16] As with other alms, the mass stipends cannot be

11. Ignaz von Born, *Joannis Physiophili Specimen Monachologiae Methodo Linnaeana Tabulis Tribus Aeneis Illustratum, Cum Adnexis Thesibus E Pansophia P.P.P. Fast ... Quas Praeside... Capistranoa Mulo Antonii ... Defendent P. Tiburtius a Vulnere Theresiae Et P. Theodatus a Stigmatibus Francisci, Etc.*, Augustae Vindelicorum, Aloysius Merz, 1783, unpaged.

12. See: Tomáš Malý, *Smrt a spása mezi Tridentinem a sekularizací: Brněnští měšťané a proměny laické zbožnosti v 17. a 18. století*, Brno, Matice moravská, 2009.

13. *Liber Ratiociniorum*, passim.

14. *Ibid.*

15. NA Prague, Bohemian Franciscan Province Archives, reg. no. 2982, carton 175, *Alms of the friary*, unpaged.

16. The friary managed to meet its obligations towards the faithful only thanks to the high number of priests (at the expense of lay brethren). The priests thus – unlike in the early Franciscan times – not only created the majority within the order, but also significantly contributed to the economy of the individual houses.

Fig. 20. Chalice with enamel images of Franciscan saints. Commissioned by the friary with the permission of Minister Provincial Severinus Wrbczansky for the sum of 158 fl. Wolfgand Rossmayer, 1735. Roman Catholic Parish Hněvotín, today in the permanent exhibition of Archdiocesan Museum in Olomouc, photo: Markéta Ondrušková.

reduced to their economic function. They formed an important part of the web of relationships between the friary and society. The mass stipends were tied to other activities, and their acquisition depended on the credibility and popularity of St Bernardino and its priests.[17]

The Franciscans always emphasized that these were voluntary alms, whose acquisition depended on the favour of people and God's mercy. Mass stipends were indeed received mostly on an irregular and occasional basis. And yet they did include one source of regular income. These were mass stipends wherein the donor bequeathed a fixed amount to the friary – a capital from which the annual interest was to be drawn. The will also specified on what the interests were to be spent. Usually this was a requiem mass said for the sponsor or their family. At times, though, other purposes were also stated. The city council foundation financed the purchase of candles for the Forty Hours' Devotion (300 fl.); the foundation of Matthias Kniebandl, Apostolic Syndic, donated 10 fl. for a mass for the dead Third Order members and 30 fl. to be divided among the poorest Tertiaries. Two other stipends had no purpose defined. At the time of its closure, the friary recorded eighteen bequests, the total capital of which was 10,491 fl. The largest was Kaspar Klementis' foundation (2,000 fl.), generating 3.5% interest, which bound the Franciscans to say 94 masses a year. While most sponsors were burghers, and a few were members of the nobility, there was also a peasant, Matyáš Macháček, who donated 100 fl. for requiem masses on the condition that they were said in the Scala Sancta Chapel. About half of the total capital was

17. Cf. Veronika Čapská, *Představy společenství a strategie sebeprezentace: Řád servitů v habsburské monarchii (1613-1780)*, Prague, Scriptorium, 2011, p. 171.

deposited in public funds, and the rest was tied to a variety of real estate. With the exception of two foundations with a 3.5% return, capital was deposited at an interest rate of 4%. The Franciscans thus received approximately 400 fl. a year to say more than 650 masses.[18]

Interest from the mass-stipend foundations was the only truly regular and guaranteed income. It was a relatively small sum which did not interfere with the otherwise strict mendicant principles of the Franciscan Order. Yet, the foundations – and other mass stipends – constituted an essential problem for the Franciscans.[19] The Rule of St Francis strictly forbade the acceptance and use of money. The friars, of course, were well aware of this prohibition and, given its gravity within the Franciscan ideal of poverty, they obviously sought to observe it. And indeed, most of the monetary alms probably were never touched by Franciscan hands. The brothers avoided direct contact with money at the cost of using highly complicated measures (sometimes risking being accused of hypocrisy).[20] They had to search for ways to combine nearly five-hundred-year-old demands with the dramatically changing reality of the new era. What may have been possible in the thirteenth century was entirely unrealistic in the eighteenth century. Besides, the mere fact that the friary kept its own accounting books (*Liber Ratiociniorum*), which converted the value of the alms into money, testifies to the fact that even the Franciscans could no longer ignore the existence of the monetary system.

Francis of Assisi was very aware that the issue of money use would be particularly tricky with respect to the ideal of poverty:

> I strictly command all my brothers **not to receive coins or money in any form** [my emphasis], either personally or through intermediaries. Nevertheless, the ministers and custodians alone may take special care through their spiritual friends to provide for the needs of the sick and the clothing of the others according to places, seasons and cold climates, as they judge necessary, saving always that, as stated above, they do not receive coins or money.[21]

However, the provisions of the Rule of St Francis allowed, to a certain extent, for concessions if a life was threatened. Asking the question “Are there any circumstances at all which would allow Friars Minor to receive and use Money?”, Joannes Damasus Charvath in his interpretation of the Rule replies as follows:

> … if there arose a Need that would be extraordinary, utmost, and final, where life could not be started or saved without using things that could only be procured with Money, in such an Event the Brother would be free both through himself and through another

18. NA Prague, Bohemian Franciscan Province Archives, reg. no. 2983, carton 175, *Mešní nadace*, unpaged. Cf. Moravian Land Archive Brno, Fund B 2, Moravian Authority – Ecclesiastical Department, sign. K 20/36, inv. no. 1446, carton 101, *The dissolution and reduction of the Franciscan friaries in Znojmo and Olomouc*, 1784-85, unpaged.

19. For example, in the montane district where some commodities were deficient and local people still intended to provide the alms, it was allowed to collect cash instead, for a total of 90 fl. for grain and 60 fl. for butter. Opava Land Archive, Olomouc office, Olomouc Archdiocese, inv. no. 2020 (sign. Bb 38), carton 412, *Franciscans in Olomouc*, 1610-1804, unpaged.

20. Charvath, *Fractio Panis*, pp. 168-177.

21. *Francis of Assisi: Early documents,* vol. 1, p. 102.

> Person to receive and use Money. The cause being: As this utmost Need, according to all Teachers, is free from every Right and Law [...], every one according to the same Law is obliged to begin his life in every possible way; as Right, and the Law of Nature is a stronger obligation than the commandment of the Rule.[22]

Such extreme situations could not (with respect to efforts to preserve the ideal of poverty) serve as a pretext for re-evaluating the Rule, not even in the changing conditions of early modern society.

2. *Spiritual friends*

The solution lay in those "spiritual friends" (*amici spirituales*), mentioned by Francis in the Rule. According to Nicholas III's decree *Exiit qui seminat* (1279), the "spiritual friends" could be officially appointed by the pope or cardinal protector, and in rare cases by the local bishop. A mere four years later, though, the Bull *Exultantes* issued by Pope Martin IV extended this competence to the Franciscan authorities (minister general, provincial ministers and custodians), who could, if necessary, designate esteemed men in the provinces or religious houses to receive donations from benefactors on behalf of the Apostolic See and then use them in favour of Friars Minor. *Constitutiones Martinianae* (issued by Pope Martin V in 1430) confirmed that these "apostolic syndics" could handle monetary alms, enter into contracts and represent the brothers in litigation. In practice, the syndic ensured all financial transactions for the religious. If someone wished to donate money to the Franciscans (whether a mass stipend or a regular gift), the monks asked the person to see their syndic, who "received and handled money on behalf of the Apostolic See".[23] He then used the money to cover some of the friary's expenses: the purchase of commodities that the brothers had failed to secure through begging, and royalties to artists and craftsmen. The friars thus never owned the money, nor did they come in contact with it. The apostolic syndic was consequently a general benefactor who provided the Franciscans with alms on behalf of other benefactors: "The Spiritual Father or someone else with whom money intended for the needs of the Brothers is deposited, is no improper person but the Deputy of the Brother, of the Benefactor himself, and a Spiritual Friend to whom the Brothers may come in times of need according to the Rule".[24] The syndic, as well as his wife and children, are granted all the indulgences and privileges of the members of the order in return for his help.[25] The apostolic syndic was clearly a key person who influenced the relationship of the friary and the community.

The function of the apostolic syndic was naturally criticized by supporters of the strict adherence to poverty. The fact that the Observants ultimately decided to preserve the function in the fifteenth century was the main reason why they were criticised by other radical friars – particularly after the division of the order in

22. Charvath, *Fractio Panis*, pp. 190-191.
23. Wrbczansky, *Quodlibetum Regulare*, p. 190.
24. Charvath, *Fractio Panis*, pp. 158-159.
25. Holzapfel, *Handbuch der Geschichte*, pp. 37-38.

1517. The institution of the apostolic syndic was rejected by most of the reformist movements opposing the Observance. These included the Spanish Alcantarians, the offshoot branch of Capuchins, as well as the Italian Reformed. For them, the absence of syndics was, at that time, one of the fundamental differences which separated them from the Observants. The disputes between the Franciscan factions had to be resolved by the popes again (Clement VII in 1530, Paul IV in 1555, and then Innocent X and Innocent XI), who explicitly confirmed that the existence of syndics was fully in line with the strict observance of the Rule. Papal intervention – and perhaps the considerable difficulties caused by the absence of the syndics in some regions – made the Reformed and some other radical movements adopt a more conciliatory approach. Even the Capuchins were eventually forced to abandon their stance and appoint apostolic syndics for their friaries.[26]

By the time the Reform had spread around Central Europe in the mid-seventeenth century, it was common for friaries to have their apostolic syndics.[27] Local Franciscans could thus build on the previous Observant tradition. This is also the case of the Olomouc house, although apostolic syndics were rarely mentioned prior to 1620.[28] A continuous string of syndics is documented only from the mid-1620s, when the office was taken by Councillor Johann Mandelius, one of the leading Catholic representatives of the city. Following his death in 1640, the new syndic became Joachim Lerschmacher, who probably held the office even in the first stage of the Swedish occupation.[29] The failed conspiracy of Michael Jahn and the ensuing plundering of the friary, which was subsequently inhabited by a single lay brother for years, made the office of syndic unnecessary. It was only at the end of the occupation that another important man became the syndic – Tobias Schwonauer of Retz, the son-in-law of Johann Mandelius.[30] He too was a leading Catholic burgher, who had held the offices of councillor and mayor several times.[31]Along with Mandelius and Schwonauer there was also Magnus Brandel of Brandenfels, the first imperial bailiff appointed following the defeat of the Rebellion of the Estates in 1621. Although sources never officially refer to him as a syndic, his significance for the friary is evidenced by the fact that while the church was undergoing a major restoration in 1635, a third crypt was built in addition to the large crypt for brothers and the crypt for benefactors. It was erected for Bailiff Brandl – "the unrivalled benefactor of this friary".[32]

26. See: Holzapfel, *Handbuch der Geschichte*, p. 211.

27. Holzapfel, *Handbuch der Geschichte*, p. 412.

28. During the repair of the belfry above the choir in 1682 a "Gothic" parchment (*scriptura gothica in membrana*) dated 1552 was found in the cupola among other papers, in which the notary Henricus Polan confirmed the appointment of venerable burgher Thomas Knosp as the spiritual friend of the friary. *Archivum*, p. 87 and *Protocollum*, p. 347.

29. *Protocollum*, p. 347.

30. It was he who, in 1650, bribed the Swedish garrison commander to allow the new Superior Meerstein to return to the friary (see: Chapter 1).

31. Schwonauer's library, comprising 828 books and absolutely unique among the Olomouc burghers, speaks volumes of his status. See: Miller, "Zchudlé město bohatých měšťanů?".

32. *Archivum*, p. 26.

All of them had strong personal ties to St Bernardino, as evidenced by the fact that they chose the Franciscan church to be their final resting place.[33] Their relationship to the friary reflected private and public interests resulting from their personal experience and ambitions. This is evident particularly in the case of Johann Mandelius. He demonstrated his devotion to the Catholic faith (and to the Emperor) during the Estates Uprising when he was imprisoned in March 1620. In prison, he and his daughter Anna Maria (the future Tobias Schwonauer's wife) cared for the dying Jan Sarkander – a Catholic priest accused of high-treason and tortured in order to extract secrets that some Catholic lords had allegedly told him during confession. After the uprising was defeated, Mandelius began to play an increasingly important role as one of the leading Catholic burghers in the public life of the city – he became councillor and mayor. As such, he helped restore the Catholic faith in the city and, among other things, sought official recognition of the martyrdom in Sarkander's death. His efforts apparently resonated with the Franciscans – reminiscent of the misfortunes they had suffered during the uprising. Their friary allegedly housed at that time one of the oldest paintings of Sarkander's death, and probably one of the first centres of the future saint's cult.[34]

The close links between St Bernardino and the city council persisted in the following periods and were not limited to the office of syndic only. This is evident from the records of the appointment of Martin Neümann as Schwonauer's successor in 1659.[35] Like his predecessors, Neümann had been a councillor, and for many years one of the benefactors of the friary.[36] The ceremony, which was a validation of his merits and the promise of further cooperation, was attended by many other councillors. Their presence reflected obligations the city had towards the friary. St Bernardino, of course, was not the only ecclesiastical institution that councillors, whether as private individuals or representatives of the city, supported. Among those who assisted Schwonauer's funeral were, for example, the local Dominicans, which suggests he must have been their benefactor as well.[37] The city council regularly distributed alms as fairly as possible to other mendicant institutions. Nevertheless, the Franciscans seem to have enjoyed a

33. Mandelius was buried in the friars' crypt in 1640, and Schwonauer had a chapel of the Holy Sepulchre with a crypt built as part of the Franciscan church. This is where he was buried in 1659. *Archivum*, p. 31, pp. 41-44.

34. Matěj Procházka, *Žiwot Bl. Jana Sarkandra Mučeníka*, W Brně, Dědictwí sw. Cyrilla a Methodia, 1861, p. 1003. His beatification was also promoted by the Olomouc Franciscans in later periods. See: *Protocollum*, p. 638. Sarkander was eventually beatified only in 1860 and canonised in 1995.

35. Provincial Aegidius Pollein, Provincial Custos and Olomouc Friary preacher Bernardinus Latke, and Superior Celestinus Mayr had the final say. *Archivum*, p. 44.

36. One of the priests delivered a sermon at the gathering of all the brethren, in which he gave the reasons for the establishment of the office. After the Provincial's nomination decree was read, Neümann made a solemn promise in which he pledged to duly carry out all the duties. At the end of the ceremony, the friars gave him the kiss of peace as a symbol of welcoming him into the community. *Archivum*, p. 44.

37. *Archivum*, p. 44.

privileged position among the other mendicants in the city, apparently due in large part to the aforementioned filiation of John of Capistrano. Even before the arrival of the Swedes, the Franciscans were entrusted with the chaplaincy of the city hall's Chapel of St Jerome. The superior of the friary was supposed to sing mass each time the city council was reinstated and also on selected major feast days. The friary of St Bernardino then received food and other alms in return for these services.[38] This annoyed the other mendicants, as well as the spiritual administrators of parish churches. After the Swedes left in 1650, St Maurice's administrator challenged the practice by claiming the chaplaincy belonged to St Maurice Church. The councillor and future syndic Martin Neümann backed the Franciscans, ensuring that, rather than having the chaplaincy pass on to the parish church, it was preferable to temporarily suspend worship in the city hall chapel.[39] In any case, the administrator was unable to substantiate his claims and the Franciscans resumed the chaplaincy. Florian Joseph Loucky says that in the middle of the eighteenth century: "In addition to the customary holidays, the Franciscans (as the foundation stipulates) say a Mass before the meetings of the city council, on the days selected by the mayor".[40]

The connection to the Catholic elite of the city stems from the very character of the friary of St Bernardino. A mendicant religious house in a royal city would naturally have the city council as the most important patron. Similarly, though, the council saw the Franciscan friary as a significant institution. Apart from personal ties, from their official position the councillors viewed the Franciscan friary as a key actor of religious life in the city and a guarantor of consolidation of the Catholic confession. Compared to the bishop's consistory, the metropolitan chapter and the Jesuits, the Franciscans made a far better partner for the city council – also thanks to their economic dependence. Working with them, the urban elite were able to participate much more strongly in shaping the character of the local church.[41]

The mutual benefits of this alliance were still evident in the early eighteenth century. It was then that the relations between the city council and the local ecclesiastical hierarchy suffered major deterioration. The Church was represented by Dean Charles Julius Orlik, Baron of Lazisko, who substituted for Bishop Charles III of Lorrain, a chronic absentee in his diocese, as administrator. The controversy arose after the bishop consistory summoned an Italian merchant living in Olomouc to testify in a marriage dispute. He asked the city council what to do, and the council forbade him from testifying before the church court, offering instead that they could, at the request of the consistory, hear him themselves. Prompted by Dean Orlik, the consistory excommunicated two members of the council in retaliation.[42] The excommunication was announced on 26 February

38. It was 21 guilders and 20 kreuzers in 1650. *Archivum*, p. 37.

39. *Archivum*, p. 37.

40. Loucký, *Popis Královského hlavního města Olomouce*, p. 44.

41. Marc R. Forster, "With and Without Confessionalization. Varieties of Early Modern German Catholicism", *Journal of Early Modern History*, 1, 4 (1997): p. 335.

42. Rudolf Zuber, "Poslední exkomunikace laiků v olomoucké diecézi", *Ročenka Státního okresního archívu v Olomouci* (1992), 20 (1993): pp. 162-169.

1702 from the pulpit at St Maurice and its wording was nailed to the church door. The excommunication naturally caused turmoil and much misunderstanding in the city. The local Franciscans, led by Superior Hieronymus Veit, also played a role: they were soon accused of deliberately failing to observe the excommunication. This provoked an outrage among the Olomouc clergy and others. Two letters sent by Gaudentius Mols and Leopold Prušák, two Franciscans from a friary in nearby Opava, are dated 20 April.[43] Alarmed, they both ask their Olomouc-based confreres whether there was any truth to the news spread around Opava by certain otherwise trustworthy men. The said men allegedly claimed that the Olomouc Franciscans did not observe the excommunication, and that the father superior even visited and dined with the excommunicated councillors. Later, Veit defended himself in the chronicle, arguing that the excommunication applied to two councillors only, not the entire council. He said the whole affair was a misunderstanding caused by the fact that some of the friars (he explicitly mentioned the Jesuits) had mistakenly assumed the excommunication concerned the entire council. The maids of selected councillors, as well as some of the burghers seen holding an official conversation with the excommunicated, were allegedly physically forced to leave St Maurice Church. Veit stated that this was why he had provided all the wronged with sanctuary in St Bernardino.[44]

Whatever the explanation, his attitude was sharply criticised by the Olomouc clergy. The relationship between the Franciscans and the other church institutions was already very tense. At the beginning of the year, Veit had declared his plan to build at the friary a chapel of Scala Sancta (Holy Stairs) – the first copy of this shrine in the diocese. The consistory and particularly the other orders were none too pleased about this ambitious project. They feared the new shrine would draw all the attention of the faithful and upset the religious "balance of power" in the city. With his attitude to the excommunication, he only added fuel to the flames and made a number of irreconcilable enemies. The following events, however, showed that the risk that Veit had taken paid off. The city council lodged a complaint with the Moravian Tribunal, and on 8 March 1702, the regional governor (*Kreishauptmann*) announced an imperial decree. Referring to the papal Bull – according to which no secular official could be excommunicated without the emperor's consent – Orlík was ordered to revoke the excommunication, otherwise his prebend would be requisitioned. The dean refused to obey this order and asked the emperor to reverse his decision. In response, the emperor threatened to extend the sequestration to other ecclesiastical estates. The dean and the other canons had to surrender, ingloriously cancelling the excommunication on May 7.[45] Veit admitted in the chronicle that the Franciscan attitude in the affair earned them the gratitude and appreciation of the city council. The superiors of St Bernardino became the city council notaries and the friary received compensation for alms denied to them by the clergy. Also, the friars received support in the construction

43. Olomouc State District Archive, Olomouc Archives – fragments of the registries, reg. no. 401, carton 13, *Holy Stairs at St Bernardino* (1701-1802), fol. 201-202.

44. *Archivum*, pp. 132-135.

45. Zuber, "Poslední exkomunikace", p. 166.

of the Scala Sancta Chapel. Once again secular authorities turned out to be a far better patron and partner than church authorities.

3. *Tertiaries: Franciscan exclusivity and its export*

With the sole exception of the builder Matthias Kniebandel, all the other apostolic syndics of St Bernardino were members of the city council.[46] Thanks to their economic and political influence they greatly contributed to the friary's integration into the city organism. Besides the syndics, the Franciscans also strove to target other distinguished persons who could become major benefactors of the friary. They worked to strengthen these relationships and build them on firmer and more durable foundations. An illustrative example of said efforts is a letter sent by Superior Victorinus Pohl to the provincial definitorium.[47] In the letter, he informs the provincial representatives about cooperation with the architect and master stonemason Wenzel Render. Render was building Scala Sancta Chapel for St Bernardino, and as Pohl highlights, he did not want any remuneration for the work. The friars only needed to acquire the building material and pay the wages of Render's partners. Besides that, Render had given the friary other donations in the past. Pohl proposes (he is surprisingly straightforward) to further encourage the builder's partiality. As Render is a bachelor and "a man of considerable means, [...] with a lot of potential", Pohl suggests taking steps "to make him still better-disposed to us". He therefore asks provincial authorities to issue a decree that would guarantee Render his final resting place in the crypt under the Scala Sancta (if it is ever built) or in the crypt of the friars. It remains unknown whether the definitorium accommodated Pohl's suggestion or how it responded. In any case, Wenzel Render was ultimately buried at the parish church of St Maurice after he bequeathed much of his wealth for the construction of the Trinity Column on the Olomouc Upper Square instead of to the Franciscan friary.

The Render case shows that the individual "care" for patrons (although often successful) had its limits – specifically when multiple institutions competed for the same benefactor. A much more stable and promising tool used to reinforce the ties between the friary and the community was collective institutions, whether filiations or religious confraternities (Render did not seem to be a member of any Franciscan confraternity).[48] The Bohemian Franciscan province comprised

46. See: *Protocollum*, Section F.

47. NA Prague, Bohemian Franciscan Province Archives, reg. no. 2980, carton 175, *Václav Render, etc.*, unpaged.

48. For more on religious confraternities, see: *Early Modern Confraternities in Europe and the Americas: International and Interdisciplinary Perspectives*, ed. by Christopher F. Black and Pamela Gravestock, Aldershot, Ashgate, 2005. For more on the situation in Bohemia, see: especially Jiří Mikulec, *Barokní náboženská bratrstva v Čechách*, Praha, Lidové noviny, 2000; *Zbožných duší úl: Náboženská bratrstva v kultuře raněnovověké Moravy [Muzeum umění Olomouc – Arcidiecézní muzeum Olomouc: Galerie, 29. ledna – 25. dubna 2010: Katalog]*, ed. by Vladimír Maňas, Zdeněk Orlita and Martina Potůčková, Olomouc, Muzeum umění Olomouc, 2010; Vladimír Maňas, Tomáš Malý and Zdeněk Orlita, *Vnitřní krajina zmizelého*

several confraternities, of which the arch-confraternity of Francis's cord (*Archi-Confraternitas Chordigerorum S. Francisci*) had long been the most significant (until the beginning of the eighteenth century).[49] Unlike other local confraternities, this one had a universal and supranational character similar to the Jesuit sodalities. The individual communities of the confraternities associated with local friaries were linked to the maternal confraternity in Rome. The arch-confraternity was founded by Pope Sixtus V in 1585. It reached the Bohemian province in 1629 and fifty years later, fifteen of the twenty-four friaries of the province had established their own confraternities.[50] It never spread to Olomouc or the other large cities (Prague, Brno, Wrocław and Opava).[51] The reasons for this absence are not entirely clear, but may have involved stronger competition, competency disputes and a different structure of ties between the friary and its supporters.

The first lay brotherhood at St Bernardino was thus the Third Order. It was the most significant and most successful Franciscan corporation for the lay people, and in the early eighteenth century it began to spread to the Transalpine provinces. In the meantime, the Third Order had had a long and very complicated history. Its origins date back to 1209 and were closely linked to the birth of the Franciscan movement. There were a number of similar groups of lay penitents, whether the Humiliati associations or Waldensian communities. Even Francis of Assisi presented himself as a lay penitent, whose conversion had transferred him from "life in sin" to "life of penance". Similar to other communities, the "Penitents of Assisi" faced two scenarios of possible development: either to accept church structures and create an order, or to reject them and become a heretical sect. As the Franciscan movement transformed into a religious order, the need to define the position of penitents was increasingly urgent. This also concerned supporters who professed Francis's ideals of penitent life, but for various reasons could not or did not want to join the developing communities of Friars Minor or Poor Clares.

města: Náboženská bratrstva barokního Brna, Brno, Statutární město Brno a Archív města Brna, 2010. An overview of the Bohemian Province friaries that were home to the arch-confraternity of the cord is available in Elbel, *Bohemia Franciscana*, pp. 126-129.

49. The members of the arch-confraternity wore a rope cingulum and had nearly the same rights and duties as other confraternities. Moreover, every month they had to attend a procession with the cingulum visibly worn (it could be worn under clothing the rest of the days). "*Hora Zlatá Seraffická, Aneb Naučenj Spolu-Bratrůw a Sester, Arcy-Bratrstwa Swatého Otce Frantisska, W Němž Se Odpustky, Regule, Dowolenj, a Modlitby Obsahugj, K Tomu Kterak Přigatj Do Toho Bratrstwa Odpustkůw Aučastnj Býti Mohau. Cum Licentia Superiorum*", Wytisstěna w Holomaucy, U Jana Jozeffa Kyliána, 1680.

50. See: data in Wrbczansky, *Nucleus Minoriticus*, and in friary chronicles in the National Archives of Prague, Bohemian Franciscan Province Archives.

51. In the Bavarian province, for example, there were arch-confraternities of the cord at all the friaries. See: Egid Börner, *Dritter Orden und Bruderschaften der Franziskaner in Kurbayern*, Werl, Dietrich-Coelde Verlag, 1988. The only "Franciscan" brotherhood found in Olomouc in the seventeenth century was the St Anthony of Padua confraternity allied to the Conventual Church. Polykarp Gudtkindt, *Seraphische Zuflucht, Dess Wunderthätigen Und Glorwürdigen H. Antonii Von Padua. Allen Betrübten Und Nothleydenden Seelen, Besonders Einer Andächtigen Und Würdigen Bruderschafft Welche Unter Dieses H. Namen in Unterschiedlichen Provincien Auffgerichtet*, Olmütz, Gedruckt bey Veit Heinrich Ettel, 1669.

Francis apparently addressed them in his *Letter to All the Faithful* (1209-1215) and its revised version of 1221, where he calls for the adoption of a penitent life based on inner conversion, not on the appropriation of external characteristics.[52] In the second version, Francis warns the penitents to observe the church hierarchy (show respect for priests) and practice (regular attendance of mass and confession). Cardinal Hugolino wrote *Memoriale prepositi* in the same year, where he strove to set clear rules for secular penitents: to wear a penitent robe, to pray canonical hours (the illiterates a given number of Paternosters), to make confession at least three times a year, to fast more often than others and to avoid carrying weapons or making unnecessary oaths.[53] These penitents were not bound by religious vows and could continue to live at home and with their families. The outlines of the movement of the lay penitents grew gradually clearer and it soon established itself as the Third Order (*Tertius Ordo*) next to the communities of the Friars Minor (*Primus Ordo*) and Poor Clares (*Secundus Ordo*).[54]

The year 1221 thus marks the official beginning of the Third Order. The first members of the Third Order blessed by Francis were said to be the once greedy merchant Luchesio and his wife Bonnadona. They were soon followed by others, and before long the Third Order spread around the entirety of Italy and beyond the Alps. Tradition has it that a number of eminent persons became Tertiaries, including many saints: Elizabeth of Hungary, King Louis IX, Ivo of Kermartin and Rochus.[55] Despite this considerable success, the relationship of the First Order to the Tertiaries was constrained after Francis's death, because the Franciscans were reluctant to take over the administration of the Tertiary communities. Their guarded attitude was largely due to the borderline position the Tertiaries held between friaries and society. Some of the guidelines of the Tertiary Rule were also considered problematic in relation to secular authorities, in particular the prohibition to take an oath or carry weapons and thus participate in the defence of cities and other military duties. The Third Order, nonetheless, enjoyed the support of several popes. In 1247, Innocent IV ordered the Franciscans to assume the role of spiritual administrators of the Tertiaries.[56] The Franciscan Pope, Nicholas IV, issued the Bull *Supra Montem* in 1289, which became the Rule of the Franciscan Third Order. Based on Hugolino's *Memoriale*, the Bull directly charged the Friars Minor with the administration of the Tertiary communities; specifically with the obligation of regular visitation.[57]

52. "Earlier Exhortation to the Brothers and Sisters of Penance", in *Francis of Assisi: Early documents*, vol. 1, pp. 41-44.

53. "Memoriale propositi fratrum et sororum de poenitentia in domibus propriis existentium". See: Holzapfel, *Handbuch der Geschichte*, p. 440. Also Iriarte, *Franciscan History*, pp. 477-486.

54. Ingrid Peterson, "The Third Order", in *The Cambridge Companion to Francis of Assisi*, ed. by Michael J.P. Robson, Cambridge, New York, Cambridge University Press, 2012, pp. 193-207.

55. Iriarte, *Franciscan History*, p. 492.

56. Holzapfel, *Handbuch der Geschichte*, p. 441.

57. Robert M. Stewart, *"De Illis Qui Faciunt Penitentiam": The Rule of the Secular Franciscan Order : Origins, Development, Interpretation*, Roma, Istituto Storico dei Cappuccini, 1991.

Fig. 21. Admission of new members of the Third Order. Jarolim Veith, *Regule aneb spůsob života bratrův a sester Třetího řádu Svatého Otce Františka potvrzená od papeže Mikuláše Čtvrtého pro ty, kteří by v svých domech kající život vésti chtěli* (V Starém Městě Pražském: u Anny Voršily Hamplový, 1708).

Thanks to papal sanctification the Third Order survived and blossomed in the following centuries until it was hit by a serious crisis in the sixteenth century.[58] Humanism (Italy) and the Reformation (the Transalpine region) led to a decline in membership and the Third Order disappeared from most of the countries. The only, but significant, exceptions were Spain, Portugal and their overseas territories, where the Third Order remained extremely popular. A gradual change took place only in the following century. The General Chapter of Toledo ordered

58. A part of the Tertiaries began to associate and live in shared houses during the Middle Ages. Their way of life resembled the First and Second Orders – except for the fact that they did not take religious vows. These communities gradually gave rise to Religious Tertiaries (mostly female). The following text will discuss the secular Tertiaries: those who became Tertiaries but continued to live "in the world". For female Franciscan convents, including those of Religious Tertiaries in the Bohemian Province, see: Jarmila Kašpárková, *Kláštery klarisek a františkánských terciářek v českých zemích v raném novověku*, Dissertation, Faculty of Arts UP Olomouc, 2014.

all provinces to strive to restore the Third Order following the Spanish model in 1633.[59] These efforts eventually proved successful – the order had several hundred thousand Tertiaries at the end of the century.[60] In Bohemian Lands, the first Tertiary communities appeared in Olomouc in 1700, followed by Jindřichův Hradec (1701) and Prague (1702) – earlier records only speak of individual Tertiaries. After these three friaries, the Tertiaries began to associate with other friaries as well, so much so that by the 1730s there were Tertiary communities at twenty-one of the thirty Franciscan friaries within the Bohemian province.[61]

The Third Order was ceremonially established in Olomouc on 13 May 1700, in the presence of Provincial Antonius Hartmann and Superior Hieronymus Veit. The cloth merchant and apostolic syndic Laurentius Benisch and his wife Justina – the Olomouc followers of Luchesius and Bonnadona – put on the Tertiary habit after completing a year-long novitiate.[62] They were followed by others – while in 1701 only eight people joined the ranks, in 1702 they numbered forty-five, and a year later there were forty-three new members. A total of 673 people (511 women and 162 men) registered with the Third Order in Olomouc (1700-1777). The number of individuals wishing to join the Olomouc Third Order naturally varied over the course of eighty years.[63] After the first years, the interest in membership logically declined, only to be revived again in the late 1730s. This new wave seemed to be closely related to the 1726 opening of the Scala Sancta Chapel (see the following chapter). Another wave of increased interest occurred in the mid-century. This time, there was apparently an interplay of multiple factors – the war and Prussian occupation of the city, the re-consecration of the Holy Stairs with new indulgences, and the two-hundred-year anniversary of Capistrano in Olomouc.[64] This particular wave of interest is marked by one interesting detail pointing to the social significance of being a member of a religious confraternity. There were only three people from nearby Prostějov registered with the Olomouc Tertiaries

59. Iriarte, *Franciscan History*, p. 494.

60. Holzapfel, *Handbuch der Geschichte*, p. 444. The flourish was stained by the internal problems of the Franciscan Order and its fragmentation. Tertiary communities developed at Franciscan, Conventual and Capuchin friaries, and at times there were serious disputes. Benedict XIII attempted (not quite successfully) to subordinate all the Tertiaries to the minister general of the Franciscans in 1725. See: "*Sanctissimi in Christo Patris Et Domini Nostri Benedicti XIII. Pont. Max. Constitutio Pro Tertiariis Ordinis Sancti Francisci: Universa Privilegia Toti Tertiariorum Coetui, in Tres Status Distincto, a Summis Pontificibus Concessa, Confirmantur; Ipsique Tertiarii Omnimodae Iurisdictioni, Et Regimini Ministri Generalis Totius Ordinis Minorum, Pro Tempore Exstituri, Denuo Subiiciuntur, Et Commendantur. Romae M.DCC.XXV*", Romae, 1726.

61. Wrbczansky, *Nucleus Minoriticus*, passim. The list of Tertiary communities Wrbczansky provides on page 65 is incomplete – later in the text he adds Tertiary communities allied to friaries in Nysa, Dačice, Hostinné, Wroclaw and Racibórz.

62. *Matrica*, unpaged, the section titled: *"Nahmen und Zunahmen, das Jahr und der Tag, deren, So in den Dritten Orden S. Francisci die H. Profession lauth ihrer Regel gethan, wie folget"*.

63. While 201 Tertiaries were accepted in the first decade of the eighteenth century, in the following decades it was: 73, 89, 62, 69, 61, 73 and 45 (the incomplete decade of 1770 to 1777) people.

64. Cf. *Archivum*, pp. 252-263 and *Protocollum*, pp.183-184.

until 1749. That year, though, four noble ladies living in the town received the Tertiary habit. They were soon followed by ten more inhabitants from Prostějov that year, apparently burghers trying to keep pace with local social elites. The last major wave of interest in the Third Order took place in the mid-1760s. In 1765 alone, thirty-seven people received the Tertiary habit, which was the third highest number after 1702 and 1703. The vast majority of these Tertiaries, however, were recruited from a narrow social group – the servants of the Bishop's residence, or Curia, and their families.[65]

Social status is specified in the registry only for some of the people. The same applies to the place of origin – although most people came from Olomouc (a minimum of 203 people) or the immediate surroundings. Other towns included Svitavy, Lanškroun, Šumperk, Šternberk, Opava, Fulnek, Nový Jičín, Hranice, Přerov and Prostějov – all places within a seventy-kilometre radius from Olomouc. In the majority of cases, though, the origin is not recorded at all, but we can assume a vast majority of the Tertiaries came from an area within the friary's collection district – the minister provincial ordered in 1731 that the local Tertiaries could not accept new members coming from outside the district without his permission.[66] Data on the Tertiaries' social status or profession are even less complete. Twenty-four people among the Olomouc Tertiaries were of noble origin. The vast majority of the members were recruited from various strata of the urban population.[67] The list includes patricians and city officials, mostly names mentioned in the chronicle among the leading benefactors. These are followed by most craftsmen (often millers and fishermen) and the poor classes, particularly a large group of servants. Another major group besides the urban population was the officials of the neighbouring estates. Their strength was not in numbers (thirteen members in total), but in importance. The Franciscans probably came into contact with them quite often – noble manors were often used as temporary depots by friars making collections in the country, from which the victuals were then transported on a cart into the friary. The rural population formed a minor part. A small but noteworthy group was four hermits who accepted the Tertiary habit.[68]

65. *Matrica*, passim.

66. This decision was motivated by the efforts to keep track of the Third Order's communities and their members more efficiently. *Matrica*, Section "Directorium pro Patribus", art. VII.

67. There were twenty confraternities altogether in Olomouc in the eighteenth century. See: Vladimír Maňas, "Náboženská bratrstva na Moravě do josefínských reforem", in *Bratrstva. Světská a církevní sdružení a jejich role v kulturních a společenských strukturách od středověku do moderní doby (III. pardubické bienále, 29.-30. dubna 2004)*, ed. by Tomáš Jiránek and Jiří Kubeš, Pardubice, Univerzita Pardubice, 2005, p. 71.

68. As semi-religious, the Third Order was ideal for attracting (and supervising) hermits. The Olomouc registry embraced four Tertiary hermits, who inhabited the hermitages at Bludov (1720), Jívová (1757), Suchdol nad Odrou (1770) and Úsov (1772). *Matrica*, passim. See also: Opava Land Archive, Olomouc office, Olomouc Archbishop Consistory (1657-1847), sign. H8, carton 5107, *Hermits* (1657-1847). Hermits as members of the Third Order at some of the Franciscan friaries are also documented by other sources – as of 1712 a certain Antonín Klimb, a Tertiary, lived, for example, in a hermitage on Mount Říp (Prague National Archives,

Fig. 22. Front page of the register of Olomouc Tertiaries. Moravian Land Archive Brno, E 21 Franciscans of Dačice, book no. 11.

The beginnings of the Third Order at St Bernardino date back to when the superior was Hieronymus Veit, one of the most active and most prominent representatives of the Olomouc friary. Although Tertiary communities also emerged at other Franciscan houses after 1700, and this was not (unlike the construction of the Scala Sancta Chapel – see the following chapter) his own isolated project, Veit significantly contributed to the restoration of the Third Order throughout the province. He wrote a handbook for Tertiaries in the Bohemian Franciscan province with comments on the Tertiary Rule, selected prayers (litanies of St Francis and St Peter of Alcantara) and a list of indulgences available to Tertiaries.[69] Veit's handbook shows that the eighteenth century's Third Order was quite different from the original penitent communities and probably did not entirely correspond

Bohemian Franciscan Province Archives, inv. no. 3131, carton 186, *Třetí řád všeobecně*, unpaged). Another Tertiary hermit minded the Holy Sepulchre in Slaný for the Franciscans. Wrbczansky, *Nucleus Minoriticus*, p. 260.

69. Hieronymus Veit, *Regel oder Weiss dess Lebens, Der Brüder und Schwestern dess dritten Ordens S. Francisci*, Ollmütz, Johann Joseph Kylian, 1701. The handbook was also published later in Czech: Jarolim Veith, *Regule aneb způsob života bratrův a sester Třetího řádu Svatého Otce Františka potvrzená od papeže Mikuláše Čtvrtého pro ty, kteří by v svých domech kající život vésti chtěli*, V Starem Měste Pražském, u Anny Voršily Hamplový, 1708.

to Francis's original idea. Now it was a tightly organized institution, whose duly registered members met at regular monthly meetings with a fixed agenda. The Olomouc Tertiaries were allowed to hold the meetings at the Chapel of St Anthony of Padua. Every meeting opened with prayer and interpretation of one of the articles of the Rule. This was followed by the brothers' confession of their sins against the Rule and by rectification (*satisfactio*). Afterwards a collection was made for the joint treasury. The meetings also served for the admission of novices and voting on allowing the novices to take vows. Those who received the habit of the Third Order of Saint Francis were recorded in the registry. The Third Order was, like regular friaries, subject to provincial visits every three years. Every year on the eve of the Feast of Saint Francis of Assisi (4 October), each Tertiary said a hundred Paternosters and Hail Marys and attended the Requiem for deceased confreres. The dead Tertiaries were buried wearing their habits and rope cingulum. Poor confreres were given these items from the joint treasury. The requirements for the wearing of the Tertiary habit had been lowered in the meantime. The original restrictive, long and narrow tunic inconvenienced both craftsmen and nobility. In 1508, Julius II introduced instead a scapular that could be worn (tied with a cingulum) under the outer garment. Clement XI made yet another concession in 1704, allowing the use of a small scapular (consisting of two pieces of cloth hung on the straps and worn again under the outer garment).[70] The ban on carrying weapons was likewise relaxed – nobles were free to carry weapons as a sign of their social status, soldiers and gamekeepers as a "working tool", and all the others for defence purposes.[71] The Tertiaries thus wore the full habit (the tunic without the hood) only for gatherings and celebrations – and then at their own funeral.[72] Yet, or perhaps for this very reason, the habit and cingulum play a crucial role in the external presentation of the Third Order. The image on the front page of the registry of the Olomouc Third Order community (1731) portrays two Tertiaries, a noble cavalier and a lady kneeling on pillows, to whom Saint Francis is handing a cingulum from his heavenly glory. This motif of the cord as a "rescue rope" is, together with the motif of Noah's three-deck ark, one of the most popular motifs of Tertiary iconography.[73]

The above indicates that while the Third Order was based on medieval tradition, it was largely influenced by other early modern confraternities. The main

70. Iriarte, *Franciscan History*, pp. 493-494.

71. Veith, *Regule aneb spůsob*, pp. 29-30.

72. Holzapfel, *Handbuch der Geschichte*, pp. 594-605.

73. Simonetta Prosperi Valenti Rodinò, "La diffusione dell'iconografia francescana attraverso l'incisione", in *L'immagine di San Francesco nella Controriforma: Roma Calcografia, 9 Dicembre 1982-13 Febbraio 1983*, ed. by Claudio M. Strinati and Simonetta Prosperi Valenti Rodinò, Roma, Quasar, 1982, pp. 163-164. The motif of Noah's Ark representing the three orders of Saint Francis is in Henricus Sedulius, "Anteloquium ad benivolum lectorem", *Historia Seraphica Vitae B. P. Francisci Assisiatis*, Antverpiae, Sumptibus Haeredum Martini Nutii, 1613, (unpaged); in Bohemia it is e.g. on the frontispiece of Gandulphus Blanik, *Thesaurus Franciscanus Nova et Vetera, Virorum ac Mulierum Tribus de Ordinibus S.P. Francisci Seraphici a Sanctitate Vitae, Probitae Morum, Zelo Fidei, Doctrinaque Illustrium, Sculpta Aere Ectypa Proferens*, Znoymae, Antonius Johannes Preyss, 1773.

emphasis was on mutual solidarity and support in the "last things of man" – the Tertiaries were supposed to attend funerals and Requiem Masses for the deceased confreres and pray for their souls. Although charity was probably an integral part of Tertiary activities, it probably did not play such a crucial role as in the case of medieval Tertiaries.[74] Some of the charity events were likely aimed primarily at solidarity with other, less wealthy Tertiaries. This much is suggested by the charter of the foundation of the Olomouc Tertiary and Apostolic Syndic Matthias Kniebandl for alms-worthy members of the Third Order of Saint Francis (1778).[75] Equally important, like in other confraternities, were social prestige and self-presentation.[76] The hallmark setting the Tertiaries apart from other confraternities in this respect was its quasi-religious character. Although the status of the Tertiary communities was not very clearly defined, the Franciscans persistently presented the Third Order as an integral branch of the Order of Friars Minor, and therefore (unlike ordinary confraternities), an exclusive community:

> There can be no doubt that this penitent Order (established by such a Holy Man, approved by some many Popes, and strengthened, enriched with so many Spiritual Graces, adorned by so many Holy Men, favoured with so many Wonders and Miracles), is no ordinary Brotherhood, or a Congregation of selected Persons, but a true Order validated in the Holy Church. Should anyone dare to trivialize, decry or oppose the Order, as if it were imperfect, not permitted and confirmed by Holy Church, know that he will fall into disgrace with the Almighty Lord and His Blessed Apostles Peter and Paul.[77]

The monastic character of the Tertiary communities was finally indirectly confirmed by Pope Benedict XIII in the constitution for the Tertiaries, *Paterna sedis apostolicae providentia*.[78] The Franciscans themselves had built the Third Order on this foundation from the very start. The mere admission of new members resembled joining an order. In contrast to the majority of confraternities, Tertiary candidates were obligated to undergo a year-long novitiate. The ceremony itself, in which the new member took vows and received the habit with the cord of St Francis, imitated classical religious institutions. With the habit, each Tertiary accepted commitments which largely exceeded the normal duties of members of

74. For more on the charitable activities of religious confraternities, see: Jiří Mikulec, *Církev a společnost raného novověku v Čechách a na Moravě*, Prague, Historický ústav, 2013, pp. 187-191.

75. Moravian Land Archive Brno, Fund B 2, Moravian Authority – Ecclesiastical Department, sign. F2/121, inv. no. 930, carton 48, *Charter concerning the fund of M. Kniebandl for poor members of the Third Order and for the poor of the city of Olomouc* (1778).

76. A certain partial decline of the penitential spirit in favour of the external aspects is, after all, mentioned by the Franciscan authors themselves. Iriarte, *Franciscan History*, p. 495.

77. Veith, *Regule aneb spůsob*, pp. 13-14.

78. Jiří Mikulec, "Náboženská bratrstva a třetí řády při františkánských klášterech v barokních Čechách", in *Historia Franciscana II.: Sborník textů: Kapitoly z dějin české františkánské provincie sv. Václava u příležitosti 300. výročí úmrtí provinčního ministra a významného učence Bernarda Sanniga (1704) a 400. výročí příchodu františkánů k Panně Marii Sněžné v Praze (1604)*, ed. by Petr Regalát Beneš and Petr Hlaváček, Kostelní Vydří, Karmelitánské nakladatelství, 2005, p. 189.

other confraternities – in particular the duty to pray the liturgy of the hours.[79] The high demands undoubtedly flattered many people and increased the attraction and exclusivity of the Third Order.[80] It was a highly appealing association from the spiritual point of view. Membership in the Third Order rendered one with more intense piety based on the Franciscan tradition, but also a share in the holiness of the whole order:

> Firstly: that they deserve to go by the name of and be the Sons and Daughters of Saint Francis and to enjoy his Fatherly protection. Secondly: that they make company and associate with three Orders of Saint Francis and participate in all their Spiritual Gifts. Thirdly: that they take part in all their contrition, flagellation, fasts, vigils, prayers, contemplation, and all good works in general. Fourthly: that he is a powerful means to eternal Salvation.[81]

Tertiary men and women practically became members of a religious institution (with all its benefits) without having to renounce their secular way of life. In addition, they found themselves in exclusive association with other illustrious persons; above all, various saints. In his book, Hieronymus Veit gives an account of a legend of how one of the Tertiaries, Tomasuccio de Foligno, was elevated to heaven for one day for his utmost holiness. There he saw, among a variety of delights, "a large and extremely glorious Crowd, People of different Status, Kings and Queens, etc. all clothed in a white-ash Apparel, which was strangely beautiful, decorated with precious Stones and Pearls..."[82] Before them the victorious banner of the Holy Cross was carried, accompanied by angels playing drums, pipes, violins, harps and other instruments. He was told that he was watching the triumph of the brothers and sisters of his order who deserved the banner and to be its guardians. Veit then warns the reader:

> Who would be so reckless and so little favouring his soul as to not be moved to conquer such magnificent Spiritual Riches? Such a Heavenly Profit, Use, and Treasure? Who could it be that (knowing that without changing his Status, he may still partake in such a magnificent Merit) would not want to connect with such noble Persons, befriend so many Saints, and be the Son of such a great Father; in particular, as no Loss, no Work is needed to achieve this Goal...[83]

The emphasis on exceptionality and the large number of saints (the Tertiaries had even more saints than some of the "regular" orders) is one of the traditional self-confirming arguments used by the First Order and additionally by the Third

79. The declining demands of the majority of confraternities on its members is described in Jiří Mikulec, "Proměny náboženských bratrstev v Čechách v raném novověku", in *Bratrstva. Světská a církevní sdružení a jejich role v kulturních a společenských strukturách od středověku do moderní doby (III. Pardubické bienále, 29. - 30. dubna 2004)*, ed. by Tomáš Jiránek and Jiří Kubeš, Pardubic, Univerzita Pardubice, 2005, p. 25.

80. Judith Pollmann, "How to Flatter the Laity? Rethinking Catholic Responses to the Reformation", *BMGN - Low Countries Historical Review*, 126, 4 (2011): pp. 97-106.

81. Veith, *Regule aneb spůsob*, pp. 73-74.

82. Veith, *Regule aneb spůsob*, p. 9.

83. Veith, *Regule aneb spůsob*, pp. 11-12.

Order of Saint Francis (from Hieronymus Veit through Heribert Holzapfel or *The Catholic Encyclopedia* to today's Wikipedia page).

The Third Order proved to be one of the most important Franciscan projects. For the Franciscans themselves, the Third Order was of undeniable significance, not only in economic terms. More importantly, the Third Order allowed them to expand and effectively export the order's spirituality beyond the friary walls; particularly when several members of a single household joined the Third Order, so the houses could be sort of viewed as lay "offshoots" of the friary. The order even drew clergy, numbered at twenty members. They were, for the most part, priests from the nearby villages (for example, the well-known preacher and writer Bohumír Hynek Josef Bílovský, and a priest in Slatenice, who received the Tertiary habit in 1713).[84] Being a part of the Third Order helped the priests deepen their own spiritual life and perhaps overcome the feeling of isolation. The regular gatherings of Tertiary communities and other meetings with Franciscan priests formed a professional platform similar to the institution of rural deaconry.[85] The priests could then become "ambassadors" of the friary in their villages and promote some of the cults and devotions initiated by the Franciscans. The Third Order thus facilitated a greater impact on believers and helped distribute the Franciscan spirituality around households and far beyond the city.

84. For more on Bílovský, see: Josef Vašica, *České literární baroko. Příspěvky k jeho studiu*, 2nd ed., Prague, Atlantis, 1995, pp. 189-199 and the study by Milan Kopecký in *Staří slezští kazatelé. Různé rozprávky a příběhy k naučení a ku potěše*, ed. by Milan Kopecký, Ostrava, Profil, 1970, pp. 92-101.

85. Marc R. Forster, *Catholic Revival in the Age of the Baroque: Religious Identity in Southwest Germany, 1550-1750*, Cambridge, Cambridge University Press, 2001, p. 179.

5. Arbiters of the Sacred

The year 1680 was quite eventful, mostly in negative terms.[1] Witch trials were gathering momentum in the nearby Velké Losiny and Šumperk regions (in the montane mendicant district of the friary). There was a great uproar when even Christopher Lautner, Dean of Šumperk, was arrested and accused of witchcraft in August of the same year. In addition, testimonies extracted from interrogated suspects began to mention honourable Olomouc burghers as participants at the Witches' Sabbaths – the wife of Councillor Meixner, one of the most notable Franciscan benefactors, being among them.[2] Bad news also arrived from other areas, such as Bohemia, struck by peasant uprisings, and the East, where the Turkish danger was coming to life again. More importantly, "the plentiful ills and lack of love in human hearts had brought the wrath of God" upon the earth and a plague broke out. Although Olomouc itself was spared the pestilence, fear and panic prevailed. Moreover, the end of this catastrophic year saw yet another horrifying event, meticulously described in the friary's chronicle. The majority of earlier records had been a few lines long – a sequence of terse bits of information, interrupted at times by a slightly longer narrative passage. Now, for the first time since Meerstein's description of the Swedish occupation, the chronicle contains a report similar to a short treatise, four full pages long. The extent of the record matched the gravity of the situation – for a comet had been spotted in the sky.[3]

The superior, and most likely also the chronicler, was Amandus Hermann, one of the most learned priests in the Bohemian province (he later wrote an almost one-thousand-page hagiography on John of Capistrano).[4] Considering Franciscan standards, the author flaunts his erudition too much: he writes the names of the

1. See: Ivana Čornejová, Iva Čornejová, Jiří Kaše, Jiří Mikulec, and Vít Vlnas, *Velké dějiny zemí Koruny české, VIII (1618-1683)*, Prague and Litomyšl, Paseka, 2008, pp. 186-192.

2. The citizens of Olomouc learned about the accusations in time and complained to the emperor about the manipulation and abuse of power by Judge Boblig of Edelstadt. Boblig was not allowed to move his tribunal to the city and the names of the Olomouc citizens were exonerated. František Spurný, Vojtěch Cekota, and Miloš Kouřil, *Šumperský farář a děkan Kryštof Alois Lautner, oběť čarodějnických inkvizičních procesů*, Šumperk, Městský úřad Šumperk, 2000, passim.

3. *Archivum*, pp. 78-81

4. Amandus Hermann, *Capistranus Triumphans: Seu Historia Fundamentalis de Sancto Joanne Capistrano*, Coloniae, apud Balthasarum Joachimum Endterum, 1700.

Fig. 23. Horror caused by the apparition of the Kirch Comet in 1680. From Christophorus Wegelius, *Ethica Naturalis seu Documenta Moralia e Variis rerum Naturalium proprietatibus Virtutum Vitiorumque symbolicis imaginibus collecta* (s.l.: s.n., 1700).

months not only in Latin, but also in Greek and Hebrew. He added a precise description to the comet report, which included his own observations and reports from other places. We learn that the comet first emerged above Nuremberg in early November in the sign of Leo. On 12 November, however, the view was obscured by thick clouds that hid the comet for several weeks. When it first appeared above Olomouc, it stretched over a considerable part of the sky – it was 54 (arc) degrees long. Then the sky again became overcast and the comet was only visible in Silesia. Hermann was able to keep track, though, thanks to his confrere from the Nysa friary in Silesia. The comet appeared once more, early in the following year, after it sped around the Sun and started moving away (this reappearance confounded even Isaac Newton, who initially thought that these were two different comets). Eventually, it would be named Kirch's Comet and its observations would go on to provide the basis for modern comet research.[5]

5. Tofigh Heidarzadeh, *A History of Physical Theories of Comets, From Aristotle to Whipple*, Dordrecht,Springer Science & Business Media, 2008, pp. 89-93.

Kirch's Comet, however, also inspired a tremendous amount of prints and reports from all over Europe interpreting the sight from a more traditional point of view – as a portent of (rather ghastly) things to come.[6] This ambiguity is manifested also in the friary chronicle. While the first page of the relation contains a fairly factual and precise description of the comet, the following three pages are dedicated to a historical account of comets and disasters. The author made a chronologic list of all known comet sightings (a hundred and fifty cases altogether) along with corresponding events the comets were supposed to presage. Those included the assassination of Julius Caesar, the persecution of Christians by Emperor Nero, the death of Charles IV, and, more recently, the Bohemian Revolt against Ferdinand II. The author was nevertheless fair to comets. He acknowledges that sometimes, comet sightings were accompanied by events that could be considered, from his point of view, positive (he mentions, for example, the birth of Aristotle and the crusader conquest of Jerusalem). He even admits there had been cases when a comet appeared, and nothing significant happened (in 1470, for example).

The list illustrates the fact that comets were usually viewed as omens of disaster. There is one important circumstance, however, which granted this particular event a deeper meaning. The comet appeared in the Olomouc sky at a time which is special in itself and is associated with a variety of signs and interpretations – Christmas Eve. The arrival of the traditional harbinger of doom on a special day, moreover in a particularly disastrous year, must have inspired much panic. The fact that it appeared on the day commemorating the Nativity of Jesus Christ might have even led to speculations whether the comet could not herald his second coming, as described in Apocalypse. At least one comment made on the second page of his treatise suggests that those fears might have indeed appeared. At one point, as the inventory of ancient comets and disasters reached the beginning of the Christian calendar, the list is interrupted by a note, written in a different font. Bigger and notably neater, the words say: "Jesus Christ was born, and a star appeared but it was not a comet".[7] The emphasized reassurance "quae non fuit cometa" suggests that the author might have been responding to the panic among the believers. The theme of the "celestial sign" was likely incorporated in Christmas sermons, both at St Bernardino and other city churches.

The story of the 1680 comet highlights the fact that the Franciscans – like other clergy in the city – played an essential role in the interpretation of important events, specifically regarding their religious significance. Apart from that, they performed many other functions related to interactions with the sacred. Their church held regular masses, devotions, sermons, and prayers, during which the friars operated as mediators between God and the believers. As Meerstein's chronicle (see Chapter 2) showed, the Franciscans presented themselves as a holy community protecting and sanctifying the city space and its inhabitants. At the

6. See: e.g. Johann Boediker, *Christlicher Bericht Von Cometen, Als Der Große Comet 1680 Und 1681 Geleuchtet Dem Christlichen Deutschen Leser Zu Dienst Aus Den Vornehmsten Meynungen Alter Und Neuer Lehrer Zusammen Gezogen*, Cölln an der Spree, Druckts Georg Schultze, 1681.

7. *Archivum*, p. 79.

same time, they mediated between different traditions and played an important role in introducing new forms of devotions from abroad. The Franciscans had a considerable advantage in this area, not only thanks to their supranational nature (an advantage shared with other religious orders) but, above all, because of their privileged position as custodians of the Holy Land. Additionally, the friars were also mediators between ecclesiastical structures and society, specifically between ecclesiastical and municipal institutions. Their role was complex and multi-layered, and they contributed fundamentally to the religious and social life of the city.

1. *Sacred space*

The friary was organized so as to fully enable the friars to perform the above functions. Firstly, the community mostly consisted of priests who had been systematically trained for their future profession from the very moment they joined the order.[8] They were supported by lay brethren who not only did most of the begging, but also frequently interacted with residents and promoted the order's spirituality in less formal ways. The rich and varied body of sources related to the activities of the Olomouc friars unfortunately contains one significant gap. There is practically no information available about the sermons which were preached every day in the church. We do know that the friary had, as a rule, four officially appointed preachers: the weekday morning, the weekday afternoon, the holiday morning, and the holiday afternoon. The Franciscans also preached away from the friary, both occasionally (festivities, canonizations, pilgrimages) and regularly (they took over the preaching office at St Maurice from the Jesuits in 1775).[9] Thus, the Olomouc Franciscan preachers gave annually more than seven hundred sermons, what makes a staggering number of over one hundred thousand sermons delivered during the period under consideration. Yet, out of this immense number, only a single sermon has survived, and a highly specific one: a solemn sermon delivered at the nearby pilgrimage shrine of Svatý Kopeček on the occasion of the coronation of a local miraculous image.[10] Nothing is known about the everyday sermons at St Bernardino, their topics, actual performance, or about their form or impact.

8. The Bohemian Franciscan Province had its own system of schools for clerics and priests. Individual, specialised schools were located in Prague and other bigger friaries. Olomouc first hosted philosophical studies (in the seventeenth century), and later the studies of speculative and moral theology). *Archivum*, p. 231.

9. *Protocollum*, p. 438.

10. The sermon was delivered by Fr. Nicefor Kaurzil before the noon of the fifth day of the festivities (12 September 1732), on the topic of "The Arch of the God's Mercy, that is the Virgin Mary, Queen of the Heavens, depicted as the Arch of Covenant", in *Enthronisticum Parthenium: Sive Gloria Et Honor Neo-Inauguratæ ... Reginæ Mariæ ... ; Prope Metropolim Olomucensem in Marchionatu Moraviæ ... Et Prima in Orbe Marcomanno Corona Regali Aurea De Urbe Missa Ritu Vaticano, Solemnissimóque Applausu Coronata*, Olomucii, typis Francisci Antonii Hirnle, 1733, unpaged.

Although the daily sermons were an important interaction between the convent and the burghers, these were part of a much broader whole. Systematic preaching could only have the desired effect when supplemented and supported by other means, often with a distinct visual component: images, symbols, rituals, and liturgies. Sources are less taciturn in this case, providing at least a partial picture of how the sacred was negotiated and mediated. The crucial factor, naturally, was the space where most of these activities took place. As already mentioned, the friary was built on a site sanctified by Capistrano's sermon in the third quarter of the fifteenth century.[11] The church had a three-aisle nave with an elongated, slightly misaligned presbytery. The northern side of the nave was adjoined to the cloister of the friary leading to the refectory and the upper floor with the dormitory. To the east, there was a spacious garden – actually, one of the largest plots within the city walls. Later, the cloister was extended and more structures were erected (sacristy, infirmary, etc.). Both the church and the cloister were vaulted with simple groin vaults. The most prominent architectural feature was the tall pyramidal roof with a spire over the nave of the church. Otherwise, the friary was a relatively unassuming structure built in deliberately "old-fashioned" style (particularly in contrast to the parish church of St Maurice, which was built at the same time by the same workshop), reflecting the ideals of the order's poverty.

The church was consecrated on 28 August 1468 by the Papal Legate Lorenzo, Bishop of Ferrara, in honour of the Immaculate Conception of the Virgin Mary and in honour of St Bernardino.[12] It seems that apart from the presbytery, the skeleton of the nave was also already standing, because the following day Bishop Rudolph of Wroclaw sanctified eight other altars: of the Virgin Mary and the Holy Cross, of St John the Baptist, of St Francis, of St Anthony of Padua and Anthony the Great, of St Barbara and St Margaret, of St Mary Magdalene, of St Ursula and her companions, and finally of St Catherine. Later, two more altars were added. The altar of the Holy Trinity was built in the cloister of the monastery in 1480.[13] After the storm on the feast of St Anne, an altar dedicated to the same saint was built in the church in thanksgiving, in 1495.[14] The church was decorated with many frescoes throughout the first half of its existence. In the presbytery there was a large black-and-white mural depicting the victory at Belgrade and several other frescoes, of which only fragments have survived (St Francis, St Bernardino, the Carrying of the Cross, and the figure of a female saint). The nave was richly decorated, too. Besides two Passion images (the Carrying of the Cross and the Deposition of Christ) on the sides of the triumphal arch, there was also a fresco of the Virgin Mary with a Franciscan rosary (1500) and a sizable fresco of St Christopher (1520), protector against sudden death – strategically placed to catch

11. Slavomíra Kašpárková and Tomáš Vítek, "Klášter bernardinů s kostelem Neposkvrněného početí P. Marie", in *Od gotiky k renesanci výtvarná kultura Moravy a Slezska 1400-1550, III. díl, Olomoucko (katalog výstavy)*, ed. by Ivo Hlobil and Marek Perůtka, Olomouc, Muzeum umění Olomouc, 1999, pp. 208-210.

12. *Archivum*, p. 3.

13. *Archivum*, p. 6.

14. *Archivum*, p. 11.

the eye of those entering the church. Both the dedication of the altars and the fresco decoration were focused on the popular late medieval saints, the Passion cult, and the order's tradition.

The larger part of the interior, including the altars, survived the Reformation and the Swedish occupation. In the seventeenth century, the friars sought to restore the sacred space they inherited from their predecessors. Yet, at the same time, they started introducing new elements which would gradually transform the entire sacred space of the friary. One of the first projects following the restoration of the house in 1650 was the construction of a new high altar which separated the brothers' choir from the rest of the church. The original altar had been moved several times at the beginning of the seventeenth century, due to the changes in the size of the religious community and the ensuing spatial demands of the choir. It also had been re-consecrated twice: first in 1615 when the relics of St Vitus and Lawrence, along with a piece of St Francis's habit, were placed inside; and again in 1635, when the dedication was extended to the Immaculate Conception of the Virgin Mary, St Bernardino, St Louis of Toulouse, and Blessed John of Capistrano.[15] The new high altar consecrated in 1653, however, reflected some of the fundamental dilemmas of the post-war restoration and the ongoing internal reforms. This included the fact that the friary or its benefactors probably lacked the funds to have the new altar decorated and, above all, gilded. At the same time, however, Meerstein claims in his chronicle that the friars were concerned that the new altar might look too splendid "nimis splendidum".[16] The altar was, in the end, left unfinished, and remained so for thirty-seven years, representing the poverty of the order. As the position of the friary strengthened and the external and internal restrictions gradually faded, the altar was finally gilded at the costs of two hundred guilders.[17] The work was carried out by the lay brother Fr Benedictus Seeblumer (*Laicus Noster Pictor*), who saved the friary a considerable amount, as secular painters demanded five hundred guilders. The altar was, nevertheless, torn down in 1765 and replaced with a new one, paid for by benefactors.[18]

The other major project after 1650 was the Chapel of the Holy Sepulchre, built by Tobias Schwonauer. The chapel was to become the symbolic climax of Schwonauer's long-term cooperation with the Franciscans – apart from sponsoring the chapel, he also asked for permission (which was promptly granted) to build a

15. *Archivum*, p. 25. Interestingly, it was one of the first dedications (if not the very first) to the Immaculate Conception in Bohemian Lands, but was largely left out in the name of the church and monastery – perhaps because the dogma had not been approved yet. The Olomouc friary was strictly referred to as St Bernardino, particularly in the early modern sources of the order. Dedication to the Virgin Mary began to be used more often, paradoxically only after the monastery was transferred to the Dominicans, who traditionally opposed the teaching of the Immaculate Conception of the Virgin Mary.

16. *Archivum*, p. 42. The choir side of the altar was furnished in the following decades with images of the order's saints, a cross, a pulpit with a liturgical bookcase, and a statue of the Virgin Mary.

17. *Archivum*, p. 102.

18. *Protocollum*, pp. 185-188.

crypt under the chapel for himself and his family.[19] The chapel, consecrated by the Olomouc Suffragan Joannes Chobar on 1 June 1653, was the first major attempt to expand and develop the existing sacred space.[20] It also highlighted what would continue to be one of the cultic and visual dominants of the temple – the cult of the Passion of Christ. When the Holy Sepulchre was being built, the original Passion Cycle frescoes (the Carrying of the Cross and the Deposition of Christ) on the sides of the triumphal arch were probably still exposed and visible. Likewise, there was probably still a beam in the triumphal arc at that time, holding the statues of the Crucified, the Virgin Mary, and John the Evangelist. The new shrine, the entrance of which was next to the frescoe capturing the Deposition, built on and developed the existing cycle. The chapel was an attractive feature that undoubtedly drew the attention of believers. It was, after all, one of the earliest imitations of the Jerusalem shrine in Bohemian Lands (following the Holy Hill near Mikulov and the Zderaz monastery of Discalced Augustinians).[21] The popularity of the site is evident from gifts (silver lamps, candlesticks), mass stipends, and the fact that the space around the chapel became a sought-after place for funerals, besides Schwonauer's crypt, where other people were also later buried (probably with the permission of the sponsor's family). This is where another councillor, Matthias Hanfstengel, was buried in 1659, the same year as Schwonauer. Five years later the body of Felix Smirowsky was laid there, too.[22]

As burials moved outside the church in the eighteenth century, a small churchyard was established around the chapel, surrounded by a wooden fence.[23] Although the mass and other services were held in the chapel on a regular basis, the chapel drew attention mainly during Easter, when the statue of the dead Christ was placed there. One custom seems to be proof of the popularity of the chapel. A number of deep longitudinal scratches run along the sandstone pilasters around the chapel and the relief of the Crucified (originally located on the outer wall of the chapel). Such scratches can be seen in other sacred objects, both in Olomouc and around Europe. They were apparently caused by attempts to scrub sand or

19. NA Prague, Bohemian Franciscan Province Archives, reg. no. 2981, carton 175, *Sacristy, Holy Sepulchre, etc.*, passim. Schwonauer himself was buried in the crypt in 1659, later followed by his wife and children, as well as other people.

20. The altar inside the chapel was dedicated to St Francis and St Anthony of Padua and contained the relics of St Paul and St Maurice. The chapel, adjoining the southern wall of the presbytery, was entered through a portal from the south nave aisle. Etched above the entrance were the words S. S. SEPULCHRUM IESU CHRISTI HIEROSOLITANUM and the trigram for Christ's name, this time as **IHS**. The design itself was based on the Jerusalem chapel rather loosely. The interior consisted of a barrel-vaulted vestibule and a square tomb chamber – the chapel probably did not have any windows (hence the name "black chapel"). The exterior was adorned with a blind arcade, and the roof of the chapel featured the typical aedicule. *Archivum*, p. 41.

21. See: Tomáš Řepa, *Kaple Božího hrobu v Čechách a na Moravě v období baroka*, dissertation, FF UP Olomouc, 2010.

22. *Archivum*, p. 44 and p. 50.

23. The fence around the churchyard is mentioned in *Archivum*, p. 210. The records of the first burial date to 1716 and the last burial to 1781. *Protocollum*, 595-598.

Fig. 24. Relief with scratches (originally placed on the wall of the Holy Sepulchre chapel, today on the northern interior wall of the church). Photo: Martin Elbel.
Fig. 25. Chapel of St Anthony of Padua. Museum of Arts Olomouc. Photo: Markéta Ondrušková.

dust from the stone parts. The resulting powder was used as a remedy – probably mixed with butter or lard and used as an ointment.[24] The healing power lay in the sympathetic relation of the powder and the venerated sacral object. In the case of the Olomouc Holy Sepulchre, the powder was likely obtained mainly during Easter, when the sacred character of the place was enhanced by the sacredness of the time and the presence of the consecrated host within the chapel. The size and number of the scratches suggest that the scraping was performed repeatedly with knowing and eventual consent by the friars. The powder from the Holy Sepulchre thus complemented other remedies – water from Capistrano's well and the slips of Salvador of Horta – the friary offered to Olomouc residents.[25]

24. Eduard Wondrák, "Otazníky kolem "záhadných" rýh na některých olomouckých stavbách", in *Okresní archiv v Olomouci: zpráva o činnosti Okresního archivu v Olomouci za rok 1979*, Olomouc, 1980, pp. 62-69. For the use of powder from consecrated objects, see also: Mikulec, *Náboženský život*, pp. 121-122

25. See: e.g. *Archivum*, p. 4.

Another major alteration of the Franciscan Church came with the construction of the Chapel of St Anthony at the south side of the church. The foundation stone of the chapel was laid in the presence of the fort commander, the bailiff, seven councillors, and twelve senators on 21 March 1675 (it was the last event attended by Modestus Meerstein – he died two days later).[26] The chapel, however, did not serve its function very long. It was destroyed in a storm in 1700, as the wind knocked the top turret of the church onto the chapel during the disaster described earlier in the text (see Chapter 2). It was decided after some time that the chapel would be rebuilt and expanded further into the street to obtain a roughly square plan, which would enable the construction of a dome. The new chapel was consecrated on 8 November 1709 by the Olomouc Suffragan Francis Julian of Braida, and the first mass was said by Abbot Bernard Wancke of the Premonstratensian monastery Hradisko. While the Holy Sepulchre had accentuated Passion motifs, the Chapel of St Anthony of Padua was focused on the elements of the order's tradition. So far, the church only had two altars dedicated to Franciscan saints (besides the high altar): the altars of St Francis and of St Anthony of Padua. The new chapel had a total of three Franciscan altars: the altar of St Anthony, of St Bonaventura, and of the newly canonised (1669) St Peter of Alcantara. The tradition of the order was also emphasized by stucco and frescoes on the inner dome of the chapel (glorification of Anthony of Padua).[27]

There were nine secondary altars in the nave of the church in the seventeenth century. The altar of the Virgin Mary and the Privileged Altar of the Holy Cross were on the gospel side next to the triumphal arch, and the altars of Our Lady of Mariapócs and of St Catherine stood along the northern wall. The altar of St John the Baptist and St Barbara, along with the altar of St Ursula, were placed by the columns on the gospel side. The altar of St Francis (Portiuncula) was on the epistle side of the triumphal arch, joined by the altar of St Anne and the altar of Mary Magdalene next to the columns. There was also the altar of the Holy Trinity in the cloister of the monastery, in the part that was accessible to the public. Starting in the 1680s, the altars were gradually rebuilt and refined so that at least the paired altars were as uniform as possible. Most of them were railed in, their sculptures and paintings were glazed. The altars were furnished over time with other statues, paintings, and relics.[28] Of great importance was the acquisition and exhibition of the relics of the holy martyrs Clement and Florian in 1682.[29]

26. *Archivum*, p. 63.

27. Josef Prucek, "K renovaci barokní, tzv. růžencové kaple v kostele Neposkvrněného početí Panny Marie v Olomouci", *Zprávy Vlastivědného muzea v Olomouci*, 28-35, 266 (1991): pp. 29-34; Leoš Mlčák, "K ikonografii, autorství a restaurování malířské a sochařské výzdoby kaple sv. Antonína Paduánského v Olomouci", *Vlastivědný věstník moravský*, 44 (1992): pp. 58-64.

28. In particular, the friars sought to promote the cults of new Franciscan saints. The altar of St Ursula was additionally dedicated to the seven Franciscan martyrs of Japan, and the altar of St Catherine re-consecrated as the altar of St Catherine of Bologna.

29. In 1681, Superior Amandus Hermann was given two boxes full of small relics by the bishop, brought from the Roman catacombs. He also received the relics of the holy martyrs Clement and Florian. Hermann had glass-covered reliquaries made for them and convinced

The canonisation of John of Capistrano in 1691 was an important landmark for the friars. In 1697, a statue of the new saint was commissioned (and sponsored by the commander of the city garrison, Heinrich Tobias de Hasling), and placed under an ornate canopy at the northern wall beside the entrance into the cloister.[30] At the same time, the friars also strove to locate any objects commemorating the visit of their founder in Olomouc. Unlike Brno, which housed the alleged habit of Capistrano, the Olomouc friary lacked such a relic.[31] Although the high altar stored an unspecified relic of Blessed John of Capistrano since 1635, the main vestige of the saint was Capistrano's well (repaired in 1699 and 1765).[32] The Franciscans caught a glimmer of hope in March 1699 as the Carthusians of the Vallis Josaphat Monastery in Olomouc sent them a message saying they had found in their archives an old filiation charter given to the monastery by John of Capistrano.[33] The charter promised the friars would pray and say masses for the Carthusians, in return for their material support. The Carthusians suggested the old agreement be revived and observed. They even specified the form of their material support – they promised to brew beer for the Franciscans in their brewery and to supply the friary with fresh fish from their ponds every three months. The discovery of the filiation caused a sensation among the Franciscans, as the charter had reputedly been penned by Capistrano himself. The Carthusians, however, did not want to part with the valuable relic. They nonetheless allowed the Franciscans to make a copy of the charter, and, as a gesture of goodwill, they promised to lend the original to the Franciscans occasionally so that the latter could put it on display in their church.[34]

the bishop to grant him the permission to celebrate the feast of the two martyrs. In July of the following year, the remains were solemnly transferred from the friary to the church and placed on the paired altars of the Virgin Mary and St Francis, on the sides of the triumphal arch. The church was decorated with scarlet candles and green branches, and the floor was covered with grass and flowers. The solemn mass, as usual followed by Te Deum, was celebrated by Petr Rehramont, Canon in Brno and the Bishop's Master of Ceremonies. Music was provided by seminarians and the subsequent banquet by the city council. *Archivum*, pp. 83-84. For more on the translation of relics from the Roman catacombs, see: Hansjakob Achermann, *Die Katakombenheiligen Und Ihre Translationen in Der Schweizerischen Quart Des Bistums Konstanz*, Stans, Verlag Historischer Verein Nidwalden, 1979, and Simon Ditchfield, "Martyrs on the Move: Relics as Vindicators of Local Diversity in the Tridentine Church", in *Martyrs and Martyrologies, Studies in Church History, Vol. 30*, ed. by Diana Wood, Oxford, Blackwell, 1993, pp. 283-294.

30. *Archivum*, p. 113.

31. "*Historia Franciscana. Katalog výstavy pořádané k 400. výročí příchodu bratří františkánů do kláštera Panny Marie Sněžné v Praze (1604-2004)*", Prague, Provincie bratří františkánů, 2004, catalogue entry no. 24, p. 31.

32. *Archivum*, p. 123 and *Protocollum*, p. 111.

33. *Archivum*, p. 116.

34. The deed is stored at the Moravian Land Archive Brno, Fund E 40, Olomouc Carthusians, sign. 1451 VII 25, *Filiation given to the Carthusians of Olomouc by John of Capistrano*, 25 July 1451. Its photograph is available at http://monasterium.net/mom/CZ-MZA/E40/1451_VII_25/charter [vid. 20. 9. 2015].

Fig. 26. Filiation charter of John of Capistrano issued for the Olomouc Carthusians (25 July 1451). Moravian Land Archive in Brno, E 40 Carthusians of Olomouc, sign. 1451 VII 25.

The sacred space of the church, of course, did not develop unilaterally, but it was continuously co-created by believers. This was probably the case of the popular cult of John of Nepomuk, whose introduction to the Olomouc Franciscan Church is credited to the apostolic syndic Michael Baum and his wife, Eva. The Baums and the merchant Antonín Habel procured a statue of the heretofore uncanonised saint for the church in 1696.[35] The statue was placed on the southern wall next to the Chapel of St Anthony of Padua and decorated with a canopy. It soon attracted the attention of other believers, who donated numerous gifts such as silver ex-votos, chalices, and lamps. Based on the permission of the bishop's office, a small gilded altar was added to the statue in 1703, followed by a new, more decorated altar in 1719, both funded by Michael and Eva Baum.[36] Eva Baum also had a crypt built under the altar. The image of Our Lady of Mariapócs, for which a new separate altar was built in 1698 on the gospel side between the altars of the Virgin Mary and St Catherine, enjoyed even greater attention and support from the faithful.[37] The image was a copy of a miraculous image (allegedly shedding tears) kept in St Stephen's Cathedral in Vienna. In the last quarter of the seventeenth century and the first quarter of the eighteenth century, it was apparently one of the most popular devotional objects in the church. This is evident from the large number of pious gifts (particularly decorated garments and crowns for the Madonna and Jesus), which did not escape the notice of thieves in 1677.[38]

35. *Archivum*, p. 112. For the manifestations of the cult prior to the beatification of the saint, see: Vít Vlnas, *Jan Nepomucký. Česká legenda*, Prague, Mladá fronta, 1993, pp. 98-100.

36. *Archivum*, p. 186.

37. For more information about the Vienna image, see: *Funftzig-Jähriges Jubel-Fest des Gandenbildes Maria von Pötsch*, Wien, Johann Peter von Ghelen, 1747.

38. After matins on the feast of St Procopius, they entered the church, broke the glass protecting the statuette, and took two silver bracelets and several other silver votive donations which were hung on the Madonna's clothing, along with a silver lamp hanging in front of the altar. *Archivum*, p. 68.

The sacred space was not only in the interior of the church. Its exterior, the surrounding area, and links to the entire city were also important.[39] Although the only statue decorating the frontage of the church was that of St Bernardino over the porch (erected in 1709), there were other visual signs that manifested the Franciscan presence in the city.[40] These were mainly the trigrams **yhs**, traditionally associated with Capistrano: a gilded one on the top of the church spire, believed to be as old as the church itself, another supposedly made by Capistrano himself on the old city gate leading to the friary, and at least four other similar symbols on civic houses. Yet, the most impressive, albeit temporarily, exports to the public space of the city were various festivities – whether they were organized by the Franciscans themselves or the friars attended as guests. The most significant of them were celebrations of the canonization of new Franciscan saints: triumphal gates were usually built in front of the church and processions starting from the cathedral were attended by all the local clergy.[41] The celebration of the canonization of Peter of Alcantara in 1669 was particularly momentous. By then, the pompous Jesuit celebrations of the canonisation of Ignatius of Loyola and Francis Xavier in 1622 (the same year that marked the beatification of John of Capistrano, and so the Franciscans probably also celebrated) had been forgotten. The Franciscan celebrations were the first of such events to take place after the war and, being something new, attracted a lot of attention among the local population.[42] The subsequent Franciscan celebrations were equally pivotal. The year 1691 finally saw the canonization of John of Capistrano (and Paschal Baylon), a man inherently linked with the tradition of the order as well as the history of the city. The traditional eight-day celebration highlighted the connection of the friary with the city and its inhabitants. However, it also underlined the fact that entering the public space of the city (as in the case of funeral processions) may cause tension and conflicts.[43]

The celebration was spoiled by the fact that the local Conventuals and Dominicans refused to take part in the ceremonial procession, though they did not sabotage the celebrations honouring Capistrano completely. Their preachers accepted the invitation to preach in honour of Capistrano in the Franciscan Church in the following days; the problem was the procession itself. The two

39. Cf. Simon Ditchfield, "Reading Rome as a Sacred Landscape, c. 1586-1635", in *Sacred Space in Early Modern Europe*, ed. by Will Coster and Andrew Spicer, Cambridge, Cambridge University Press, 2005, pp. 190-191.

40. *Archivum*, p. 165.

41. Apart from the two celebrations above, there were also the eight-day celebrations of the canonization of Catherine of Bologna (1713), James of the Marches and Francis Solanus (1727), Margaret of Cortona (1728), and Peter de Regalado (1747). The three-day celebrations of the beatification of John of Prado (1728) and of Benedict S. Philadelpho (1744) were more modest. *Archivum* and *Protocollum*, passim.

42. *Archivum*, p. 56. For the "multimedia" aspect of the cult of saints, see: Simon Ditchfield, "Tridentine Worship and the Cult of Saints", in *Cambridge History of Christianity, Volume 6: Reform and Expansion 1500-1660*, ed. by R. Po-chia Hsia, Cambridge, Cambridge University Press, 2008, pp. 201-224.

43. *Archivum*, pp. 104-106.

orders would have to give up their traditional position in the procession and line up in front of the Franciscans. The order in which the participants proceeded reflected their social status in the city. The religious communities lined up based on how old and thus how dignified their monasteries were. The youngest institutions were to go first and the oldest and most important were to go last, as close as possible to the "symbolic centre" of the procession. This seemingly petty setback is a reminder that the Catholic Church in the early modern period was far from being homogeneous.[44] This is especially true of the closed city space, where church institutions were constantly interacting with other institutions. Each of them had their own (often diametrically different) ideas and interests, which led to latent tensions. And events organized in the public space of the city provided an opportunity to ventilate this tension. Similar rivalry in the demarcation and use of public space was witnessed, of course, primarily in confessionally divided cities and specifically in the case of a sudden change in the power balance.[45] However, similar problems also persisted in spaces which were entirely Roman Catholic. Even here, the relationships between individual actors, and their position in the sacred topography of the space, needed to be redefined and renegotiated.

2. *Balance of power*

On 15 September 1698, the provincial chapter assembled in Prague and elected new superiors for the individual friaries. The man appointed to St Bernardino in Olomouc was Hieronymus Veit, "Praedicator et Missionarius Apostolicus Regni Aegypti".[46] About a year later, he was briefly replaced by Paulinus Veit (probably a relative), while Hieronymus remained in Olomouc as a morning preacher. He resumed the position of the superior on 5 September 1700, holding the office for another three years. Veit was undoubtedly one of the most prominent (and the most controversial) men who ever lived in the Olomouc friary – among other issues, his name was linked to the beginning of the Third Order in Olomouc, and to the scandal of the excommunicated city council. As his honorary title suggests, Veit was a highly experienced missionary. He had spent nine years mostly in Egypt, but also in Palestine, Cyprus, and elsewhere in the Mediterranean. He came to Olomouc with a wealth of experience, but probably also a great deal of self-confidence. This much is clear from records in the chronicle, which undergo a change with Veit's arrival. Terse testimonies written in the third person ("The following was built under the superior..." or "Father Superior had ...built...") were replaced by extensive and often expressive passages written in the first person.

44. For more on the conflicts between parties involved in the post-1620 developments, see: esp. Alessandro Catalano, *Zápas o svědomí: Kardinál Arnošt Vojtěch z Harrachu (1598-1667) a protireformace v Čechách*, Prague, NLN, Nakladatelství Lidové noviny, 2008.

45. Will Coster and Andrew Spicer, "Introduction: the Dimensions of Sacred Space in Reformation Europe", in *Sacred Space in Early Modern Europe*, ed. by Will Coster and Andrew Spicer, Cambridge, Cambridge University Press, 2005, p. 8.

46. *Archivum*, p. 115.

His records even contain a harsh criticism of Emperor Leopold and his son Joseph concerning the new meat tax. Allegedly, the duty also affected poor peasants (*pauperculi rustici*), who used to donate the first-born calf to the Franciscans, and the friary thus suffered severe losses from the "tyrannical tax policy". Veit ranted that it was unheard of to tax charity and that the poor were exempted from taxes everywhere, "even among the Turks, as I know from my own experience". The entire passage was later crossed out (though it remained legible).[47]

Veit's other records are also outstandingly varied and vivid. It was he who penned the testimony of the tragic storm of 13 August 1700 (when the friary was briefly run by Paulinus Veit), which culminated with the collapse of the Chapel of St Anthony. This record alone demonstrated a talent for dramatic storytelling (chaos in the church), but also self-presentation (depicting the brave behaviour of the religious community).[48] Although the storm killed three people, Veit was willing to see the calamity as a miracle of sorts – as an intact picture of the Virgin Mary was found under the debris.[49] His passages generally speak of miracles more often than other writers of the chronicle. When describing the renovation of the high altar (1699), for example, he notes that St Bernardino was given an unexpected and miraculous gift from a certain burgher from Ostrava, who had been urged to make the donation by two Franciscans who appeared to him in a dream.[50] Another time, Veit writes about strange phenomena which labelled the Olomouc friary *Sanctuarium Provinciae*. The opening and closing door of a cell, bells, music, or lit candles appearing at night on the altars – these were all signs usually followed by a letter announcing the death of one of the former Olomouc brothers living in another monastery.[51] Veit is, however, considerably biased in his perception of miraculous events and signs. On one hand, he describes how one night, shortly before matins, the organ could be heard playing by itself in the church – which was seen as another harbinger of death – and how the community waited in vain for news of the death of one of the confreres. On the other hand, he dismisses a bell cracking while it was ringing during a procession as a minor accident and focuses instead on the description of the newly cast bell.[52]

Lurking in the background of all the descriptions is the effort to present St Bernardino as a sacred place – to the extent unparalleled both within the Saint Wenceslas Province and the city itself. When depicting the papal jubilee celebrations of 1700, for example, he stressed that it was his friary who organized the very first procession, which the other religious communities then imitated.[53] Veit brought the original Franciscan/Observant notion of exclusivity back to life.

47. *Archivum*, p. 119.

48. While describing another storm (5 June 1699), which reputedly smashed almost all of the windows in the friary and damaged a large part of the roofs, he focused on the hail and even drew two hailstones – thus enriching the chronicle with its only illustration. *Archivum*, p. 121.

49. *Archivum*, p. 127.

50. *Archivum*, p. 122.

51. *Archivum*, p. 122.

52. *Archivum*, p. 120.

53. *Archivum*, p. 126.

He spent his entire term of office improving the house. His building projects included the repair of the well of St John of Capistrano, the construction of a new infirmary, granary, and water supply, the renovation of the shingle roofing on the whole friary, and the redevelopment of the choir, particularly by adorning the back of the high altar (facing the choir) with new paintings "to enhance the devoutness of the friars". Equally important for him was to strengthen good relations with the burghers, whether it was his risky support of the city council during the conflict with the Consistory or the establishment of the Third Order community at St Bernardino. Some of the data in the chronicle point to the fact that the friary indeed enjoyed increasing popularity under his management. Veit introduced yet another new feature to the chronicle – he began to record the number of people who received Communion. While in 1699 there were 18,286 communicants, in 1701 there were as many as 25,656, and the year 1702 saw a total of 27,946 communicants.[54] The church held as many as seven to eight thousand masses a year at that time, and there were countless penitents. As his successors did not keep a count of the religious participant numbers, there are no data available for monitoring the long-term trend. The significant increase in communicants between 1699 and 1702, nevertheless, suggests that Veit's activities met with an enthusiastic response from the people.

Veit's main undertakings were aimed at enhancing the sacred reputation of St Bernardino and improving its position in the city's sacred topography. His endeavours culminated in an ambitious project to build a new Chapel of the Holy Stairs on a vacant lot near the friary gate.[55] He summarized his plan (and the complications he encountered) in a memorandum which he penned into the chronicle in mid-1702. The first (incomplete and abbreviated) sentence of the memorandum reads as follows:

> May the future people know that I, Father Hieronymus Veit, p.t. Superior of the Friary, returning from Jerusalem and Egyptian missions, from the city of Cairo or New Babylon, once called Memphis – after spending nine years in the various kingdoms and lands of Palestine, Egypt, Cyprus, Candia, Corsica, Sicily, Naples, Malta, Spain, and Italy – and arriving in our lands, I set out to build Scala Sancta at any convenient part of our friary, and model these on the stairs which are venerated and visited in Rome with great devotion; after my appointment of the Superior of this place, I saw a vacant, highly convenient plot near the portal of our friary, towards the city street [...] I asked the honourable city council for the plot for the above-mentioned purposes, and soon found my request graciously granted...[56]

54. *Archivum*, p. 125, p. 131, and p. 145. This is why Veit had a new silver ciborium holding 1,000 hosts made. *Archivum*, p. 125.

55. For more on the Olomouc Holy Stairs (older literature), see: Václav Nešpor, "Svaté schody v Olomouci", *Časopis Vlastivědné společnosti musejní v Olomouci*, 37 (1926), pp. 101-103; Bohuš Vybíral, "Ještě jednou o olomouckých Svatých schodech", *Časopis Vlastivědné společnosti musejní v Olomouci*, 39 (1927), pp. 109-117. More recently, Martin Elbel, "Budování poutního místa: Svaté schody při františkánském klášteře v Olomouci", *Folia Historica Bohemica* 20 (2004), pp. 215-239.

56. *Archivum*, p. 136.

Fig. 27. Front façade and the high altar of the Holy Stairs chapel. Originally from *Andacht der Heiligen Stiegen nechst an der Kirchen dess Heil. Bernardini der WW.PP. Franciscanern in der Königlichen Haubt-Stadt Ollmütz auff der Bielten*. Ollmütz: gedruckt und zu finden in der Buchdruckerey allda, 1726. State District Archive in Olomouc, Collection of litographs and photographs, sign. 998/XXXII, 5. Photo: Muzeum umění Olomouc.

The design of the sanctuary was modelled after the Scala Sancta chapel at the papal Lateran Palace. That chapel consisted of twenty-eight marble steps which, according to the tradition, were originally the stairway leading to Pilate's palace in Jerusalem, on which Jesus Christ supposedly started his last journey to the Calvary. These stairs had been purportedly brought to Rome by St Helena, in 326, as a precious relic consecrated by Christ's footprints and blood. Already revered in the Middle Ages, they became truly renowned only after the reconstruction in 1589 when Pope Sixtus V ordered the construction of twenty-eight marble steps into a staircase in front of the chapel of Sancta sanctorum, which contained some of the most precious relics. The lateral staircases were built on either side of the "Pilate's stairs", as these were used only for devotion, and believers could only climb them on their knees.[57] The new sanctuary began to attract the attention of visitors to Rome and inspired numerous imitations. As there was no such chapel

57. Devotions were endowed with rich indulgences. For devotions at the Lateran Holy Stairs, see: Josephus Maria Soresinus, *Della Scala Santa Avanti Il Sancta Sanctorum Nel Laterano Venerata*, Roma, Per Giacomo Dragondelli, 1674.

in the Bohemian Lands so far, the Friary of St Bernardino would acquire a unique, prestigious shrine with attractive devotions and rich indulgences.[58]

The first mentions of the plan to build the Holy Stairs in Olomouc date back to 25 June 1701, when Veit asked the Olomouc city council for the vacant lot by the main gate of the friary, in the direction of the neighbouring Ursuline convent.[59] The area used to be baths, abandoned and demolished in the Thirty Years' War. The neighbouring Ursulines, however, filed a protest against the Franciscans' intent, claiming they had been considering building an extension to their church on the vacant lot. The city council sided with the Franciscans and granted them the lot on 20 October. Six days later, Veit and his confreres put a large stone on the parcel, supposedly the remnant of an ancient column, to mark the Franciscan claim. Toward the end of the year, he asked the bishop's consistory for a building permit, which was granted on 2 January 1702. The smooth start of the construction, however, soon became complicated. It was then that the conflict between the consistory and the city council, which led to its excommunication on 26 February, began to intensify. Veit's boycott of the excommunication enraged the local ecclesiastical hierarchy, and Dean Orlík in particular. Response was not long in coming. Orlík took up the Ursulines' cause and intervened against the Franciscans regarding the construction of the Holy Stairs. The consistory consequently vetoed the building project on 24 April.[60]

Fortunately for Veit, Orlík's position became increasingly weak. Following the emperor's intercession, he was forced to cancel the excommunication on 7 May. The grateful city council stepped in and negotiated a compromise with the Ursulines. The consistory had no other option but to approve construction again on 22 June. The Franciscans were free to ceremoniously commence the foundation works. What followed is perhaps best conveyed by Veit's record in the chronicle, validated by the subsequent reaction of the other Olomouc religious orders:

> Then, on 3 July around six o'clock in the evening, in the presence of a large crowd I began to dig the foundations with a hoe. And lo and behold, the wonder! I only had to dig about three times into the ground before the onlookers hurried over. Everyone tried to get hold of a hoe and start digging, while venerable ladies and virgins rushed over to empty loaded carts, young children collected earth with their hands, scarves, hats, and baskets, and there was such a zeal to the people that I can only attribute it to God, who thus moved the people's hearts to complete this work. This went on for days and nights for they sacrificed sleep, staying up and working. As I said, venerable ladies, including baronesses and countesses, were not ashamed to carry the soil out in baskets, day and night. Thanks to the enthusiasm, the foundations were excavated two and a half fathoms deep within three days, something which ten workers would hardly complete in four weeks.[61]

58. Augustinians at Karlov, Prague, had their holy stairs built between 1708 and 1710. Pavel Bělina, Jiří Kaše, Jiří Mikulec, Irena Veselá, and Vít Vlnas, *Velké dějiny zemí Koruny české, IX (1683-1740)*, Prague and Litomyšl, Paseka, 2011, p. 188.

59. *Archivum*, p. 128.

60. For details on events surrounding the chapel project, see: the Olomouc State District Archive, Olomouc Archives – fragments of the registries (1426-1786), reg. no. 401, carton 13, *Holy Stairs at St Bernardino* (1701-1802). Elbel, "Budování poutního místa", pp. 215-239.

61. *Archivum*, p. 139.

This colourful scene, as if adopted from the early Franciscan legends, speaks volumes of Veit's character and the position the Franciscans had in the city. The event became a sensation and exasperated the other religious orders in the city, specifically the Capuchin friars, who sharply criticized Veit's practices. They went so far as to accuse the Franciscans of simony, wryly asking people who helped dig the foundations how many days of indulgences Father Superior had promised them for their work. The outrage caused is understandable. Capuchins and other mendicants had a good reason to worry that a new sanctuary, endowed with many indulgences, would upset the "balance of power" in the city, and the Franciscans would monopolize the attention and favour of the burghers.[62] The other mendicant orders would probably lose the alms they depended on. Other church institutions joined in the opposition. The abbot of the Premonstratensian Hradisko Monastery, Norbert Želecký of Počenice, was outraged by both the behaviour of the Franciscans during the excommunication of the city council and during the construction of the chapel. He allegedly also feared that the Franciscans were building competition for the nearby Svatý Kopeček (Holy Hill) pilgrimage site, which was under Premonstratensian administration. He decided that his monastery would not give the Franciscans the annual alms of bread and beer but divide them among the other mendicants as compensation for the wrongs.[63] Veit complained in the chronicle that "no work is holy enough not to have its detractors", but promptly added that "the impoverished friary" was more than compensated for the damages caused by defamation and slander. The friary was given plenty of bricks, building stone, and sand by a number of benefactors – it seems that the fears of other mendicants were not entirely unjustified. On Sunday, 9 July, Veit himself stepped to the pulpit to deliver a speech in which he emphasized the importance of building objects commemorating the passion of Jesus Christ as opposed to the vanity of flamboyant secular buildings. Two days later, with the permission of the consistory – and of course in the presence of the venerable city council – the cornerstone of the chapel was solemnly laid and dedicated to Our Lady of Sorrows.[64]

Veit's activities caused a considerable upheaval, spreading beyond the city and lingering long after. The provincial authorities, however, backed Veit – the provincial congregation of 1702 acknowledged him as the Olomouc superior. Veit remained in Olomouc until the end of his three-year term of office. Before he left Olomouc, he at least succeeded in finishing another project: the renovation of the Holy Sepulchre chapel.[65] He was eventually replaced by Cajetan Faulhaber

62. *Archivum*, p. 140. The chronicle of the Olomouc Capuchins does not mention the conflict. See: Opava Land Archive, Olomouc office, Olomouc Capuchins, book 5, *Liber memorabilium notatu dignorum quae contingerunt a prima Nostri Olomucensis Fundatione* (1685).

63. Moravian Land Archive, Brno, Fund E 55, Premonstratensians of Klášterní Hradisko, sign. 210 II no. 11, *Diaries of the canonry of Klášterní Hradisko* (1702-1705), fol. 21a.

64. *Archivum*, p. 141.

65. New acquisitions for the chapel included the statue of the dead Christ in a "beautiful grotto", sculptures of Our Lady of Sorrows, a seated angel and Roman soldiers, and several silver lamps. Calvary was painted above the entrance to the chapel, with a crucifix with Virgin

in September 1703. This was when the neighbouring Ursulines managed to stop construction once more; the Franciscans reached a final agreement with them only in 1705. And yet, the chronicle falls silent on the Holy Stairs for many years. Veit's successors probably turned their attention to the restoration of the demolished Chapel of St Anthony of Padua. Records of ongoing construction reappear only in 1714. Superior Viktorín Pohl noted to the provincial definitorium that the stonemason Wenzel Render was building the chapel without any claim for compensation, and even donated another thousand guilders.[66] The chronicle also mentioned that, in 1719, the chapel had a roof and an upper vault as timber had been donated by the prior of the Olomouc Carthusians and bricks had been donated by the city council.[67] In 1723, the Franciscans managed to procure indulgences for the future chapel from Pope Innocent XII. Two years later they were significantly scaled up by Benedict XIII.[68] At about the same time, the Olomouc Franciscans wrote a book for visitors on the chapel, which, besides describing the chapel of the Holy Stairs and its significance, provided information about indulgences, instructions for performing devotion, and all the necessary prayers. The introduction to the book is dated to 2 January 1726.[69] The works on the chapel were finished, and the Holy Stairs were finally – ten years after Veit's death – ready for consecration and a ceremonial opening.

The chapel was incorporated into the premises of the friary and separated from the neighbouring Ursuline convent by an alley. The facade, as the result of a compromise reached after protracted disputes with the Ursulines, faced the street. The area in front of the facade was paved, and – to protect the faithful

Mary and John the Evangelist placed in the front and the statues of St Veronica and Mary Magdalene on both sides of the entrance. The total cost was 230 fl. *Archivum*, p. 145.

66. NA Prague, Bohemian Franciscan Province Archives, reg. no. 2980, carton 175, *Václav Render, etc.*, unpaged.

67. *Archivum*, p. 186.

68. On 5 May, Pope Innocent XII granted 100-day indulgences to those who, any Friday of the year in the chapel dedicated to the Passion of Our Lord Jesus Christ (the upper chapel of the Holy Stairs), said the prayer of the suffering of the Lord and begged God for general concord among Christian sovereigns, the extinction of heresy, and the elevation of the Roman Catholic Church. Benedict XIII, the successor to Innocent, considerably expanded the indulgences in 1725. First, on 27 January, he offered plenary indulgence and redemption of all sins to believers who, after confession and communion, truly repented and visited the Chapel of the Passion of the Lord on Passion Sunday (between the first vespers and the sunset of the next day) to say the necessary prayers. Moreover, whoever attended the Marian litany in the chapel once a week, on a day set by the local spiritual authorities (later Thursday was selected as the day) and on Marian feasts, would also be granted a 100-day indulgence. That same year (28 September) Benedict XIII offered plenary indulgence to all visitors of the Holy Stairs who, four times a year, on their days of choice, performed due devotions. Hundred-day indulgences were promised for other days. "*Andacht der Heiligen Stiegen nechst an der Kirchen dess Heil. Bernardini der WW.PP. Franciscanern in der Königlichen Haubt-Stadt Ollmütz auff der Bielten*", State District Archive in Olomouc, Ollmütz: gedruckt und zu finden in der Buchdruckerey allda., sign. 998/XXXII, 1726, collection of litographs and photographs, p. 5. Photo: Muzeum umění Olomouc pp. 7-8. Hereafter cited as "*Andacht der Heiligen Stiegen*".

69. *Andacht der Heiligen Stiegen*, p. 9.

from passing wagons – surrounded with a balustrade. The facade was designed as "Pilate's house", which is how the Holy Stairs are sometimes referenced in sources. Upstairs there was a balcony with an *Ecce Homo* sculpture, while the top of the facade held the Calvary sculpture. Inside the building were three flights of stairs leading up to the Chapel of the Passion. The middle staircase was the "Holy Stairs" themselves, imitating the Lateran original.[70] It was comprised of twenty-eight marble steps holding a total of fifty-nine relics inside – relics were placed on both sides of each step.[71] Three important steps were highlighted with special relics in the middle: the relic of St Maurice in the second step commemorated the place where, according to tradition, a drop of Christ's blood fell on the original steps of Pilate; the relics of St Vitus in the eleventh step and of St Jucundinus in the twenty-second step marked the other two places where Christ had fallen and bled. Visitors to the chapel were supposed to climb these stairs on their knees, pray, and honour each of the relics (or at least each step) with a kiss. The upstairs Chapel of the Passion housed an altar with a copy of the icon of Christ from the Lateran Sancta Sanctorum Chapel. The believers were to pray shortly here and then descend down one of the side stairs. The side staircases also served the old and the sick who were unable to climb the middle staircase on their knees. There were two more pictures hung along the side stairs – Christ carrying the cross on the left side and the flagellation of Christ on the right. Moreover, there was a stone column down by the entrance, containing an alleged fragment of the column where Jesus had been scourged. Kissing the column concluded the entire devotion.[72]

The Holy Stairs ceremoniously opened on 26 January 1726. The chapel was consecrated by Count Turri, a canon of Olomouc and the mitred provost of Brno. He put a fragment of the Holy Cross inside the altar and celebrated the first mass. The chapel finally, after many unforeseen events, began to serve its purpose – at the end of the passage depicting the ceremony, the keeper of

70. The frescoes were made by the Olomouc painter Johann Christopher Handke. Handke dates the work to 1723 in his autobiography. Given that he wrote his autobiography at the end of his life, the date may not be accurate. Jan Kryštof Handke, *Vlastní Životopis: 1694-1774*, ed. by Leoš Mlčák, Olomouc, Muzeum umění, 1994, p. 32.

71. The left hand side of the stairs, bottom up, held the relics of the following (mostly) martyrs: St Alban, Revocata, Jucundus, Aurea, Manilius, Fructuosa, Optatus, Theodora, Crescentia, Jucundinus, Digna, Benedict, Severina, Bonus, Felicity, Marcialus, Urabanus, Innocent, Felicissima, Victor, Bonosus, Aletus, Constance, Donatus, Vincentia, Florus, Inocencia, and Nominandus. The relics on the right side included: St Fortunatus, Severus, Felix, Perpetua, Boniface, Victoria, Vitalis, Gaudentia, Maxima, Pantaleon, Emerentiana, Pius, Cleophy, Justin, Illuminata, Florida, Klemencie, Lucius, Restituta, Constantius, Simplicie, Juvenalise, Candida, Fidelis, Christina, Amator, Leontia, and Tranquilinius. It is not clear whether the position of the relics followed a hierarchy similar to the one of the Holy Stairs in Karlov, Prague. Cf. Jiří Mikulec, "Klášter a barokní společnost: K vlivu řeholního prostředí na spiritualitu laiků", in *Locus pietatis et vitae: Sborník příspěvků z konference konané v Hejnicích ve dnech 13. -15. září 2007*, ed. by Ivana Čornejová, Hedvika Kuchařová, and Kateřina Valentová, Prague, Charles University Prague, Scriptorium, 2008, pp. 281-300, here 287-288.

72. *Andacht der Heiligen Stiegen*, pp. 43-56.

Fig. 28. The later view of the Holy Stair chapel. Oil on wood, nineteenth-century. Regional Museum in Olomouc, collection Olomuciana, inv. no. O 46. Photo: Pavel Rozsíval.

the chronicle remarked: "How many arguments emerged before the chapel was finished?!" Several months after the Holy Stairs opened, it was visited by Cardinal Schrattenbach, Bishop of Olomouc, and his court. The guests first attended mass in the friary church, and after the superior blessed them with the Eucharist, they visited the Holy Stairs. The cardinal, followed by several canons of the metropolitan chapter and other distinguished guests, climbed the stairs on his knees to perform all the devotions. Afterwards, Schrattenbach and his retinue visited the Capuchins.[73]

We have no record whether the Capuchin community shared Schrattenbach's enthusiasm about the chapel, which had caused such an uproar among the Olomouc mendicants twenty-five years ago. Generally, records about the fate of

73. *Archivum*, p. 194.

the finished chapel are rather terse.[74] The friary chronicle limits itself to a few phrases about the public veneration of the passion of Jesus Christ and the chapel itself.[75] Florian Joseph Loucky, municipal syndic and chronicler, mentioned in 1746 that "in summer, numerous processions stop" at the Holy Stairs.[76] On the other hand, Consignatio Processionum, the list of major pilgrimage processions in the diocese from 1771, does not mention the Olomouc Holy Stairs at all.[77] The Scala Sancta at St Bernardino eventually remained in the shadow of Svatý Kopeček – by far the most popular pilgrimage site in the region.[78] Within the city itself, however, the chapel was one of the most important and regularly visited shrines. One indication can be found in the registry of new members of the Third Order at St Bernardino. After the introduction of the order and the initial wave of interest in the membership, the number of novices gradually declined. The opening of Scala Sancta, however, seemed to provoke a new uptick in interest: while only 23 people joined the order in the first half of the 1720s, in the second half of the decade the number suddenly grew to 63.[79]

The construction of the Holy Stairs underlines one important aspect of the changes made in St Bernardino's sacred space after 1650. While the friars continued to uphold the widely popular cult of the Virgin Mary and the cults "inherited" from the medieval period, at the same time they introduced new, specific devotions which gradually transformed the entire sacred space of the friary. In that process there are two major, discernible tendencies. The first one was to emphasise the holiness of the order. It was particularly strong in the cloister itself, where countless images of Franciscan saints adorned the refectory, the dormitory, and even the infirmary. It was, however, quite clearly manifested also in the church, where the old altar of St Francis was newly supplemented with the statue of Capistrano and the chapel of St Anthony of Padua with the altars of St Bonaventure and St Peter of Alcantara. The other tendency (which included the construction of the Holy Stairs) was to promote and emphasise the cult of the Passion of Christ. This one eventually became the main motif unifying the sacred space of the church and the friary as a whole.

74. A new altar mensa, twelve consecration crosses, and iron candlesticks were made in 1751. The chapel and the altar were newly consecrated by Count Scherffenberg, the Olomouc Suffragan, on 5 September of the same year. The sermon once again highlighted the significance of the sanctuary and reminded believers of the indulgences available during the Holy Stairs worship. The list of the indulgence was placed inside a display case, and hung on the walls of the chapel. *Protocollum*, pp. 183-184.

75. The book *Andacht Der Heiligen Stiegen* was reputedly revised and published again in the 1740s. Viz: *Archivum*, p. 235. Not a single copy of the new edition is available, though.

76. Loucký, *Popis královského hlavního města Olomouce*, p. 56. Loucký incorrectly states, however, that the Olomouc Holy Stairs were founded by Superior Apolinarius Khytribius (who was the Olomouc superior from 1705 to 1707). Veit's merits were then probably forgotten.

77. Opava Land Archive, Olomouc office, Olomouc Archbishop Consistory (1452-1949), sign. C 9, carton 2212, *List of the pilgrimage shrines in Moravia and Silesia* (circa 1760), passim.

78. Another Chapel of the Holy Stairs was eventually built, also at Svaty Kopeček.

79. *Matrica*, passim.

Fig. 29. Statue *Ecce Homo* (originally the façade of the Holy Stairs chapel, today Senici na Hané). Philip Sattler, Museum of Art Olomouc. Photo: Zdeněk Sodoma.

3. Pietas Franciscana

Information about what became of Veit after he left Olomouc is clear only partly. His next stop was the friary in Moravská Třebová. After some time, he was transferred to the Kroměříž friary, where he spent the last years of his life. There, he held the office of the superior from 1708 until 1710, and between 1714 and 1715 he was listed as a preacher. Referred to as *Missionarius Apostolicus, Verbi Dei famosus Praeco, olim Guardianus ac multorum meritotum Pater* in the necrology, he died in Kroměříž in 1716 and was buried in the friars' crypt.[80] Although he did not live long enough to see the completion and consecration of Olomouc's Holy Stairs, his efforts to build a copy of one of the most sacred shrines eventually yielded results. While serving in Moravská Třebová, Veit got in touch with the nobleman Francis Michael August Šubíř of Chrobyně and inspired him to transform a hill above the town of Jaroměřice on his estates into "Calvary Mountain". A complex of shrines was to be built on the top, based on Veit's instructions and drawings; the proportions, layout, and appearance of which were to imitate Jerusalem's Via Dolorosa. The shrine was consecrated on 14 September

80. Moravian Land Archive, Brno, Fund E 21, Dačice Franciscans, book 5, *Protocollum Conventus Cremsiriensis ad SSS. Trinitatem,* Section Sepulturae Fratrum, 1716, unpaged.

1713, with Hieronymus Veit delivering the first Czech sermon.[81] The shrine soon became an immensely popular pilgrimage shrine; its arch-confraternity (initiated by Veit as well) had more than a thousand members within a year.[82] Veit's ambitious plans were apparently more likely to succeed on a nobleman's estates than in complicated urban settings.

Veit's successors, however, continued to strengthen the Passion motifs in the Olomouc church. In 1707, the Holy Sepulchre was furnished with "theatrum novum cum duplici mutatione" – theatre sets for two different scenes.[83] A much more important addition to the Passion concept of the church turned out to be the initially inconspicuous image *Ecce Homo!* painted or printed on paper. The image is first mentioned in 1701, while it was still in the possession of a townswoman. At that time, an incident occurred involving three soldiers staying in her house on Mittergasse. One of them, allegedly a non-Catholic from Silesia, lost all his money playing cards. He started yelling, daring the devil to either give him money or take him away. Having no response, he reputedly lashed out at the image *Ecce Homo!* glued to the wall, shouting that if there were a real God, he should give him money. Scandalized, the owner of the house chided him to stop the blasphemy lest he should be punished for the insult. And so, the Franciscan chronicle claims, he was. The following night, the three soldiers broke into the Loretto Chapel of the cathedral and stole silver votive gifts from the image of the Virgin Mary. Eight years later, all the three of them were captured near Olomouc and taken to the city, where two of them (the third one escaped) were beheaded. Meanwhile, sometime around 1706, a certain Franciscan lay brother Onuphrius noticed the image while begging for alms. He found it extremely venerable and managed, after a while, to exchange it with the owner for another picture. He brought *Ecce Homo!* to his cell and put it up on the wall. It allegedly gave him immense spiritual solace. After Onuphrius died, the image was transferred to the church (on the Maundy Thursday of 1729) and immediately drew the attention of believers.[84]

81. The premises were dominated by the Church of the Exaltation of the Holy Cross. Surrounded by an ambit, the area also included imitations of the chapel of the tomb of the Virgin Mary, the Holy Sepulchre, the Bethlehem Chapel, and later also Stations of the Cross. Pastoral care was provided by the Franciscans of the Moravská Třebová friary, until Šubíř established a foundation for a permanent priest in 1718. In order to enhance the importance of the complex, Veit had a copy made of the image of Christ's icon from the Lateran chapel Sancta Sanctorum. Karel Eichler, *Poutní místa a milostivé obrazy na Moravě a v Rakouském Slezsku*, vol. I, Brno, Nákladem Dědictví ss. Cyrilla a Methoděje, 1887, pp. 174-179.

82. It was an offshoot of the Lateran Arch-Confraternity of the Most Holy Saviour. The renowned preacher and writer (and also a Tertiary at the Olomouc Franciscan friary) Bohumír Hynek Bílovský became a notary of the arch-confraternity and wrote a handbook detailing the importance of the organization and the duties of members of the arch-confraternity. Although the confraternity was officially founded in 1712, it was not until 17 September 1715 that it truly "opened" and acquired its first members. Gottfried Joseph Bilowsky, *Societas Jesu Salvatoris, Das ist die Hochlöbliche Ertz-Bruderschafft oder Gesellschaft der Allerheiligsten Bildnuss dess Erlösers der Welt unsers Herrn Jesu Christi [Etc.]*, Brün, Jacob M. Swoboda, 1720.

83. *Archivum*, p. 159.

84. *Archivum*, unpaged section, fol. 301a-301b.

As the image grew increasingly popular, the Franciscans moved it to new places, connecting it to other sacred objects within the church. First, the picture was placed by the statue of John of Nepomuk, then it was transferred to the altar of Our Lady of Mariapócs (where there was another venerated picture of the Virgin Mary), and afterwards it was placed below the statue of John of Capistrano. The picture was by then hung with numerous votive gifts and embellished with expensive canopy and silver lamps. In addition, it bore the following inscription:

> This holy picture was shamefully defiled by a vainglorious heretic and his heartless curses and blasphemy, and stained and disgraced by shameful, ignominious blows (insolently prompted by the evil Satan). You Christian souls, erase the presumptuous ignominy inflicted upon Your Redeemer with your veneration and piety.[85]

The call did not go unheard. The simple paper image became one of the most venerated items in the church. As the friary chronicler says: "it became famous for many wonders and miracles, and no pious worshiper of this image was left unheard, if what he asked for served to save his soul". Due to the great popularity of the picture, the superior asked the Bishop Consistory in 1735 for permission to celebrate the Eucharist at the picture. A few years later, in 1748, a decision was made to build a separate marble altar for the picture. It was consecrated on 5 August 1750 by Olomouc Suffragan John Charles of Scherffenberg in the honour of Jesus the Saviour and Our Lady of Sorrows (a picture of the Pieta was placed on the altar next to the image *Ecce Homo!*).[86]

The Franciscans, of course, had no monopoly in introducing new cults and items related to the Christological worship.[87] However, their privileged position in the Middle East – which enabled them to mediate "authentic" contact with sacred places in Jerusalem and elsewhere – gave them a clear advantage. The Province of the Holy Land was formally established in 1217, when the Crusader states were spiralling into decline. The kingdom of Jerusalem was reduced to a narrow strip of coastal land, and not even St Francis, during his visit to the Middle East, was able to make it to the holy places associated with the life and passion of Jesus. And yet, the Franciscans managed to settle in Jerusalem in 1229. In 1272, the sultan allowed them to settle in the Cenacle (*Cenaculum*) on Mount Sion, which became the headquarters of the Franciscan mission in the region. The Franciscans retained their position, in spite of many twists and turns, even after the Latin kingdom fell in 1291. Although the original province was reduced to a mere *custodia*, its importance grew. It was the only representative of the Western Church in the Holy Land – the *custos* (the superior of Mount Sion) became the formal holder of the title of the Latin Patriarch of Jerusalem.

85. *Archivum*, 301b.

86. *Ibid.*

87. Lieselotte Kötsche, "Das Heilige Grab in Jerusalem und seine Nachfolge", in *Die Reise nach Jerusalem*, ed. by Hendrik Budde and Andreas Nachama, Berlin, Argon, 1996, pp. 64-75. See also: Colin Morris, *The Sepulchre of Christ and the Medieval West: From the Beginning to 1600*, Oxford, Oxford University Press, 2005, 328-362.

Moreover, the Franciscans managed to obtain the administration of the Church of the Holy Sepulchre in 1309, which earned them a privileged position among other Christian groups in Jerusalem, and, simultaneously, among other religious orders in the West. In 1342, Pope Clement VI confirmed the Franciscans as administrators of the sacred places in Palestine, instructing them to look after Christian pilgrims coming from the West. In 1517, Jerusalem was taken over by the Ottomans, and the continuing military conflicts between the Ottoman Empire and the Christian states weakened the Franciscan position (so much so that the Franciscans lost their friary on Mount Sion in 1552). In the early modern period, the Custody of the Holy Land thus depended on continued diplomatic and economic support from the Western powers (Venice, the emperor, Spain, and later largely France).[88] In spite of the difficulties, the Franciscans managed to hold ground in Jerusalem, Bethlehem, and other cities. Their mission was twofold: on the one hand, they cared for Christian pilgrims from the West (including non-Catholics); on the other hand, their order mediated contact with these places for those who could not make the pilgrimage.[89]

The Bohemian Franciscans were also linked to custody of the Holy Land. Like all Franciscan provinces, the Province of Saint Wenceslas was obliged to collect alms for the Holy Land.[90] Moreover, as the Bohemian province and the Holy Land custody were both members of the Cismontane ("Italian", Eastern) branch of the order, the Bohemian friars were allowed to apply for a missionary position in the Middle East. The missionary past of Hieronymus Veit was thusly no exception. At least twenty missionaries left the Bohemian province in the seventeenth and eighteenth centuries for Egypt, eleven for the Holy Land, and fifteen for the Balkans. The friars of the Bohemian province served in the Holy Land mainly in the seventeenth century; later they were usually assigned to Egypt. The reason was that in 1697 the Egyptian missions were removed from the jurisdiction of the Holy Land Custody. From that year on, solely Observant friars could serve as missionaries in the Holy Land, while Reformed friars (e.g. Bohemian ones) could be sent only to Upper Egypt, Nubia, and Ethiopia.[91] Many of the missionaries

88. The Franciscan chronicles celebrated the promise of Leopold I to liberate Jerusalem or to at least ensure Franciscan administration of the Church of the Holy Sepulchre and hence access for Catholic pilgrims to the holy places. See: Bernhard Sannig, *Chronica de origine & constitutione Provinciae Bohemiae Ordinis Fratrum Minorum S. Francisci Reformatorum & ejusdem conventuum*, vol. 2, Prague NA, Bohemian Franciscan Province Archives, book 21, entry of 1685, unpaged.

89. Glenn Bowman, "Christian ideology and the image of a holy land: the place of Jerusalem pilgrimage in the various Christianities", in *Contesting the Sacred: The Anthropology of Christian Pilgrimage*, ed. by John Eade and Michael J. Sallnow, London and New York, Routledge, 1991, pp. 98-121.

90. The collections had initially been made by foreign (Italian) friars. Emperor Leopold I, however, considered it an unnecessary interference on his territory. He ordered that the alms could be collected by local friars only. Minařík, "Provinciál P. Bernard Sannig", 62 (1921): p. 65.

91. Marek Dospěl, "The Annotationes in Aegyptum (c. 1799): A manuscript penned by a Czech Franciscan missionary", *Archivum Franciscanum Historicum*, 104 (2011): p. 287.

wrote compelling travel accounts, others published descriptions of Jerusalem and other holy places. The publications clearly illustrate the abovementioned twofold role of the Franciscans as mediators: the prints served as a guide for pilgrims, and at the same time as a pious reading for those who could only travel in their imagination. This also resulted in the book by former Commissary to the Holy Land, Elector Zwinner, titled *Blumens-Buch dess Heiligen Landts Palestinae*, which became (also thanks to engravings of selected objects) one of the most important sources of information on Palestine in the German language.[92] Another "guidebook", *Fasciculus Myrrhae in Campis Palestinae Collectus* by Jan Cantius Solik, also provides useful travel advice (along with a detailed list of all indulgences) and inspiration for readers regarding places connected with the life and passion of Jesus Christ.[93]

One of the most important products of Franciscan mediation between the Holy Land and other parts of the Catholic world were the Stations of the Cross (*Via Crucis*). The devotion has its roots in the veneration of places associated with the life and death of Jesus Christ. Pilgrims travelling to the Holy Sepulchre began, roughly in the fourteenth century, to pay more attention to the path Jesus walked up to Calvary after the trial. Although the Gospels described the route in very vague terms, the whole of Via Dolorosa and its individual stations were, over the next two hundred years, gradually "reconstructed". Meanwhile, in Europe the first imitations of the route began to emerge as sets of chapels built outdoors, or as paintings or sculptures inside churches, as early as the fifteenth century. The copies facilitated similar experiences and devotions for Christians who could not afford pilgrimage to the original in Jerusalem. Particularly captivating (in this first stage of the Via Dolorosa transfer) were large-scale imitations on hills, whose shape was thought to resemble Golgotha in Jerusalem. The places are typically accompanied by legends which claim that the site was built after an accurate design and descriptions brought by a pilgrim (often a Friar Minor) from Jerusalem.[94] It seems it was these pilgrimage sites (such as the Sacred Mountain of Varallo,

92. Franciscus Electus Zwinner, *Blumen-Buch, Dess Heiligen Lands Palestinae: So in Drey Bücher Abgetheilt*, München, durch Johann Wilhelm Schell, 1661. The book contains a detailed geographic and historic description of the Holy Land (Book One) and the locations divided into twenty-three pilgrimage routes, including due prayers and devotions (Book Two), and the description of major sites in Syria, etc. (Book Three). Zwinner was from the Bohemian province and served as Commissary of the Holy Land. He wrote the book upon his return from the third trip (see: the preface dated 1661 in Plzeň). He died in Bethlehem in 1668 while visiting the Holy Land for the fourth time. See: NA, ŘF, book 104, *Cathalogus patrum et fratrum in alma provincia Bohemiae ab anno 1590 usque ad praesens tempus*, f. 129v.

93. Joannes Cantius Solik, *Fasciculus Myrrhae in Campis Palestinae Collectus: Seu Sacrorum Locorum Ibid.em Existentium (Prout Nunc Sunt) Brevi Methodo Descriptio*, Brunae, Typis Joannis Francisci Svoboda, 1716.

94. Other orders also played their part, specifically the Jesuits. Martin Gaži and Jarmila Hansová, *Svatyně za hradbami měst: Křížová hora u Českého Krumlova v jihočeských a středoevropských souvislostech*, České Budějovice, National Institute for Monuments, 2012, pp. 126-128.

instigated by Franciscan Bernardino Caimi), not Jerusalem, which played a key role in the formation of the devotions of the Stations of the Cross – the reason being that during Ottoman rule the possibilities for ostentatious Christian piety in public spaces was rather limited.[95]

The exact route of the Via Dolorosa in Jerusalem, along with its individual stations and devotions, were eventually codified in the seventeenth century. At that time, however, pilgrimages to the Holy Land continued to be costly and dangerous, and the number of pilgrims was strictly limited.[96] For most Christians, friars included, Jerusalem's shrines were practically unattainable. This was one of the reasons why in 1686 Pope Innocent XI offered the same indulgences one could acquire at the Jerusalem Via Dolorosa at the Stations of the Cross erected in Franciscan churches. Initially, these indulgences were reserved exclusively to the Franciscans, but given the high demand Benedict XIII extended them to all believers attending Franciscan churches. Eventually, in 1731, Pope Clement XII granted permission to establish the Stations of the Cross to parish churches and other places. This exported the devotion outside the Franciscan churches; the Friars Minor, nonetheless, retained their privilege to consecrate the Stations of the Cross and remained leading promoters of the devotion.[97]

By then, the Stations of the Cross (*Via Crucis*) were a codified and unified devotion. The number of the stations settled at fourteen.[98] The stations could be works of art (statues or paintings) or simple wooden crosses. Although private worship was possible, emphasis was placed on public, community devotion, which usually took place once a month on Friday. Unlike the traditional Passion processions, this devotion was simple, yet powerful.[99] The priest led the procession of believers from one station to another (if there was not enough room, only the priest and servers walked around the stops while the believers kept standing).

95. Leonhard Lemmens, *Geschichte der Franziskanermissionen*, Münster, Verlag der Aschendorffschen Verlagsbuchhandlung, 1929, pp. 61-78.

96. Solik, *Fasciculus Myrrhae*, Directorium Itinerarii, unpaged.

97. In Italy, for example, their propagation was associated with the name Leonard of Port Maurice (later canonized), who had the Stations of the Cross erected in the Roman Colosseum and other places around Italy. Leonard also wrote a concise manual which explained the importance of the devotion and contained basic prayers, songs, and meditation themes for individual stations. The book was translated into many languages, and often included an illustration annex which stimulated personal piety and helped to codify iconography of the stations of the cross. See: Leonardo da Porto Maurizio, *Via Sacra Spianata, ed Illuminata*, Roma, Nella Stamperia di S. Michele, per il Puccinelli, 1749. See also: Gianvittorio Signorotto, "Lo spazio delle devozioni nell'età della Controriforma", in *Luoghi sacri e spazi della santità*, ed. by Sofia Boesch Gajano and Lucetta Scaraffia, Torino, Rosenberg & Sellier, 1990, pp. 315-326.

98. The stations included the following: 1. Jesus is condemned to death; 2. Jesus carries his cross; 3. Jesus falls for the first time; 4. Jesus meets the Virgin Mary; 5. Simon of Cyrene helps Jesus carry the cross; 6. Veronica wipes the face of Jesus; 7. Jesus falls for the second time; 8. Jesus meets the women of Jerusalem; 9. Jesus falls for the third time; 10. Jesus is stripped of his clothes; 11. Jesus is nailed to the cross; 12. Jesus dies on the cross; 13. Jesus is taken down from the cross; and 14. Jesus is placed in the tomb.

99. For more on Passion processions and their diverse forms, see: Vojtěch Ron, *Lidové pašijové divadlo v českých zemích*, Prague, Vyšehrad, 2009, pp. 179-197.

Prayer, singing, and meditation were held at each station, and a blessing with the Eucharist concluded the devotions. Prints and sermons encouraged further private meditation and prayers related to the main devotion.

The Stations of the Cross were a late, yet crucial, Franciscan contribution to the religious life of early modern times. This devotion stemmed from the Franciscan traditions and its exclusive ties to the Holy Land.[100] It also reflected the changing priorities and needs of the Roman Catholic Church. While pilgrimage played an important role in the mobilization and subsequent consolidation of Catholic society at the time of confessional conflicts, later the problems associated with pilgrimage practice became increasingly evident. The devotion focused on spectacular ceremonies and popular cults often outshone more fundamental elements of the Christian faith. Although the clergy were far from united on this issue, many of them complained that "wherever the Lord has a church, the devil will build a chapel" and "many a [pilgrim] bring back greater sins from their pilgrimage than what they started the journey with".[101] The critical voices were joined by secular authorities, who pointed out the social and economic impacts of excessive pilgrimage practices. Eventually, in the second half of the eighteenth century, in many countries the number of feasts and pilgrimages was gradually reduced, overnight pilgrimages forbidden, and devotions simplified.[102]

The Stations of the Cross to some extent offered an alternative to traditional, much more pompous and spectacular pilgrimage festivities.[103] Their structure and content was based directly on the text of the Gospels. Emphasis was placed primarily on the sacrifice of Christ, the Eucharist (the final blessing), and the basic tenets of the Christian faith. In addition, the ritual allowed for a balance between public and private piety.[104] It was a simple and unified piety under the direct control of the clergy – the stations could be erected only with the permission of the bishop, consecrated exclusively by the superior of the nearest Franciscan friary, and led by a local priest. Superstitious beliefs and habits (as in the case of major pilgrimages) seemed to be eliminated – after all, the main motivation for participation was to meditate the suffering of Christ, not to seek divine intercession and a miracle. The devotion, nevertheless, retained the allure of a highly exclusive pilgrimage. The believer, as a member of the community led

100. The Passion cult was an important part of Franciscan spirituality, and as such was accentuated in the Franciscan devotional literature – see, for example, a Tertiary guidebook containing instructions on how to meditate on Christ's suffering while praying the Lord's Prayer. See: e.g. *Regule a Kssafft*, p. 198.

101. Jestřábský, *Vidění rozličné sedláčka sprostného*, p. 125.

102. Opava Land Archive, Olomouc office, Olomouc Archbishop Consistory, sign. C9, carton 2213, *Processions and pilgrimages in Olomouc and at Sv. Kopeček* (1617-1897), no. 1.

103. A similar shift "from the militant, glorious sainthood of the Jesuits to a model inspired by Franciscan spirituality" was also seen in the case of the cult of saints in the eighteenth century. Ronnie Po-chia Hsia, *The World of Catholic Renewal, 1540-1770*, Cambridge, Cambridge University Press, 1998, p. 137.

104. The character of the devotion corresponded to the trends of the eighteenth century – a shift to personal and private devotion. Forster, *Catholic Revival*, p. 61.

by the priest, almost literally complied with Jesus' call to "take up the cross, and follow me" (Mark 10:21). And, more importantly, participants in the devotion could receive practically the same indulgences as pilgrims to the Via Dolorosa in Jerusalem.[105] The richness of the indulgences – no other devotion seemed to be endowed with a similar quantity – indicates the support lent to the new devotion. As a moderate devotion void of superstitions and the excesses, it was better suited to meet the needs of a confessionally stable society and was closer to the ideals of the Catholic Enlightenment.[106]

This codified form of the Stations of the Cross reached Bohemian Lands later than the Mediterranean.[107] The Stations of the Cross began to be erected at Franciscan friaries in the Saint Wenceslas Province as late as the 1730s.[108] St Bernardino had its first Stations of the Cross made in 1736. It was located in the upper cloister and accessible only to the brothers. Only later were new Stations of the Cross built for the public. The opening ceremony took place on the first Sunday of Lent (3 March) in 1743. That day, Superior Amandus Kraus celebrated the first devotion, accompanied by the entire religious community and crowds of believers.[109] A resolution was adopted to hold the Stations of the Cross at St Bernardino on a regular basis, every fourth Sunday of the month, in the afternoon after vespers. The Stations of the Cross were to be preceded by a short devotion at the Holy Stairs; the devotion of the Stations itself began at the top of the steps in the Chapel of the Passion of the Lord, where the first two stations were installed on the sides of the altar. The procession then walked down the side stairs, then to the church, where the Stations of the Cross continued with three stops by the main altar (the Epistle side). The procession continued past other stations arranged around the walls of the church until they reached the last, fourteenth station – the Chapel of the Holy Sepulchre. The Stations of the Cross thus absorbed and connected the existing "Passion" objects built in the past decades into a single entity.[110] The complex of the church and adjacent chapels became a Via Dolorosa leading from "Pilate's House" (the Chapel of the Holy Stairs) to Jesus' temporary

105. Amédée (Teetaert) da Zedelgem, *Saggio storico sulla devozione alla Via Crucis*, trans. by Paolo Pellizzari, Ponzano Monferrato, Centro di documentazione dei Sacri Monti, Calvari e Complessi devozionali europei, 2003, p. 127.

106. For the clergy's attempts to control popular piety, see: e.g. R. Po-chia Hsia, *Social Discipline in the Reformation: Central Europe 1550-1750*, London and New York, Routledge, 1992, p. 183. See also: Robert Bireley, *The Refashioning of Catholicism, 1450-1700: A Reassessment of the Counter Reformation*, Basingstoke, Macmillan, 1999, p. 107.

107. The first "Stations of the Cross" emerged in Central Europe as early as the seventeenth century (Mikulov, Římov, and others). They were the older form of "holy mountains", or sets of shrines in open landscape. See: Gaži and Hansová, *Svatyně za hradbami měst*, pp. 126-129.

108. In 1731, the provincial authorities ordered all friaries to celebrate the Stations of the Cross every month. *Statuta praecipua*, p. 21.

109. *Archivum*, p. 235.

110. The altar with the image of *Ecce Homo*!, however, was not included in the complex. The reason might have been the fact that the popular "miraculous" image could disrupt the otherwise modest and sober character of the new devotion.

grave.[111] The Stations of the Cross completed the Franciscan attempts to turn their church into an exclusive sacred dominant within the city.

111. For the transformation of a monastery into a "New Jerusalem", see: June L. Mecham, "A Northern Jerusalem: The Transformation of Space at the Convent of Wienhausen", in *Defining the Holy: Sacred Space in Medieval and Early Modern Europe*, ed. by Sarah Hamilton and Andrew Spicer, Aldershot, Ashgate, 2005, pp. 139-160.

6. House No. 578

While the two-hundredth anniversary of Capistrano's visit to Olomouc went largely unnoticed due to the difficult situation following the departure of the Swedish troops, the three-hundredth anniversary was one of remarkable commemorative celebrations for the time (Hradisko Monastery celebrated the six-hundredth anniversary of its founding in the same year, albeit in a much grander style).[1] The main ceremony was scheduled for 26 August 1751, the eve of the anniversary of the day Capistrano bestowed filiation on the city. The superior celebrated a sung mass in the presence of the entire city council and a large number of burghers, concluding it with the *Te Deum*. A copy of Capistrano's filiation was displayed on a table under the saint's statue throughout the ceremony, with candles burning beside it. A requiem was held the following day for all the deceased covered by the filiation.[2] The ceremony both commemorated important events and manifested the strong ties between the friary and the city, the city council, and all the inhabitants.

This close connection was reflected in another, more permanent feat. The monumental Holy Trinity Column on the Upper Square was nearing its completion. The ambitious building started as a private project by stonemason and architect Wenzel Render after the great plague of 1714-1716. Render was, however, unable to finish the construction before his death. The project had been taken over in the forties by the city council, who charged local craftsmen and artists with its completion. They also changed the iconographic programme of the monument. While the overall structure of the building (three floors, each with six sculptures, and the Holy Trinity sculpture at the top) was preserved, selected saints on the column were replaced by others. Each of the eighteen sculptures (together with the statues of the Virgin Mary and Archangel Michael on the column shaft) now corresponded to one of the Olomouc ecclesiastical institutions: the cathedral, parish churches, monasteries, the university, and prominent chapels. Render's original concept of the apotheosis of a universal church was transformed into the glorification of the local church – the column basically catalogued local church institutions and their traditions.[3] The

1. Jana Oppeltová, "Premonstrátská kanonie Hradisko u Olomouce a její kulturní prostředí", in *Olomoucké baroko: Výtvarná kultura let 1620-1780 (3. Historie a kultura)*, ed. by Ondřej Jakubec and Marek Perůtka, Olomouc, Olomouc Museum of Art, 2010, pp. 53-65.

2. *Protocollum*, p. 638.

3. Martin Elbel, "Consolidation, 1700-1750", in *The Transformation of Confessional Cultures in a Central European City: Olomouc, 1400-1750*, ed. by Antonín Kalous, Roma,

Fig. 30. The view of Olomouc from the north, c. 1740. Friedrich Bernard Werner and Thomas Scheffler, etching. State District Archive in Olomouc, sign. VIII/48.

Franciscan friary was represented by the statue of John of Capistrano. It marked the position and importance of St Bernardino in the sacred topography of the city. This particular topography, nonetheless, was beginning to collide with another topography – one professed by state authorities. A topography based on a new order and vision for society that left little room for the existing structures, privileges, and traditions. The new position of the friary was symbolically expressed through the numbering of buildings in the city, imposed by Empress Maria Theresa in 1771. For administrative reasons, each house in the city was allotted a number. St Bernardino was given number 578.[4]

1. *Filiation*

The position of St Bernardino developed over centuries, and the old ties and structures never gave way completely to the new ones – at least not until

Viella, 2015, pp. 160-161. Cf. Howard Louthan, "Breaking Images and Building Bridges: the Making of Sacred Space in Early Modern Bohemia", in *Sacred Space in Early Modern Europe*, ed. by Will Coster and Andrew Spicer, Cambridge, Cambridge University Press, 2005, p. 292.

4. *Protocollum*, p. 437.

Fig. 31. The Column of the Holy Trinity with statues of the saint-patrons of the local church institutions. Joseph Freindt, etching, third quarter of the eighteenth century. Museum of Arts in Olomouc, G 13242, photo: Zdeněk Sodoma.

the friary was abolished. The strong ties to the urban community had their roots in Capistrano's filiation of 1451, in which he symbolically affiliated the Olomouc residents and their offspring with the order of the Friars Minor and its Observant branch. In return for supporting the friars, the inhabitants of Olomouc were promised a share in "all spiritual benefaction" of the order, such as masses, devotions, prayers, fasts, repentance, pilgrimages, sermons, and contemplation.[5] This general definition of filiation was implemented, developed, and consolidated by the daily interaction between the friars and burghers: by attending the friary church, providing mass stipends, alms, and in some cases, joining the Third Order. Every day, there was a mutually beneficial exchange of services and goods, in which the Franciscans demonstrated and confirmed their usefulness and contribution to the urban community. The friary was thus connected with the city and its inhabitants by a network of ties – both spontaneous and institutional.[6]

5. *Archivum*, p. 198.

6. Apart from the notary post, held by the Olomouc superiors from the time Hieronymus Veit was in office, and pastoral care provided in the city spital of St Job and Lazarus, it was, above all, the prestigious role of the chaplains of the City Hall Chapel of St Jerome.

Fig. 32. Statue of John of Capistrano on the Column of The Holy Trinity. Photo: Martin Elbel.

Moreover, the city and its inhabitants were willing to invest in the friary. When a costly (in Franciscan terms) renovation of the friary was launched in 1739, sponsors were recruited from all the classes of the local population. Besides the main benefactor, Norbert Umlauf, Abbot of the Hradisko Monastery, the Prior of the Olomouc Carthusians, Anthelmus Fournier; several aristocrats (including Josef von Petrasch, leading local protagonist of the Enlightenment and founder of the learned society *Societas Incognitorum*); the city council; and several other officials funded the construction. The project would not have been realized without support from countless other people from the city and the greater area. As the chronicle indicates, these were not just wealthy burghers: the donors include a certain widow from Prostějov who donated 17 kreutzers for the construction, and even a pauper who contributed half a kreutzer.[7]

The relationships of the friary were not limited to the city. Links to the surrounding area were somewhat looser, but equally important, primarily with towns and villages in the mendicant district. The links were not only shaped by the regular collections of alms; much stronger and more permanent ties resulted from Third Order membership. Tertiary parish priests, noblemen, and local administrative officials in particular were major points of support, which allowed the Franciscans to go beyond the city boundaries and operate on a much wider area. The above ties were joined by one more network in the 1740s, which

7. *Protocollum*, p. 349. Benefactors were similarly diverse in the case of other major projects, such as the construction of a new high altar in 1765. *Ibid.*, pp. 350-351.

allowed the Franciscans to export the elements of their order's spirituality. It was the Stations of the Cross devotion – until then reserved exclusively for the Franciscan churches – which had begun to expand to other areas thanks to papal approval and recommendation. Almost five hundred Stations of the Cross were consequently built in the Bohemian Lands alone – in churches, cemeteries, and in the open countryside.[8] The Franciscans, however, maintained the privilege to consecrate new stations – usually by the superior in whose mendicant district the location was.[9] The Olomouc superior consecrated the first "external" Stations of the Cross at the cemetery in front of the filial Church of the Birth of the Virgin Mary in Hranice (Weisskirchen), as early as 1744 – a year after the Olomouc Franciscans built Stations of the Cross in their own church. By 1785, the Olomouc friars had consecrated a total of thirty-one stations in their district, thus bolstering their links with the countryside.[10]

The friary, naturally, faced some difficulties along the way. The event that most influenced the life of the city as a whole was the War of the Austrian Succession. The war put a halt to the ongoing remodelling of the friary and greatly affected the character of the city and, inadvertently, the position of St Bernardino, for years to come. On 25 December 1741, around ten o'clock in the morning, the Prussian army led by General Schwerin arrived and immediately took over Hradisko Monastery and the Olomouc suburbs. The city fortifications were in a sorry state, the fort garrison was weak and inadequately armed, and so, following brief negotiations, the commander surrendered. The Prussians entered the city on 28 December – Olomouc was once again, after nearly a century, occupied by an enemy, whose soldiers, to make matters even more complicated, were mostly non-Catholic. The army was accommodated in burgher houses and monasteries, and a high *contributio* was imposed on the city. The enemy soldiers remained in the city until mid-April, when the Prussian army left.[11]

The city was spared any great harm thanks to the capitulation, and whatever damage had been caused was quickly repaired. The developments of the war itself had a much graver impact on life in the city. As Frederick II annexed most of Silesia, the border with the Prussian enemy was suddenly much closer, and Olomouc became a key point on the route between the Prussian Silesia and Vienna.

8. The list of the Stations of the Cross consecrated by the superiors of the Bohemian and Moravian friaries between 1735 and 1786 is in "*Communicationes Viae S. Crucis*", Prague National Archives, Bohemian Franciscan Province Archives, book 352). Pages concerning Silesian friaries were cut out – probably after the division of the province in 1755.

9. NA Prague, Bohemian Franciscan Province Archives, book 353, *Benedictio Viae S. Crucis*.

10. See also: Martin Elbel, "Pilgrims on the Way of the Cross: Pilgrimage Practice and Confessional Identity in Early Modern Bohemian Lands", in *Frontiers of Faith: Religious Exchange and Constitution of Religious Identities (1400-1700)*, ed. by Eszter Andor and István György Tóth, Budapest, CEU Press, 2001, p. 281.

11. *Archivum*, pp. 242-243. See also: Vítězslav Prchal, "Války s Pruskem a přeměna Olomouce v pevnost", in *Olomoucké baroko: Proměny ambicí jednoho města (1. Úvodní svazek)*, ed. by Martin Elbel and Ondřej Jakubec, Olomouc, Olomouc Museum of Art, 2010, pp. 285-292.

Fig. 33. The community of the Olomouc Franciscans paying homage to Cardinal Troyer, Bishop of Olomouc, during his inauguration entry in 1747. Francis Lawrence Korompay-circle, 1783(?), oil on canvas, 104x641 cm, detail. Archbishopric of Olomouc, AMK, KE 2988, O 410, today in the exhibition of the Archdiocesan Museum in Olomouc, photo: Zdeněk Sodoma.

The rapid surrender of the city in 1741 was even more alarming given the new situation. Therefore, Olomouc was declared *Königliche Haupt- und Grenzfestung* in 1742, and work on a large modern fortress commenced. Although Olomouc was granted fortress status already in 1655, it had obsolete and absolutely insufficient fortifications. Now the suburbs were razed to the ground, and the city surrounded by a system of bastions, ravelins, ditches, and other fortification elements.[12] Construction work was also carried out close to St Bernardino; behind their northern wall the massive bastion Number XII was built. During construction, the friary's beer cellar was accidentally flooded (the friars even had to buy a pump), and the latrines needed to be moved and a new sewer built.[13]

12. Vladimír Kupka, "Olomoucké fortifikace na plánech a ve skutečnosti", in *Olomoucké baroko: Proměny ambicí jednoho města (1. Úvodní svazek)*, ed. by Martin Elbel and Ondřej Jakubec, Olomouc, Olomouc Museum of Art, 2010, pp. 293-300.

13. *Protocollum*, pp. 109-110.

The fort was completed just in time to repel another Prussian attack in 1758.[14] In this case, the city was able to prepare for the siege more thoroughly, by increasing the garrison size and complementing supplies, but also by evacuating part of the population. The community of St Bernardino was reduced to seventeen brothers. The other friars were hastily moved to country vicarages or to the houses of selected benefactors. The Prussian army advanced to the city in late May and immediately began siege work. The first parallel opened on 30 May and the city began to be shelled. St Bernardino was at a relatively safe location and suffered only negligible damage, unlike the Capuchins, the Dominican nunnery, the Dominican friary, and many burgher houses. This is also why the semi-empty friary became a refuge for many burgher families (including the family of Councillor Johannes Kniebandl), whose homes had been damaged by bombardment. The safety of St Bernardino reputedly led Olomouc's citizens to attend Franciscan services instead of worshipping at other, more threatened churches.[15] The recently completed fort withstood the Prussian siege. After General Laudon intercepted and dispersed the Prussian convoy delivering ammunition and supplies for the siege army, the Prussians were forced to end the siege on 2 July. The successful defence was jauntily celebrated. The victory largely rectified the military reputation of the city, which had been damaged by rapid surrenders in 1642 and 1741. The city crest was promoted by Maria Theresa and several leading burghers were granted a noble title. The victory was to be commemorated annually with shooting festivities, for which the empress committed to contribute eight hundred guilders.[16]

Olomouc was slowly becoming a fortress city, whose life was subordinated to military needs. The importance of the military gradually increased – often at the expense of ecclesiastical institutions, which had to cooperate with the military authorities and make available all their capacities during war.[17] For example, the Franciscans had to accommodate a troop of soldiers and a military pharmacy in 1778, during the War of the Bavarian Succession.[18] These were temporary inconveniences that complicated life in the friaries, but were no major threat. Conversely, the ongoing changes posed challenges and new opportunities, at least for some of the religious houses (notably the mendicants). The new fort and the reinforcement of the permanent garrison re-introduced a long forgotten element

14. "*Diarium oder: Gründliche Anzeige von dem gänzlichen Vorgange der Belagerung und Bombardirung der neuen Gränzvestung Olmütz...*" Wien und Prag, Trattner, 1758.

15. The Franciscan chronicler pointed out that the feast of Anthony of Padua had only been celebrated that year by the Franciscans, because neither Conventuals nor Capuchins offered masses at that time (13 June). The only victim at the friary was a Croatian who was killed by a cannon ball which flew in through the windows of the Chapel of Holy Stairs. *Protocollum*, p. 436.

16. Alois Chytil, *Obležení Olomouce a zničení pruského dovozu u Domašova*, Olomouc, R. Prombergr, 1900, p. 109.

17. This was reflected in the construction of an artillery armory in the immediate vicinity of the bishop's palace, and after the abolition of the Jesuit college and later of the other monasteries, when many buildings were handed over to the army.

18. *Protocollum*, p. 438.

to the life of St Bernardino – conversion to Catholic confession and admission to the church.

After the Swedish soldiers left, the Franciscans had a century to work in a confessionally homogeneous environment. Although it was possible that during the first decades there still were citizens whose affiliation to the Catholic Church was questionable, the friary chronicle does not report any accounts of working with non-Catholics or of their conversion. The chronicle speaks of isolated blasphemers and individuals with dubious morals (such as the thieves who broke into the church in 1677 to steal a silver lamp and several silver votive donations from the statue of the Virgin Mary) living in the otherwise orthodox city.[19] The Franciscan activities were thus targeted solely at the Catholic population throughout the entire period. The only exception was the baptism of a few non-Christians. A Turkish woman, the maid of the wife of the fort commander, was baptized in the Franciscan church in December 1690 (her godparents were the chapter provost and the commander's wife). Another Turkish woman and her son were baptized in February of the following year.[20] Two Jewish youths were christened in 1706 and 1707 respectively.[21] The five individuals were the only people of different faith to enter the Franciscan Church for a long time. Nonetheless, starting in the 1740s, the fort garrison was gradually reinforced with troops recruited from other countries of the monarchy or even abroad. The new units brought a number of Lutheran and Calvinist soldiers to Olomouc, so the local clergy focused their missionary activities on them. Before long, on 2 November 1749, a Hungarian Calvinist was admitted to the Catholic Church at the Holy Trinity altar in the cloister of the Franciscan friary.[22] He was followed four months later by a Silesian Lutheran, and still later by others. Over the next thirty-five years, more than a hundred and thirty people were admitted to the Roman-Catholic Church at the Trinity altar – mostly soldiers and their families from Hungary, Silesia, and the Empire. The highest number of conversions took place in the last decade of the existence of the house (twenty-two people converted in 1779 alone).

Successful involvement in pastoral care during the construction of the fortress suggests that the Franciscans responded flexibly to changing conditions. There did not seem to be any signs of crisis in religious life – at least not in the case of the Franciscans. St Bernardino was functioning at full capacity. Franciscan services were in high demand and the friars found it quite easy to live on alms and mass stipends. Both the city council and the city's inhabitants

19. The chronicle does not provide any details about the thieves or their possible subsequent apprehension. See: *Archivum*, p. 68.

20. *Archivum*, p. 104.

21. *Archivum*, pp.153-154.

22. The altar of the Holy Trinity was built in 1480 in the lower cloister of the friary. In 1744, the bishop consistory refused to confirm the indulgences relating to this altar on the grounds that the altar was in the cloister, not in the public space. The superior retorted that the altar was in an area excluded from the cloistered area, and that the altar was regularly sought by penitents and Tertiaries, who held their exhortations there. Canon Giannini was dispatched to visit the friary, and after seeing that the cloister was safe from disruption, the consistory issued the permit. *Protocollum*, pp. 483-484.

Fig. 34. Plan of the Olomouc fortress in the nineteenth century. State District Archive in Olomouc.

regarded the friary as an important part of the city, and they also appreciated the fact that the Franciscans upheld the demanding ideals of poverty. As the city syndic Florian Joseph Loucký remarked in his description of Olomouc in 1746: "At present, there are 48 brothers, subordinate to the Superior, and although they themselves live from alms only, they compassionately divide the alms among others".[23]

2. *Reduction*

As secure as the existence of St Bernardino was locally, and although most of the population approved of its existence, the second half of the eighteenth century saw a rise of views that ultimately led to its dissolution. Although these opinions were rather isolated and limited to a relatively narrow social class, they belonged to influential people and found a sympathetic ear at the court of Mary Theresa and, above all, of Joseph II. Their criticism was partly based on traditional anti-religious or anti-mendicant stereotypes, transferred under the influence of Enlightenment rationalism. The main themes of these views were the social uselessness of religious orders, their economic exploitation of the population, and

23. Loucký, *Popis královského hlavního města Olomouce*, p. 56. Loucký himself was one of the foremost benefactors of the Olomouc Franciscans. He, for example, gave them an electric apparatus and thirty books on electricity in 1772. *Protocollum*, p. 351.

the propagation of obscurity and superstitions.[24] The reproaches are catalogued in two satirical works written from the perspective of Enlightenment intellectuals.[25] The first of them is *Monachologia* by Ignaz von Born – "a natural history of monks" described according to the system of Carl Linnaeus.[26] Born portrays monks as a distinct animal species forming the connecting link between the ape and the human. Despite being more mature than the apes, monks, unlike humans, lack reason and free will – they only do what they are told by their superiors. The monk is, moreover, generally characterized as a vile, stinking, and constantly thirsty animal that would rather die of starvation than work. In the preface, the author said that he was driven to describe this species before it becomes extinct, for many rulers had taken the action (the introduction of the book is dated 28 December 1782) to eradicate them – like any other vermin. The twelve chapters describe individual subspecies, their anatomy (notably the habit, footwear, and hair and beard), and behaviour. The fourth chapter deals with the *Monachus Franciscanus*, an animal of especially impertinent and coarse morals. It emits an unpleasant odour, despises gold and silver, and only cares for stuffing itself. The habit has many pockets, where the monk hides the things he has begged, as well as rosaries and snuff – which he also offers in return for alms. A Franciscan also has a unique skill to turn pictures, pieces of paper, and amulets into wine and meat.[27]

The other satire is *The Picture Gallery of Monastic Ills* by Joseph Richter, which is an addendum to his previous book, *The Picture Gallery of Catholic Ills*. Twenty pictures depict the specifics of the religious environment, from joining the order to religious vows, administration, monastic prisons, and pharmacies. The twentieth picture – which, as the author claims, is like those that usually hang in the darkest corner of painting galleries – is devoted to mendicants and their collections of alms. Richter emphasises that mendicants are a burden on society, especially for peasants and the state. He says that mendicants acquire alms through sweet talk and threats, yet many peasants are afraid to refuse donating alms so as not to be badmouthed in the village or branded as heretics. For Richter, mendicants were nothing but vampires who sucked the blood of simple folk.[28]

These and other critical voices began to manifest in full in the second half of the eighteenth century, and found the most receptive audience during the reign of Joseph II, when monastic institutions were diminished considerably. The

24. In this context, it was not a very good idea for Wrbczanský to enrich his description of the Olomouc friary with the legends of a skeleton wandering the halls and of a spirit (*spiritus malus, seu genius personatus*) forced to serve the Franciscans. Wrbczansky, *Nucleus Minoriticus*, pp. 144-145.

25. Cf. Jiří Mikulec, "Poznámky ke vnímání řeholního života mezi barokem a osvícenstvím", *Theatrum historiae*, 3 (2008), pp. 275-287.

26. Born, *Joannis Physiophili Specimen Monachologiae*, unpaged.

27. Count Walerian Krasiński, who translated the *Monachologia* into English in the mid-nineteenth century, is more lenient toward the Franciscans, claiming to know a few Franciscans who could be described as human beings. Ignaz von Born, *Monachologia: or, Handbook of the Natural History of Monks, Arranged According to the Linnean System*, Edinburgh, Johnstone and Hunter, 1852, p. 58.

28. Richter, *Bildergalerie klösterlicher Misbräuche*, p. 251.

state had, nonetheless, began to intervene in the order's operations much earlier. Initially, there were conflicts of competence, in which the emperor interfered in order to limit the influence of foreign subjects. A good example was the first major conflict between the province and the order superiors in Rome in the second half of the seventeenth century. At that time, it was decided that each province would be visited every three years by an appointed *visitator*, who would inspect the affairs of the province and chair the provincial chapter. Those visitators, however, were almost exclusively Italians – to the great dismay of the representatives of Northern provinces. Eventually, Leopold I intervened, as he agreed that visitations by Italian friars were an unwarranted interference in the affairs of his territory. He helped enforce the decision that only members of the transalpine provinces would visit the transalpine provinces (Bohemian, Austrian, Bavarian, and both Polish and Hungarian).[29] A much greater intervention took place in 1706, when Joseph I prohibited the officials of provinces within his territory from taking part in the general chapter held in Vitoria, Spain – then a hostile country.[30]

The imperial interventions mentioned above foreshadowed a trend that fully manifested after the middle of the eighteenth century: the weakening of ties to the order centres and the gradual reduction of autonomy from other institutions. Religious orders became increasingly subject to episcopal, and later, state control. The state control initially focused on two basic areas, the first being the number of monasteries and their members. Although there were not as many monks and friars in the Bohemian Lands as in other parts of the monarchy (Lombardy, South Netherlands), it was still a considerable problem which the representatives of the orders themselves were aware of.[31] This was also the case for the Bohemian Franciscan Province, whose superiors were repeatedly requested in the eighteenth century (in 1738 and again in 1753) to curb the recruitment of new members and thus regulate the situation in individual houses – to enable each friar, in accordance with the statutes, to have his own cell (this goal was never achieved, though).[32] Thus, for example, it was ordered in 1754 that St Bernardino could house a maximum of 51 friars. When asked ten years later by the regional authorities, the superior was forced to admit there were 54 resident friars in the house. There were also two Tertiaries (although in their case, the superior claimed that these were not genuine friars, somewhat contrary to the previous tradition). The regional office immediately ordered the friary to cut the number of men by three, who, following consultations with the provincial, were moved to other houses.[33]

29. The decrees of Leopold I and Joseph I against foreign visitators were published in Wrbczansky, *Nucleus Minoriticus*, pp. 53-57.

30. Moravian Land Archive Brno, Fund E 21, Dačice Franciscans, book 3, *Archivum Conventus Brunensis*, p. 78.

31. Derek Beales, *Prosperity and Plunder: European Catholic Monasteries in the Age of Revolution, 1650-1815*, Cambridge, Cambridge University Press, 2003, p. 2 and p. 180.

32. NA Prague, Bohemian Franciscan Province Archives, book 68, *Acta et Statuta Praecipua*, p. 21 and p. 29.

33. *Protocollum*, p. 485.

Fig. 35. The siege of Olomouc by the Prussian army in 1758. Johann Martin Will, etching. State District Archive in Olomouc, sign. I/27.

The other area that the bishop and later the state authorities began to investigate was the management of the friary, namely the revenue from alms and mass stipends. For example, on 28 July 1749, the gubernium ordered the Franciscans and Capuchins to determine the times, places, and type of alms they planned to collect – they were forbidden to collect donations outside the given timeframe.[34] In 1769, the gubernium issued a decree requesting the superiors of the houses to submit an inventory of all the existing mass stipends.[35] The state institutions also sought to limit the autonomy of the orders and subordinate them to the bishop consistories, which would continue to control their economic activities, among other things. For example, in the 1770s, the Olomouc bishop consistory ordered the superiors of local mendicant friaries to submit detailed records of alms, mass stipends, and other income (see Chapter Three).

The state was now increasingly intervening in the life of mendicant institutions and their relationship to the community. While in the earlier period the friary depended primarily on the local population, now the interests of the state (and the processes taking place across society under the Habsburg monarchy and throughout the Catholic world) had the upper hand. The first major event indicating the dramatically changing status of the religious orders was the abolition

34. Jaksch, *Gesetzlexikon*, 1, pp. 65-66.
35. *Protocollum*, p. 485.

of the Jesuit Order in 1773. The chronicle of the Olomouc Franciscans reflects the dissolution of the Jesuit Order, conveying a detailed record of how the bishop commission proceeded while closing the Olomouc college. The record is neutral, avoiding any evaluation. While the dissolution of an influential and respected religious institution may have been shocking for many friars, St Bernardino was not directly affected by that act. The Olomouc Franciscans did not have any immediate economic ties to the Jesuits – whether in the form of regular alms or significant occasional donations. On the contrary, in the short term, the dissolution of the Jesuit College only reinforced the local standing of the Franciscans: the Franciscans took over the Jesuits' preaching position in the largest parish church of St Maurice in 1775. This provided them with more regular alms in the form of fees and an opportunity to address the city's population more effectively (sermon dates and collisions had previously been the subject of disputes between the Franciscans and the St Maurice priests). With this, the Franciscan friary became even more involved in the functioning of the city organism in the last ten years of its existence.

Unlike the dissolution of the Jesuits, the new wave of reductions in the early 1780s had a direct economic impact on the friars. When the Olomouc Carthusians were abolished on 18 January 1782, the Franciscans lamented having lost regular alms in the form of bread and beer from the Carthusian brewery, which they used to receive for requiem masses offered for deceased Carthusians. The friars – not very wisely – asked the Moravian Land Chamber to compensate for this loss. Soon, however, other religious houses were dissolved: the Poor Clares, the Dominican nuns, and the Canons Regular. Tension mounted. When the Premonstratensian at the Hradisko Monastery were abolished on 18 August 1784, the author of the chronicle, in the very last record in the *Memorabilia Conventus* section, limited himself to but a brief statement.[36]

Meanwhile, the friars had been witnessing other changes that were radically altering the character of their religious life. Many of the changes were radically limiting the autonomy of religious institutions. The stricter episcopal control of the regular clergy was particularly significant. Until then, the priests had typically undergone studies at schools in selected friaries of the province. A directive issued at the beginning of 1782 ruled that all regular priests had to be tested in dogmatic, polemical, moral, and pastoral theology, along with ecclesiastical law, at the consistory. The Franciscan priests were examined at the consistory on 12 March.

36. *Protocollum*, p. 441. In total, 118 monasteries (97 friaries and 21 nunneries) were abolished in the Bohemian Lands, of which 74 monasteries were in Bohemia, 41 in Moravia, and 3 in Silesia (Austria). Pavel Bělina, Jiří Kaše, and Jan P. Kučera, *Velké dějiny zemí Koruny české X (1740-1792)*, Prague and Litomyšl, Paseka, 2001, p. 102. A slightly lower number (94 friaries) is given by Ondřej Bastl, "Rušení klášterů v Čechách a na Moravě za Josefa II.", *Historická geografie*, 28 (1995), pp. 155-182, see: chart p. 158. Cf. Karel Beránek and Věra Beránková, "Rušení klášterů za Josefa II.", in *Pražské arcibiskupství 1344-1994. Sborník statí o jeho působení a významu v české zemi*, ed. by Zdeňka Hledíková and Jaroslav V. Polc, Prague, Zvon, 1994, pp. 209-224. About 700 monasteries were abolished in the entire monarchy; the number of friars dropped by 14,000, while the number of secular clergy grew by 5,000. Beales, *Prosperity and Plunder*, p. 194.

But this was not the end of the episcopal supervision. On 4 April, the friary was visited by the consistory assessor, who summoned all the appointed confessors (except three ill priests) and gave them several questions to which they had to write answers without using books.[37]

The order to examine the regular clergy – even though it interfered with what was traditionally considered the internal affairs of the order – did not pose a significant threat to the Franciscans, nor did it considerably limit their activity. The following measures, however, fundamentally affected the basic aspects of religious, specifically mendicant, ways of life.[38] First, royal decrees issued at the turn of 1783 abolished all third orders in the monarchy.[39] This was a particularly hard blow to the Franciscans: the measure affected the carefully nurtured ties of the friary to the local population, and violated the order's tradition, which saw Tertiaries as an important and integral part of the Franciscan community. Another royal decree from 9 February 1784 prohibited the nativity scenes, Holy Sepulchres, rosaries, rogation processions, as well as the Stations of the Cross – one of the major Franciscan contributions to early modern Catholic spirituality.[40] This last ban significantly shattered the sacred space of St Bernardino, where the church and adjacent chapels were linked by the Stations of the Cross. The next intervention targeted the religious community itself: the regulation, issued in the same year, prohibited burials in church crypts. This seriously disrupted the traditional notion of the communion of the living and deceased friars within the walls of the friary.[41]

Yet the most serious interference for the Franciscans was the prohibition of mendicancy, which banned friars from collecting alms in any form. Instead, the religious houses were to receive a regular allowance from the state for each

37. The test results are not available, unfortunately. The same year, the Olomouc mendicants were ordered to designate a priest to help the military chaplain (the Franciscans had also assisted with pastoral care in the Olomouc prison from 1774). *Protocollum*, p. 440.

38. In 1781, the regional authority ordered the friary to pay a horse tax under the threat of seizure of property. The friary sent a plea to have the tax decreased. In the end, the friary was spared the tax for good (for the four remaining years of its existence, in this case). *Protocollum*, p. 483.

39. Third orders were hit by limitation for the first time in 1772, after they were forbidden to accept new members. Jiří Mikulec, *Barokní náboženská bratrstva v Čechách*, Prague, Nakladatelství Lidové noviny, 2000, p. 132. The St Bernardino Franciscans, however, continued to accept Tertiaries for another five years. See: *Matrica*, passim.

40. Stations of the Cross were permitted again in 1837. Rudolf Zuber, *Osudy moravské církve v 18. století, 2. Díl*, Olomouc, Matice cyrilometodějská, 2003, p. 256.

41. An imperial order was issued as early as 1773 requesting all the church crypts in use to have an entrance from the street and not from the church. The Franciscans had to stop using their order's master crypt in front of the high altar and bury the dead only in the crypt under the Chapel of St Anthony of Padua, where it was possible to build a street entrance. *Protocollum*, p. 189. Later, burials in crypts were prohibited alltogether and friars were to be burries in public cemeteries. The first friar the measure applied to was Fr Emanuel Strzella, who died on 4 December 1784 and was buried in the public cemetery at the Theresian Gate. It was the first (and since it was the last death in the friary, the only) burial of a local Franciscan outside the church since the Great Plague in 1715. *Protocollum*, p. 542.

member of the community. As for the Franciscans, the instructions of the provincial authorities had until then requested each friary to be supported with a value of alms based on the number of inhabitants in the house, namely 150 fl per priest or cleric and 120 fl per lay brother. The Olomouc house, as mentioned above, did not always manage to reach the amount, and yet the funds collected were fully sufficient. Starting from 1 January 1785, the community at St Bernardino began to receive a regular state subsidy of 200 fl per person per year, in line with the imperial instructions. It obtained 2,600 fl from religious funds for the first three months. In total, the income from state subsidies was roughly one-third higher than the previous alms. The friary all of a sudden had a large sum at its disposal, despite the fact that it was probably still managed by its apostolic syndic, Adalbert Morawek. The regular (and last) quarterly audit in *Liber Ratiociniorum* dated 18 August indicates that by then the friary had already received over 7,000 fl, which was more than a year's worth of alms, based on the 1773 statement. After the second quarter, they still had 1,683 fl.[42]

The documents of St Bernardino do not convey any subjective evaluation of the ongoing changes. Due to the importance of alms-begging for the survival of the friary and, above all, for the development and maintenance of its relations with the public, the friars were likely upset and worried by the ongoing changes. Permanent and regular financial contributions also contradicted the order's original doctrine of apostolic poverty. The friars had to say farewell to the most distinctive feature of their religious life, which was considered to be the sacred legacy of St Francis's Rule, and for centuries had shaped and defined their position in society. Yet the Friars Minor, like other religious orders, showed considerable flexibility and adaptability at that time – finding their new *modus operandi* under the changing circumstances. Nonetheless, this was the very end of the existence of the Olomouc friary.

3. *Dissolution*

On 13 August 1785, the Moravian Land Gubernium, in cooperation with the directorship of the chamber estates, issued a decree charging Freiherr Joseph of Zwole, as the official of the regional authority, to close down the Friary of St Bernardino. The commissary visited the friary on 1 September to officially notify the superior and the entire community of the abolition of the house and to oblige them to cooperate.[43] The assembled brothers were informed that they could stay until the 9th of the same month, after which date they were obligated to move to their new posts set by the provincial. According to the list from 3 September, there

42. The number of people in the house gradually declined in the following months, and the friary still received at least some funds from the mass stipends. See: *Liber Ratiociniorum*, passim.

43. The dissolution of the friary was governed by the instructions of the royal decree issued for the entire monarchy within the first wave of the dissolution of monasteries (issued on 12 January 1782 and published four days later). See: Jaksch, *Gesetzlexikon*, pp. 436-441.

were only 36 people living in the friary at that time, roughly seventeen fewer than normal.[44] There were twelve priests, fifteen clerics, and nine lay brothers (including one Tertiary). The clerics were all to be transferred to a general seminary in the former Premonstratensian Hradisko Monastery to continue their studies. The remaining twenty-one men were moved to nearby Franciscan friaries in Opava, Brno, Kroměříž, Moravská Třebová, and Dačice. That did not put an end to the turmoil as the first three houses were later closed as well. It is possible that part of them eventually abandoned religious life, the reason being that the number of people in the individual houses was considerably restricted in the following years: only eighteen men could live in the Prague friary, while in other houses the number was limited to twelve.[45] As of 1790, the Bohemian Franciscan Province consisted of nineteen friaries housing two to three hundred friars.[46]

The commission spent the following days taking inventory of the friary's property. At first (12 September), an inventory was made of the cells, the names of their inhabitants, and the furniture they had. The cells were mostly furnished with a bed, a bedside table, a table with a chair, and in the case of the priests, also with a bookcase. The only additional objects were pictures (*Ordens Bilder*) in eight cells and a wall clock in the cells of the superior and another cleric. There was also a piano and a violin in the cell of one of the priests (whose remaining equipment, however, consisted only of a bed and an armchair). As part of the inventory, each friar had to sign a consignation in which he assumed liability for the property listed. Superior Protasius Biwald, Sacristan Carolus Strakele, and the Apostolic Syndic Adalbert Morawek had to sign an oath that none of the monastic property had been withheld.[47]

The inventory was completed on 20 October 1785. All the furnishing (including 63 paintings, 270 dishes, 94 tankards, 49 glasses, 228 items of linen, 10 chamber pots, and many other items) were estimated to be worth 472 fl. Grain, wine, and other commodities in the pantry and cellars were estimated at 207 fl. The stables were found to contain two horses (a seventeen-year-old gelding blind in the right eye and a sixteen-year-old blind in the left eye), a caleche, a wagon,

44. No information about their fate could be found. The number probably decreased gradually in the eighties, as no novices were accepted to replace the deceased confreres. Some of the friars were perhaps moved to other houses or opted for secularization and left the friary. The priests could continue as pastors at a new location. Moravian Land Archive Brno, Fund B 2, Moravian Authority – Ecclesiastical Department, sign. K 20/36, carton 101, unpaged: *Verzeichnüss über den – bey Reduzirung des Olmützer Franziskaner Klosters zum Heil. Bernardin bestanden – geistlichen personal Stand (3. Sep. 1785).*

45. Overall, the Josephinian interventions cut the monastic numbers in the Habsburg monarchy from 65,000 down to 27,000. Mario Rosa, "The Catholic Clergy in Europe", in *Cambridge History of Christianity, Volume 7: Enlightenment, Reawakening and Revolution, 1660-1815*, ed. by Stewart J. Brown and Timothy Tackett, Cambridge, Cambridge University Press, 2006, pp. 89-108.

46. Klemens Minařík and Bonaventura Wilhelm, *Dějiny klášterů františkánských v Čechách a na Moravě*, Třebíč, Františkánská provincie česko-moravská, 1909, passim.

47. Moravian Land Archive Brno, Fund B 2, Moravian Authority – Ecclesiastical Department, sign. K 20/36, carton 101, unpaged: *Consignation... (12. Sept. 1785).*

a carriage sleigh, and a work sleigh – all estimated at 36 fl. In short, the liquid property of the friary, handed over to the directorship of chamber estates, was worth a little over 700 fl. A specific category (unfortunately there is no estimate in the inventory) was the "church silver". Despite the continuing repression of friaries, people still sought friars to say mass for a given intention in exchange for monetary alms. The superior handed over the 103 fl commission in cash. The assets also included bills and securities worth 371 fl. The most important part of the friary's property by far was the mass stipend capital, whose interest was used to pay for masses said for donors. A total of eighteen legacies were worth 10,491 fl. The total sum calculated by the commission (excluding the church silver and the value of the buildings) was 11,683 guilders and 10 kreutzers.[48]

The inventories made by the commission are a careful yet distorted description of the condition and furnishing of the friary. They reduce it to its fiscal value, taking the items out of context – both the spatial context (reliquaries, images) and the social context (stipends). Still, it is obvious that the furnishings were quite modest (especially when compared to the much more luxurious interior of large monasteries) and corresponded to the Franciscan doctrine of poverty. The total profit of the Olomouc Franciscan friary, which once accommodated fifty friars, was infinitesimal.[49] When the Jesuits were abolished in 1773, the registered property of their college, seminaries, and other institutions was worth 830,000 fl. The Jesuits had naturally held an exceptional position due to being responsible for several educational institutes, among other things. However, other Olomouc monasteries also closed in the 1780s had substantially larger assets. For example, even the kindred friary of the Friars Minor Conventuals was inhabited by twenty-seven friars, yet it was endowed with mass stipend capital worth 19,000 fl (the value of the other assets could not be established). Female mendicant cloisters were much wealthier. As nuns could not collect alms due to their prescribed strict enclosure, they were fully dependent on the revenue from their own property. In the case of the Poor Clares Convent (housing twenty-eight nuns) the property was estimated at 187,000 fl, while in the case of the Dominican nuns (a convent with thirty-six nuns) it was 238,000 fl. The other two abolished "non-mendicant" monasteries were similarly wealthy: the Augustinian canons were endowed with 209,000 fl, while the sixteen Carthusians had property worth 280,000 fl. The largest sum for the religious fund was generated by the dissolution of the Premonstratensian canonry and the Hradisko Monastery (70 persons), the property of which was worth an astonishing 1,406,000 fl.[50] To put it simply, assets designated to provide

48. Moravian Land Archive Brno, Fund B 2, Moravian Authority – Ecclesiastical Department, sign. K 20/36, carton 101, unpaged: *Inventarium Über das Vermögen des aufgehobenen Franziskaner Klosters zu Ollmütz (20. Oct. 1785).*

49. The total amount which the religious fund in Moravia generated through the dissolution of monasteries exceeded 10,000,000 fl. Bělina, Kaše, Kučera, *Velké dějiny zemí Koruny české X*, p. 104.

50. Tomáš Václav Bílek, *Statky a jmění kollejí jesuitských, klášterů, kostelů, bratrstev a jiných ústavů v království Českém od císaře Josefa II. zrušených*, Prague, nákladem Františka Bačkovského, 1893, pp. 100-358. Other sources estimate the value of the Premonstratensian

for a nun in a convent equalled more than 6,500 fl, while in the case of male (non-mendicant) monasteries it was more than 15,000 fl per person. In the case of the Conventuals (solely the mass stipends are counted), property was worth 700 fl per friar; in the case of the Franciscans it was a trifling 220 fl per person.[51] Most of their regular income thus consisted of voluntary alms and "donations" for celebrated masses. In any case, compared to the other abolished houses in the city, the total value of St Bernardino was paltry. Its dissolution was not a profit but rather a financial burden for the religious fund. The reason was that for many years to come stipends needed to be paid for secularized friars and those who remained in "active service".

The fate of the Olomouc friary need not have been sealed yet, despite the completed inventory. The initial plans for the dissolution of monasteries had counted on a severe reduction of the Franciscan houses. A variety of data suggests that both female convents and at least fifteen of the twenty-two friaries were to be closed.[52] The representatives of the province immediately began to intercede with Vienna to save them. They were supported by multiple influential patrons, parish clergy, and local authorities, who highlighted the Franciscan contribution to pastoral care in the given cities. The dissolution of most of the affected friaries was ultimately suspended, despite the fact that, as in Olomouc, their property had been already catalogued. The definitive verdict was only pronounced for the two women's houses and five men's houses: Opava, Kroměříž, Brno, Znojmo, and Olomouc.[53] It seems no coincidence that it was primarily the eastern houses of the province which were sacrificed. In previous centuries, the province had been plagued by disputes between the German majority and the Czech minority. The Czech friars complained they were under-represented in provincial offices and proposed twice (in 1675 and 1701) to have the large province divided into

monastery at staggering 1,913,339 fl. See: *Encyklopedie moravských a slezských klášterů*, ed. Dušan Foltýn, Praha, Libri, 2005, p. 516.

51. Bílek, *Statky a jmění*, pp. 334-336, says that as of 1756 the Brno convent of (female) Regular Tertiaries had 156,733 fl in securities and its annual income equalled 8,905 fl. Compared to that, when closed in 1786, the securities of the Brno friary were worth a mere 16,300 fl. The amount did not differ significantly from the sums given by Bílek (p. 230, pp. 336-337, and p. 367) for the other Franciscan friaries. The Hájek and Slaný friaries had around 40,000 fl each, the Opava friary had 15,000 fl in securities, and the Znojmo friary not more than 6,000 fl.

52. The Bohemian province of St Wenceslas was comprised of thirty men's friaries, one residence, and three women's houses in the first half of the eighteenth century. After the wars of the Austrian Succession and the loss of Silesia, ten men's friaries and one women's convent were separated and regrouped under the new province of St Hedwig of Silesia in 1755. In the eighties the Bohemian province acquired two friaries under its administration. These were the Cheb friary (1782), which had formerly belonged to the Strasbourg province, and the Uherské Hradiště friary (1785), which the Bohemian province took over from the Hungarian province.

53. Minařík and Wilhelm, *Dějiny klášterů*, passim, argue that at least the following fifteen houses were to be dissolved: Opava, Olomouc, Brno, Znojmo, Kroměříž, Cheb, Kadaň, Hájek, Jindřichův Hradec, Plzeň, Uherské Hradiště, Turnov, Slaný, Morovská Třebová, and Skalka. For more on some of the permanently or temporarily closed Franciscan friaries, see: Bílek, *Statky a jmění*, pp. 228-231 (Irish Franciscans in Prague, Cheb, Hájek, Slaný), pp. 334-337 (Tertiary nuns in Brno; Franciscans in Brno, Znojmo, and Kroměříž), and p. 367 (Opava).

the western "Czech" part and the eastern "German" part.[54] The German majority, however, managed to neutralize these attempts with the help of the foreign visitators. After the secession of the Silesian (i.e. mostly "German") friaries, the balance of power tilted considerably in the favour of the Czech Franciscans. This probably played a part in the struggle to save the houses under dissolution, where the rescue efforts concentrated primarily on "Czech" friaries. All the abolished friaries (except Kroměříž) belonged to leading "German" centres of the province; the structure of the post-1785 province was strikingly similar to the 1701 proposal to separate the "Czech" part of the province. The Bohemian Franciscan Province of St Wenceslas, as a result, became even more "Bohemian" and "Czech" – both geographically and linguistically.

The verdict on the Olomouc friary remained, nonetheless, the same – whatever the background of the reduction of the Franciscan province. Freiherr Joseph of Zwole, based in Uničov at the time, completed his report of the reduction on 28 November, and together with all the inventories sent it to the Moravian Land Gubernium, where it was registered on 21 December. In the meantime, the Olomouc Dominicans were moved from their seat at St Michael to the vacated Franciscan friary.[55] This was a paradox, as the Dominicans – who had traditionally rejected and criticized the cult of the immaculate conception of the Virgin Mary (approved as a dogma only in 1854) – were now supposed to serve at a church which was one of the oldest, if not *the* oldest, dedication of this type in the Bohemian Lands.[56] Eventually, the Josephinian reduction also hit the Chapel of the Holy Stairs, which survived the local Franciscan community by

54. For sources on ethnic disputes, see: NA Prague, Bohemian Franciscan Province Archives, reg. no. 865, carton 21. See also: Minařík, "Provinciál P. Bernard Sannig", (1921-1922), passim.

55. The only other orders, besides the Dominicans, to survive the dissolution of monasteries in Olomouc were the Capuchins and the Ursulines.

56. The dedication was nevertheless preserved – unlike the consecration of St Bernardino, which was omitted from the original name of the church. The takeover of a church built for centuries by a different order naturally introduced the need for a substantial remodelling of the liturgical space. This primarily involved altars consecrated to Franciscan saints, which were gradually replaced by altars with Dominican dedications. In addition, the interior of the church altered as the requirements for the functioning of the liturgical space changed (the number of altars was reduced). The most distinct transformation was the neo-Gothic restoration of the church in the 1880s. This was when the original altar with the image of the Virgin Mary by Joseph Ignatius Sattler was removed and replaced by a pseudo-Gothic altar purchased in 1884 at a fair in Germany. In 1880, the Chapel of the Holy Sepulchre was equipped with a copy of the painting of Our Lady of Perpetual Help, to whom the chapel was also dedicated. The Chapel of St Anthony of Padua was consecrated to Our Lady of the Rosary in 1948. Another major modification was the general renovation of the church and friary after the floods in 1997. For more details on the subsequent restorations of the church and friary, see: Olomouc State Research Library, Manuscript Collection, sign. II 296.834, Theodor Divina, *Dějiny kláštera františkánů u sv. Bernardina v Olomouci a kostela N. P. P. Marie (dnes dominikánský) do roku 1783*, Olomouc, 1957; and Tomáš Černušák and Miloslav Pojsl, *Olomouc. Klášter dominikánů a kostel Neposkvrněného početí Panny Marie*, Velehrad, Historická společnost Starý Velehrad se sídlem na Velehradě, 2005.

only a few years (although it is unknown whether it remained in use). The regional authorities notified the Olomouc city council on 7 October 1799 that, based on an imperial decree, the chapel was to be handed over to the Education Fund. It was decided that the building would house the main school (*Hauptschule*).[57] The chapel needed to be rebuilt to serve the purpose. The facade with the sculptural decoration was pulled down (the statue of *Ecce Homo!* was rescued and moved to Slatinice) and the interior of the building was completely redesigned. The chapel furnishings were removed. One of the reliquaries was handed over to Olomouc goldsmith Johann Bischoff at the beginning of the year for appraisal. His report of 25 January 1799 curtly says: "The relic is of no value, for it is lined with fake glass beads and copper, silver-plated work".[58]

57. Josef Kšír, "Stavební historie budov Moravské filharmonie v Olomouci", *Zprávy Krajského vlastivědného muzea v Olomouci*, 58 (1958), p. 90.

58. Olomouc State District Archive, Olomouc Archives – fragments of the registries, reg. no. 401, carton 13, *Holy Stairs at St Bernardino* (1701-1802), fol. 240.

Conclusion

A number of other religious houses shared the fate of St Bernardino: the friars were moved to other places or retired, their abandoned buildings were handed over to other secular or ecclesiastical institutions. Libraries were inspected, valuable books transferred to public libraries, and the rest sold. The majority of the churches were preserved, and the furnishings of dissolved ones were transferred to other mostly new or poorer churches in rural areas. Although information on the social and economic impact of the dissolution of monasteries is scarce, it is evident that there were no major upheavals. Believers came to accept the new situation, supporters of the religious institutions found their way to other houses, old and broken ties were gradually replaced by new ones, and the existing friaries sought new forms of service.[1] This formed a system, which lasted with some variations until the much more drastic dissolution of monasteries by the Communist State Security in 1950.

The smooth course of the Josephinian suppression of monasteries paradoxically showcases the success and sustainability of the religious system built over the past two centuries. Importantly, the system was flexible and variable.[2] Although the Council of Trent and the popes tried to unite and mobilize the remaining parts of Europe that still laid under their sphere of influence, the result was more than ambiguous. The seemingly integrated façade of the Catholic Church with its hierarchy and unified liturgy concealed a broad network of often disparate customs and ideas. The diversity was not determined by regional differences only: far from it. Similar variety was found also at the local level, specifically where religious life was co-shaped by multiple institutions. Religious orders in particular were a major contributing factor.

They also played an important role due to the fact that some of the *Tridentine* plans never came to fruition. Although the religious life of believers was supposed to be centred in the parish church, and all of this was to be subject to episcopal

1. For more details on the religiosity of the new period, see: Zdeněk R. Nešpor, *Náboženství na prahu nové doby: Česká lidová zbožnost 18. a 19. století*, Ústí nad Labem, Albis International, 2006, pp. 459-466.

2. Cf. the brilliant study by Judith Pollmann, "Being a Catholic in Early Modern Europe", in *The Ashgate Research Companion to the Counter-Reformation*, ed. by Alexandra Bamji, Geert H Janssen, and Mary Laven, Farnham, Ashgate, 2013, pp. 165-182.

supervision, reality fell short of expectations. The parish network was inadequate, and the quality of the parish clergy was far from ideal. Some of the initially criticized ills, such as pluralism, became common practice once again. This was also true for the bishops, who, moreover, had to deal with increasingly influential state authorities. On the other hand, activities aimed at building a confessional society managed to reach the lay people and interest them in various forms of religious life. The secular clergy was not always able to satisfy the demand, which opened an immense space for religious orders and their alternative structures and approaches.

The plethora of Church institutions – both at a general and local level – were a strong motivation for all those involved. Institutions, and notably religious orders, were forced to constantly strive to secure their position. They had to compete with others, emphasize their specifics, and patiently build their own network of ties to the local population. For the common people, this situation was quite advantageous, particularly in cities. Even though, in keeping with the *Tridentine* requirements, basic worship (most of the sacraments, regular Sunday masses, and sermons) were tied to the parish church, believers could also attend many other "extra" devotions in local religious churches, whether these were masses, sermons, various devotions typical for the given order, membership in religious confraternities, requiem prayers, and funerals.

The religious orders were well prepared for these tasks. This was especially true for the mendicants who, thanks to their lifestyle, were dependent on maintaining good relations with the population. Their friaries were staffed by large numbers of priests who had undergone proper training and studies, and could be specialized in selected services, such as preaching. In addition, they could draw on the rich traditions of their order, offering the believers services which the parish clergy could hardly compete with. The mendicant way of life only boosted the friars' popularity. Despite some compromises (like the adoption of the apostolic syndics in order to be able to accept mass stipends and other monetary alms), the reformed mendicant houses managed to observe the basic principles of life in poverty. More importantly, they managed to demonstrate these principles to the public – emphasizing that their own poverty and observation of the original rule was crucial to the communication strategy of the mendicants.

The mendicant system was not important only for the practical reasons of friary sustenance and for maintaining a positive image of the friars. Alms were, in fact, far from unilateral. They were, actually, clearly reciprocal: donors were granted spiritual services in return for their material donations. Begging for alms was one of the main forms of interaction between the friary and the local community, allowing the mendicants to significantly extend their reach and address a much wider population. Although depending on alms complicated the running of the house, at the same time it was a highly positive stimulus which shaped and cultivated a network of relationships between the friary and the local community. In addition, the economic dependence of mendicants made them close to the city elites, who saw them as important allies in the negotiation and formation of religious life in cities. The coalitions of mendicant communities (with their ties to Rome and other centres) and city councils (often backed by the emperor or state authorities) were extremely powerful players, who were able to assert their interests even against episcopal authorities or other influential ecclesiastical institutions. The story of St Bernardino in Olomouc is a telling illustration of that complex and manifold process of the formation of religious life in early modern society. It demonstrates that the confessional culture of the Roman Catholic world was not built unilaterally, from the top down, but was instead the result of synergy and even conflicts between many actors.

Bibliography

1. *Archival sources*

National Archive in Prague

ARCHIVE OF THE BOHEMIAN FRANCISCAN PROVINCE (1283/1367-1950)

BOOKS

17. Bernhard Sannig, *Chronica de origine & constitutione Provinciae Bohemiae Ordinis Fratrum Minorum S. Francisci Reformatorum & ejusdem conventuum*, 1678.
20. Bernhard Sannig, *Chronica de origine & constitutione Provinciae Bohemiae Ordinis Fratrum Minorum S. Francisci Reformatorum & ejusdem conventuum*, Tomus I., second half of the seventeenth century.
21. Bernhard Sannig, *Chronica de origine & constitutione Provinciae Bohemiae Ordinis Fratrum Minorum S. Francisci Reformatorum & ejusdem conventuum*, Tomus II., second half of the seventeenth century.
67. "*Tabulae Capitulares Provinciae Bohemiae, & Acta*", 1611-1675.
68. "*Acta praecipua & notabilia conclusae in Capitulis Provincialibus et Diffinitoriis celebratis, Ab Anno 1614 ex Provinciae Protocollo excerpta–Statuta praecipua in Capitulis Provincialibus et Diffinitoriis facta ab Anno*", 1614-1759.
69. "*Tabulae Capitulares Provinciae Bohemiae, & Acta, Ab Anno Domini 1732 usque ad Annum 1889*".
104. "*Cathalogus patrum et fratrum in alma provincia Bohemiae ab anno 1590 usque ad praesens tempus*".
337. "*Fundationes Missarum Perpetuarum in Omnibus Conventus,* before 1756.
352. "*Communicationes Viae S. Crucis*", 1735-1786.
353. "*Benedictio Sacrae Viae Crucis*", eighteenth century.

DOCUMENTS

Inv. no. 851, carton 14, *Proceedings of provincial chapters and congregations*, (1681-1720).

Inv. no. 863, carton 21, *The archive of the province, inventories, instructions for chroniclers*.

Inv. no. 864, carton 21, *Apostolic syndics*.

Inv. no. 865, carton 21, *National conflicts.*
Inv. no. 2981, carton 175, *Sacristy, Holy Sepulchre, etc.*
Inv. no. 2982, carton 175, *Alms of the friary.*
Inv. no. 3131, carton 186, *Third order in general.*
Inv. no. 3142, kart 190, *Map of the Bohemian Franciscan Province.*

Archive of the Capuchin Order
Inv. no. 321, carton 345. *A., The old friary*, seventeenth and eighteenth centuries.
Inv. no. 322, carton 345. *B., Decrees, conflicts*, seventeenth and eighteenth centuries.
Inv. no. 324, carton 345. *D., Funds and alms,* seventeenth and eighteenth centuries.
Inv. no. 325, carton 345. *E., Others,* 1632-1755.

Moravian Land Archive in Brno

B 2, Moravian Gubernium – Ecclesiastical Department (1296) 1743-86
Sign. K 20/36, inv. no. 1446, carton 101, *The dissolution and reduction of the Franciscan friaries in Znojmo and Olomouc*, 1784-1785.
Sign. F2/121, inv. no. 930, carton 48, *Charter concerning the fund of M. Kniebandl for poor members of the Third Order and for the poor of the city of Olomouc*, 1778.

E 21, Franciscans of Dačice
Book 3, *Archivum Conventus Brunensis.*
Book 5, *Protocollum Conventus Cremsiriensis ad SSS. Trinitatem.*
Book 9, *Archivum Conventus Olomucensis,* 1650-1749.
Book 10a., *Protocollum Archivi Conventus Olomucensis,* 1745-1788.
Book 10b., *Liber Ratiociniorum Conventus Olomucensis ad Sanctum Bernardinum*, 1756-1785.
Kniha no. 11, *Matrica III. Ordinis S. Francisci Olomucii. ErneVertes VerzeIChnVs Deren Wertesten BrVDern VnD SChWestern / eInes preIsWVrDIgsten DrItten so erWehnten BVsser OrDens Vnseres grossen ErzVaters FranCIsCI*, 1746-1782.

E 24, Franciscans of Uherské Hradiště (1623-1950)
Carton 22, *Inheritance of P Klemens Minařík O.F.M.*

E 40, Carthusians of Olomouc (1281-1781)
Sign. 1451 VII 25, *Filiation given to the Carthusians of Olomouc by John of Capistrano*, 25 July 1451.

E 55, Premonstratensians of Klášterní Hradisko
Sign. 210 II. no. 11. *Diaries of the canonry of Klášterní Hradisko*, 1702-1705.

G 10, Manuscripts
Inv. no. 213, evid. no. 236, *Nekrology of the Franciscan friary in Olomouc and of the Bohemian Province for the years 1404-1783*, 1763-1783.

Land archive Opava, branch Olomouc

ARCHBISHOPRIC OF OLOMOUC

Inv. no. 2011, sign. Bb 29, carton 410, *Franciscans in the Diocese of Olomouc*, 1615-1815.

Inv. no. 2020, sign. Bb 38, carton 412, *Franciscans in Olomouci,* 1610-1804.

Inv. no. 2025, sign. Bb 43, carton 413, *Franciscan hermits,* 1689-1771.

Inv. no. 2030, sign. Bb 48, carton 414, *Alms for the Holy Land,* 1668-1743.

ARCHBISHOPRIC CONSISTORY IN OLOMOUC (1452-1949)

Sign. C 9, carton 2212, *List of the pilgrimage shrines in Moravia and Silesia*, c. 1760.

Sign. C9, carton 2213, *Processions and pilgrimages in Olomouc and at Sv. Kopeček*, 1617-1897.

Sign. H7, carton 5105, *Third Order*, 1773-1890.

Sign. H8, carton 5107, *Hermits,* 1657-1847.

Sign. H28, carton 5125, *Franciscans,* 1650-1782.

CAPUCHINS IN OLOMOUC

Kniha no. 5, *Liber memorabilium notatu dignorum quae contingerunt a prima Nostri Olomucensis Fundatione*, 1685.

State District Archive in Olomouc

ARCHIVE OF THE CITY OF OLOMOUC: BOOKS

Inv. no. 5701, sign. 1738, *Memorabilia Metropolis Moraviae Olomucensis. Extract aus einen uralten Manuscripto (1432-1614).–Denckwürdige Sachen, welche von einen gewissen Burger in Olmütz (lutherischer Religion) (nehmlich Valentin Ecker, ein Schlosser) beschrieben worden (1618-1715).*

ARCHIVE OF THE CITY OF OLOMOUC: FRAGMENTS OF THE REGISTRY OFFICES (1426-1786)

Inv. no. 190, carton 8, *Excommunication of the city council by Bishopric Administrator Orlik of Lažisko*, 1702-1709.

Inv. no. 251, carton 9, *Decision of the city council to cede the plot for the Holy Stairs to the Franciscans,* 1701.

Inv. no. 401, carton 13, *Holy Stairs at St Bernardino*, 1701-1802.

Inv. no. 458, carton 16, *Enlargement of the Chapel of St Anthony*, 1708.

Inv. no. 535, carton 20, *Excerpts by Florian Loucký about churches and monasteries in Olomouc* (s.d.).

Inv. no. 547, carton 20, *Divine services in the city hall chapel,* 1694-1698.

Inv. no. 548, carton 20, *Controversy between the Franciscans and the Ursulines*, 1702.

Inv. no. 558, carton 20, *Ursulines in Olomouc*, 1695-1740.

Inv. no. 825, carton 30, *Fragment of the Olomouc chronicle (fires, processions to Sv. Kopeček, etc.)*, 1709-1739.

Inv. no. 912, carton 36, *Controversy about the mass stipend for the city hall Chapel of St Lawrence*, 1736-1750.
Inv. no. 1133, carton 44, *Aid to the poor, donations to monaesteries*, 1719-1798.
Inv. no. 2153, carton 88, *Introduction of the plague from Šumperk into Olomouc*, 1714.
Inv. no. 3455, carton 121, *Superior of St Bernardino claims the restitution of the things stolen from the Franciscan church*, 1660.
Inv. no. 3482, carton 122, *City hall chapel, expenses for the divine service and decorations,* 1673-1687.
Inv. no. 3763, carton 132, *Donations to monasteries,* 1676-1698.
Inv. no. 4415, carton 160, *Mag. Daniel Cordatus describes to the mayor and the council ills and lack of discipline at St Bernardino*, 1545.

Parish office at St Maurice (1510-1952)
Inv. no. 24, *Account book,* 1727-1751.

Library of the National Museum in Prague

Collection of Manuscripts
Sign. VIII F 75: *Chronica Fratrum Minorum de Observantia Provinciae Bohemiae,* fifteenth to eighteenth centuries.

Research Library in Olomouc

Collection of Manuscripts
Sign. II 296.834., Theodor Divina, *Dějiny kláštera františkánů u sv. Bernardina v Olomouci a kostela N. P. P. Marie (dnes dominikánský) do roku 1783,* Typescript, Olomouc, 1957.
Sign. III 100., *Harmonia Unisona seu Liber Missarum pro Conventu Olomucensi Fratrum Minorum Reformatorum ad S. Bernardinum,* 1698.

2. *Printed sources and editions*

"*Andacht der Heiligen Stiegen nechst an der Kirchen dess Heil. Bernardini der WW.PP. Franciscanern in der Königlichen Haubt-Stadt Ollmütz auff der Bielten*", Ollmütz, gedruckt und zu finden in der Buchdruckerey allda, 1726.

Balbinus, Bohuslaus, *Miscellanea Historica Regni Bohemiae Decadis I. Liber IV. Hagiographicus, seu Bohemia Sancta, continens Sanctos et Beatos Bohemiæ, Moraviæ, Silesiæ, Lusatiæ*, Pragae, Typis Georgii Czernoch, 1682.
Bilowsky, Gottfried Joseph, *Societas Jesu Salvatoris, das ist die Hochlöbliche Ertz-Bruderschafft oder Gesellschaft der Allerheiligsten Bildnuss dess Erlösers der Welt Unsers Herrn Jesu Christi [Etc.]*, Brün, Jacob M. Swoboda, 1720.
Blanik, Gandulphus, *Thesaurus Franciscanus, Nova et Vetera, Virorum ac Mulierum Tribus de Ordinibus S.P. Francisci Seraphici a Sanctitate Vitae, Probitae Morum,*

Zelo Fidei, Doctrinaque Illustrium, Sculpta Aere Ectypa Proferens, Znoymae, Antonius Johannes Preyss, 1773.

Boediker, Johann, *Christlicher Bericht von Cometen, als der Große Comet 1680 und 1681 Geleuchtet dem Christlichen Deutschen Leser zu Dienst aus den vornehmsten Meynungen alter und neuer Lehrer zusammen gezogen*, Cölln an der Spree, Druckts Georg Schultze, 1681.

Bonanni, Philippus, *Ordinum Religiosorum In Ecclesia Militanti Catalogus Eorumque indumenta in Iconibus Expressa, & oblata. Pars Prima. Editio Secunda*, Romae, Typis Georgii Plachi, 1714.

Charvath, Jan Damasus, *Fractio Panis in Refectionem Fratrum Minorum. To jest: Krátký výklad na Regulu Bratří Menších*, V Uherské Skalici, u Joz. A. Skarnycla, 1765.

Conciliorum Oecumenicorum Generaliumque Decreta. Editio critica. Tomus III. The Oecumenical Councils of the Roman Catholic Church: From Trent to Vatican II (1545-1965), eds. Klaus Ganzer, Giuseppe Alberigo, and Alberto Meloni, Turnhout, Brepols Publishers, 2010.

de Bagnoregio, Bonaventura, *Doctoris Seraphici S. Bonaventurae ... Opera Omnia, iussu et auctoritate Bernardini a Portu Romatino ... studio et cura PP. Collegii a. S. Bonaventura, ad plurimos codices MSS. Emendata,* vol. 12, Quaracchi, ex typographia Collegii S. Bonaventurae, 1882.

da Porto Maurizio, Leonardo, *Via Sacra Spianata, ed Illuminata*, Roma, nella Stamperia di S. Michele, per il Puccinelli, 1749.

"*Diarium oder: Gründliche Anzeige von dem gänzlichen Vorgange der Belagerung und Bombardirung der neuen Gränzvestung Olmütz*", Wien und Prag, Trattner, 1758.

Erasmus, Desiderius, *The Colloquies of Erasmus*, trans. by Craig R. Thompson, Chicago, University of Chicago Press, 1965.

Flade, Friedrich, *Tagebuch des feindlichen Einfalls der Schweden in das Markgrafthum Mähren während ihres Aufenthaltes in der Stadt Olmütz, 1642-1650*, ed. by Beda Dudík, Wien, Gerold, 1884.

Francis of Assisi: Early documents. 3 vols., ed. by Regis J Armstrong, J. A. Wayne Hellmann, William J. Short, Hyde Park, NY and London, New City, 1999-2001.

"*Funftzig-jähriges Jubel-Fest des Gandenbildes Maria von Pötsch*", Wien, Johann Peter von Ghelen, 1747.

Gesetzlexikon im Geistlichen-, Religions- und Toleranzfache, ed. by Peter Karl Jaksch, Erster Band (von A-D), Prag, Gubernialregistratur, 1828.

Gonzaga, Franciscus, *De Origine Seraphicae Religionis Fra[n]ciscanae eiusqu[e] Progressibus, de Regularis Obserua[n]ciae Institutione*, Romae, ex typographia Dominici Basae, 1587.

Greiderer, Vigilius, *Germania Franciscana, Seu Chronicon Geographo-Historicum Ordinis S. P. Francisci in Germania, Tomus I. Germania Franciscana Orientali-Australis*, Oeniponte, Typis Joannis Thomae Nobilis de Trattnern, 1777.

Gudtkindt, Polykarp, *Seraphische Zuflucht, dess wunderthätigen und glorwürdigen*

H. Antonii von Padua. Allen betrübten und nothleydenden Seelen, besonders einer andächtigen und würdigen Bruderschafft welche unter dieses H. Namen in unterschiedlichen Provincien auffgerichtet, Olmütz, Gedruckt bey Veit Heinrich Ettel, 1669.

Handke, Jan Kryštof, *Vlastní životopis: 1694-1774*, ed. by Leoš Mlčák, Olomouc, Muzeum umění, 1994.

Hermann, Amandus, *Capistranus Triumphans: Seu Historia Fundamentalis de Sancto Joanne Capistrano*, Coloniae, apud Balthasarum Joachimum Endterum, 1700.

"*Hora Zlatá Seraffická, aneb Naučenj Spolu-Bratrůw a Sester, Arcy-Bratrstwa Swatého Otce Frantisska, w němž e Odpustky, Regule, Dowolenj, a Modlitby obsahugj, k tomu kterak přigatj do toho Bratrstwa Odpustkůw aučastnj býti mohau*", Wytisstěna w Holomaucy, V Jana Jozeffa Kyliána, 1680.

Hueber, Fortunatus, *Menologium, seu, Brevis, & compendiosa Illuminatio, relucens in Splendoribus Sanctorum, Beatorum, Miraculosorum, Incorruptorum, Extaticorum, Beneficorum, et quocumque Sanctimoniae, vel Virtutis Fulgore, Illustrium, Singularium, aut Praecellentium Famulorum Famularumque Dei, Martyrum, Confessorum, Virginum, Viduarum, Poenitentium*, Monachii, Typis Ioannis Lucae Straubii, 1698.

Jestřábský, Valentin Bernard, *Vidění rozličné sedláčka sprostného*, ed. by Milan Kopecký, Uherský Brod, Muzeum J.A. Komenského, 1973.

Kaurzil, Nyceforus, "Archa Milosti Páně: to gest Králowna Nebeská Marye Panna Premonsstratenská skrze Archu Úmluvy wyobrazená", in *Enthronisticum Parthenium: Sive Gloria et Honor Neo-Inauguratæ ... Reginæ Mariæ ... ; Prope Metropolim Olomucensem in Marchionatu Moraviæ ... et Prima in Orbe Marcomanno Corona Regali Aurea de Urbe Missa Ritu Vaticano, Solemnissimóque Applausu Coronata*, Olomucii, typis Francisci Antonii Hirnle, 1733.

Koranda, Václav, *Manualník M. Vácslava Korandy: Rukopis Bibliotheky klementinské*, ed. by Josef Truhlář, Praha, Král. česká spol. nauk, 1888.

Loucký, Florián Josef, *Popis Královského hlavního města Olomouce sepsaný syndikem Floriánem Josefem Louckým roku 1746*, ed. by Vladimír Spáčil a Libuše Spáčilová, Olomouc, Vlastivědná společnost muzejní v Olomouci a Památkový úřad, 1991.

Marek, Damascenus, *Trojí Chléb Nebeský pro lačný Lid Český,* V Starém Městě Pražském, u Karla Jana Hraby, 1728.

Meerstein, Modestus, *Hymni cum Antiphonis, qui secundum Ritum Sanctae Romanae Ecclesiae, & Seraphicae Religionis S. Francisci in publicis processionibus cantari solent ad uniformem normam relati. ut sic, in Psalmis, & Hymnis, & Canticis Spiritualibus canentes & psallentes in Cordibus Vestris*, Olomucii, Vitus Henricus Ettelius, 1666.

"*Regule a kšaft Serafínského Otce S. Františka, s počátkem, rozmnožením a rozdělením téhož Řádu, a s přiloženým některým duchovním cvičením*", Vytištěno v Novém Městě Pražském, U Anny Voršily Hamplový, 1708.

"*Relation von dem Schwedischen Abzug auss denen inngehabten Posten im Marg-*

grafthumb Mähren wie derselbe am 8. Julii zu Ollmütz seinen Anfang genommen, und noch ebenselben Tag glücklichen vollzogen worden", Gedruckt zu Ollmütz, Bey Nicolao Hradetzcky von Brusnaw, 1650.

Richter, Joseph, *Bildergalerie Klösterlicher Misbräuche: Eine nöthige Beylage zur Bildergalerie Katholischer Misbräuche*, Frankfurt und Leipzig, s.n., 1784.

"*Sanctissimi in Christo Patris et Domini Nostri Benedicti XIII. Pont. Max. Constitutio pro Tertiariis Ordinis Sancti Francisci: Universa Privilegia toti Tertiariorum Coetui, in Tres Status distincto, a Summis Pontificibus Concessa, Confirmantur; Ipsique Tertiarii omnimodae Iurisdictioni, et Regimini Ministri Generalis Totius Ordinis Minorum, pro Tempore exstituri, denuo subiiciuntur, et Commendantur*", Romae, 1726.

Sannig, Bernardus, *Rituale Franciscanum, continens varias Absolutiones, Benedictiones, Conjurationes, Exorcismos, Ritus, ac alias Caeremonias Ecclesiasticas, ad utilitatem Christi Fidelium et praxim Sacerdotum, maxime Ordinis S. Francisci ex variis Ritualibus coordinatum. a Bernardo Sannig. Ord. S. Franc. Reform. Prov. Bohemiae S. Wenceslai D. et M. Sacerdote et iterato Ministro Provinciali dictae Provinciae*, Neo-Pragae, Typis Joan, Nicolai Hampelii, 1685.

Sedulius, Henricus, *Historia Seraphica Vitae B. P. Francisci Assisiatis*, Antverpiae, Sumptibus Haeredum Martini Nutii, 1613.

Solik, Joannes Cantius, *Fasciculus Myrrhae in Campis Palestinae Collectus: Seu Sacrorum Locorum ibidem existentium (prout nunc sunt) brevi methodo descriptio*, Brunae, Typis Joannis Francisci Svoboda, 1716.

Soresinus, Josephus Maria, *Della Scala Santa avanti il Sancta Sanctorum nel Laterano venerata*. Roma, Per Giacomo Dragondelli, 1674.

"*Staří slezští kazatelé. Různé rozprávky a příběhy k naučení a ku potěše*", ed. by Milan Kopecký, Ostrava, Profil, 1970.

"*Theatri Evropaei, Fünffter Theil. Das ist außführliche Beschreibung aller denckwürdigen Geschichten die sich in Europa ... vom Jahr 1643. biß in gegenwärtiges 1647. Jahr allerseits begeben und verlauffen*", Franckfurt am Mayn, Matthaei Meriani, 1651.

Veit, Hieronymus, *Regel oder Weiss dess Lebens, Der Brüder und Schwestern dess dritten Ordens S. Francisci*, Ollmütz, Johann Joseph Kylian, 1701.

Veith, Jarolim, *Regule aneb spůsob života bratrův a sester Třetího řádu Svatého Otce Františka potvrzená od papeže Mikuláše Čtvrtého pro ty, kteří by v svých domech kající život vésti chtěli*, V Starém Městě Pražském, u Anny Voršily Hamplový, 1708.

von Born, Ignaz, *Joannis Physiophili Specimen Monachologiae Methodo Linnaeana Tabulis Tribus Aeneis Illustratum, cum adnexis Thesibus e Pansophia P.P.P. Fast ... Quas Praeside... Capistranoa Mulo Antonii ... Defendent P. Tiburtius a Vulnere Theresiae et P. Theodatus a Stigmatibus Francisci, Etc.*, Augustae Vindelicorum, Aloysius Merz, 1783.

von Born, Ignaz, *Monachologia: or, Handbook of the Natural History of Monks, Arranged According to the Linn System*, Edinburgh: Johnstone and Hunter, 1852.

Wegelius, Christophorus. *Ethica Naturalis seu Documenta Moralia e Variis rerum Naturalium proprietatibus Virtutum Vitiorumque symbolicis imaginibus collecta*, S.l.: s.n., 1700.

Wrbczansky, Severinus, *Nucleus Minoriticus, seu vera et sincera relatio originis et progressus Provinciae Bohemiae, Conventuum et Residentiarum, Fratrum et Sororum Sancti-Monialium Ordin. Minor. S. P. Francisci Strict. Observ. Reform. in Provincia sub Patrocinio Sancti Wenceslai Ducis et Martyris, per Bohemiam, Moraviam, et Silesiam existentium*, Vetero-Pragae, Typis Joannis Caroli Hrabae, 1746.

Wrbczansky, Severinus, *Quodlibetum Regulare Theologicum Canonico-Morale: Complectens Varia Religiosum Statum Concernentia*. Vetero-Pragae: typis Caroli Joannis Hraba, 1732.

Zaczkovic, Paulinus. *Chronik des Minoriten-Guardians des St. Jacobs-Klosters in Olmütz, P. Paulinus Zaczkovic, über die Schwedenherrschaft in Olmütz von 1642 bis 1650*. Ed. Beda Dudík. Wien: Gerold, 1881.

Zwinner, Franciscus Electus. *Blumen-Buch, dess Heiligen Lands Palestinae: So in drey Bücher abgetheilt*. München: durch Johann Wilhelm Schell, 1661.

3. *Literature*

A Companion to Observant Reform in the Late Middle Ages and Beyond, ed. by James Mixson and Bert Roest, Leiden, Brill, 2015.

Achermann, Hansjakob, *Die Katakombenheiligen Und Ihre Translationen in Der Schweizerischen Quart Des Bistums Konstanz*, Stans, Verlag Historischer Verein Nidwalden, 1979.

Armstrong, Megan C., *The Politics of Piety: Franciscan Preachers During the Wars of Religion, 1560-1600*, Rochester, NY, University of Rochester Press, 2004.

Armstrong, Megan C., "Jerusalem in the Reinvention of the Catholic Tradition, 1500-1700", in *Layered Landscapes: Early Modern Religious Space Across Faiths and Cultures*, ed. by Eric Nelson and Jonathan Wright, London, Routledge, 2017.

Attisani, Antonio, and Jane House, "Franciscan Performance: A Theatre Lost and Found Again", *PAJ: A Journal of Performance and Art* 25, 1 (January 2003), pp. 48-60.

Barasch, Moshe, *Giotto and the Language of Gesture*, Cambridge, Cambridge University Press, 1987.

Bastl, Ondřej, "Rušení klášterů v Čechách a na Moravě za Josefa II.", *Historická geografie*, 28 (1995), pp. 155-182.

Beales, Derek, *Prosperity and Plunder: European Catholic Monasteries in the Age of Revolution, 1650-1815*, Cambridge, Cambridge University Press, 2003.

Bělina, Pavel, Jiří Kaše, and Jan P. Kučera, *Velké dějiny zemí Koruny české, X (1740-1792)*, Praha a Litomyšl, Paseka, 2001.

Bělina, Pavel, Jiří Kaše, Jiří Mikulec, Irena Veselá, and Vít Vlnas, *Velké dějiny zemí Koruny české, IX (1683-1740)*, Praha a Litomyšl, Paseka, 2011.

Beneš, Petr Regalát, "O trojím těžkém začínání františkánů observantů v Praze (1460-68, 1482-83 a 1604-11)", in *Historia Franciscana II,* ed. by Petr Regalát Beneš and Petr Hlaváček, Kostelní Vydří, Karmelitánské nakladatelství, 2005, pp. 66-104.

Beneš, Petr Regalát, "San Giovanni da Capestrano e gli inizi dell`oservanza francescana in Boemia e Moravia", in *Cultura, società e vita religiosa ai tempi di S. Giovanni da Capestrano: Atti del V convegno storico internazionale: Capestrano, 21-22 Ottobre 2002*, ed. by Edith Pásztor, Capistrano, Centro studi S. Giovanni da Capestrano, 2003, pp. 109-141.

Beránek, Karel and Věra Beránková, "Rušení klášterů v Čechách za Josefa II", in *Pražské arcibiskupství (1344-1994). Sborník statí o jeho působení a významu v české zemi,* ed. by Zdeňka Hledíková and Jaroslav V. Polc., Praha, Zvon, 1994, pp. 209-224.

Bílek, Tomáš Václav, *Statky a jmění kollejí jesuitských, klášterů, kostelů, bratrstev a jiných ústavů v Království českém od císaře Josefa II. zrušených*, Praha, nákladem Františka Bačkovského, 1893.

Bireley, Robert, *The Refashioning of Catholicism, 1450-1700: A Reassessment of the Counter Reformation*, Basingstoke, Macmillan, 1999.

Bobková-Valentová, Kateřina, *Každodenní život učitele a žáka jezuitského gymnázia*, Praha, Karolinum, 2006.

Bolek, František, *Katolické kostely a kaple v Olomouci*, Olomouc, Lidové závody tiskařské a nakladatelské, 1936.

Bolzoni, Lina, *The Web of Images: Vernacular Preaching From Its Origins to St Bernardino Da Siena*, trans. by Carole Preston and Lisa Chien, Aldershot, Ashgate, 2003.

Börner, Egid, *Dritter Orden und Bruderschaften der Franziskaner in Kurbayern*, Werl, Dietrich-Coelde Verlag, 1988.

Bowman, Glenn, "Christian Ideology and the Image of Holy Land: The Place of Jerusalem Pilgrimage in the Various Christianities", in *Contesting the Sacred: The Anthropology of Christian Pilgrimage*, ed. by John Eade and Michael J. Sallnow, London and New York, Routledge, 1991, pp. 98-121.

Brčák, Marek, "Kapucínský řád a společnost v Čechách a na Moravě v letech 1618-1673", Diplomová práce, UK Praha, 2013.

Buben, Milan, *Encyklopedie řádů, kongregací a řeholních společností katolické církve v českých zemích. 3.2 Žebravé řády*, Praha, Libri, 2007.

Burke, Peter, *Popular Culture in Early Modern Europe*, revised reprint, Aldershot, Scolar Press, 1994.

Catalano, Alessandro, *Zápas o svědomí: Kardinál Arnošt Vojtěch z Harrachu (1598-1667) a protireformace v Čechách*, Praha, Nakladatelství Lidové noviny, 2008.

Chytil, Alois, *Obležení Olomouce a zničení pruského dovozu u Domašova*, Olomouc, R. Prombergr, 1900.

Cohen, Anthony P., *The Symbolic Construction of Community*, London, Routledge, 1985.

Communities of Devotion: Religious Orders and Society in East Central Europe, 1450-1800, ed. by Maria Craciun and Elaine Fulton, Farnham, Ashgate, 2011.

Copeland, Clare, "Sanctity", in *The Ashgate Research Companion to the Counter-Reformation*, ed. by Alexandra Bamji, Geert H Janssen, and Mary Laven, Farnham, Ashgate, 2013, pp. 225-241.

Coster, Will, and Andrew Spicer, "Introduction: The Dimensions of Sacred Space in Reformation Europe", in *Sacred Space in Early Modern Europe*, ed. by Will

Coster and Andrew Spicer, Cambridge, Cambridge University Press, 2005, pp. 1-16.

Čapská, Veronika, "Vytváření prostoru pro působení servitů v Českých zemích 17. a 18. století", in *Úloha církevních řádů při pobělohorské rekatolizaci: Sborník příspěvků z pracovního semináře konaného ve Vranově u Brna ve dnech 4.-5. 6. 2003*, ed. by Ivana Čornejová, Praha, Univerzita Karlova, 2003, pp. 152-164.

Čapská, Veronika, *Představy společenství a strategie sebeprezentace: Řád servitů v Habsburské monarchii (1613-1780)*, Praha, Scriptorium, 2011.

Černušák, Tomáš a Miloslav Pojsl, *Olomouc. Klášter dominikánů a Kostel Neposkvrněného početí Panny Marie*, Velehrad, Historická společnost Starý Velehrad se sídlem na Velehradě, 2005.

Čornejová, Ivana, Jiří Kaše, Jiří Mikulec, and Vít Vlnas, *Velké dějiny zemí Koruny české, VIII (1618-1683)*, Praha a Litomyšl, Paseka, 2008.

Čornejová, Ivana, *Tovaryšstvo Ježíšovo: Jezuité v Čechách*, Praha, Mladá fronta, 1995.

Čtrnáct mučedníků pražských: Vpád Pasovských a závěr vlády Rudolfa II., ed. by Petr Regalát Beneš, Petr Hlaváček, and Tomáš Sterneck, Praha, Univerzita Karlova v Praze, Filozofická fakulta: Filosofia, 2014.

Davis, Natalie Zemon, *The Gift in Sixteenth-Century France*, Oxford, Oxford University Press, 2000.

Deventer, Jörg, "Confessionalisation - A Useful Theoretical Concept for the Study of Religion, Politics, and Society in Early Modern East-Central Europe?", *European Review of History*, 11, 3 (2004), pp. 403-425.

Dipple, Geoffrey, *Antifraternalism and Anticlericalism in the German Reformation: Johann Eberlin Von Günzburg and the Campaign Against the Friars*, Aldershot, Scolar, 1996.

Dipple, Geoffrey, "'Si sind all glichsner:' Antifraternalism in Medieval and Renaissance German Literature", in *Defenders and Critics of Franciscan Life: Essays in Honor of John V. Fleming*, ed. by Michael F. Cusato and Guy Geltner, Leiden, Boston, Brill, 2009, pp. 177-192.

Ditchfield, Simon, "Martyrs on the Move: Relics as Vindicators of Local Diversity in the Tridentine Church", in *Martyrs and Martyrologies, Studies in Church History, Vol. 30*, ed. by Diana Wood, Oxford, Blackwell, 1993, pp. 283-294.

Ditchfield, Simon, "Reading Rome as a Sacred Landscape, c. 1586-1635", in *Sacred Space in Early Modern Europe*, ed. by Will Coster and Andrew Spicer, Cambridge, Cambridge University Press, 2005, pp. 167-192.

Ditchfield, Simon, "Tridentine Worship and the Cult of Saints", in *Cambridge History of Christianity, Volume 6: Reform and Expansion 1500-1660*, ed. by R. Po-chia Hsia, Cambridge, Cambridge University Press, 2008, pp. 201-224.

Donnelly, John Patrick, "New Religious Orders for Men", in *Cambridge History of Christianity, Volume 6: Reform and Expansion 1500-1660*, ed. by R. Po-chia Hsia, Cambridge, Cambridge University Press, 2008, pp. 162-179.

Dospěl, Marek, "The Annotationes in Aegyptum (c. 1799): A Manuscript Penned by a Czech Franciscan Missionary", *Archivum Franciscanum Historicum,* 104 (2011), pp. 285-297.

Dřímal, Jaroslav, "K brněnskému pobytu a filiačním listům Jana Kapistrána", *Časopis Matice moravské*, 63, 4 (1940), pp. 374-391.

Early Modern Confraternities in Europe and the Americas: International and Interdisciplinary Perspectives, ed. by Christopher F. Black and Pamela Gravestock, Aldershot, Ashgate, 2005.

Eichler, Karel, *Poutní místa a milostivé obrazy va Moravě a v Rakouském Slezsku*, Brno, Nákladem Dědictví ss. Cyrilla a Methoděje, 1887, díl I.

Elbel, Martin, "Pilgrims on the Way of the Cross: Pilgrimage Practice and Confessional Identity in Early Modern Bohemian Lands", in *Frontiers of Faith: Religious Exchange and Constitution of Religious Identities (1400-1700)*, ed. by Eszter Andor and István György Tóth, Budapest, CEU Press, 2001, pp. 275-283.

Elbel, Martin, *Bohemia Franciscana: Františkánský řád a jeho působení v českých zemích 17. a 18. století*, Olomouc, Verbum, 2001.

Elbel, Martin, "Dva světy? Konfesijní hranice za švédské okupace Olomouce, 1642-1650", in *Konec švédské okupace a poválečná obnova ve 2. polovině 17. století: Sborník příspěvků ze sympózia (Historická Olomouc XIII)*, ed. by Martin Elbel and Milan Togner, Olomouc, Univerzita Palackého, 2002, pp. 99-105.

Elbel, Martin, "Budování poutního místa: Svaté schody při františkánském klášteře v Olomouci", *Folia Historica Bohemica*, 20 (2004), pp. 215-239.

Elbel, Martin, "The Making of a Perfect Friar: Habit and Reform in the Franciscan Tradition", in *Friars, Nobles and Burghers-Sermons, Images and Prints: Studies of Culture and Society in Early-Modern Europe*, ed. by Jaroslav Miller and Laszlo Kontler, Budapest, Central European University Press, 2010, pp. 149-175.

Elbel, Martin, "Consolidation, 1700-1750", in *The Transformation of Confessional Cultures in a Central European City: Olomouc, 1400-1750*, ed. by Antonín Kalous, Roma, Viella, 2015, pp. 141-163.

Elbel, Martin, "Early Modern Mendicancy: Franciscan Practice in the Bohemian Lands", *Journal of Ecclesiastical History*, 96, 1 (2018), pp. 39-56.

Encyklopedie českých klášterů, E. Pavel Vlček, Petr Sommer a Dušan Foltýn, Praha, Libri, 1997.

Encyklopedie moravských a slezských klášterů, Ed. Dušan Foltýn, Praha, Libri, 2005.

Englund, Peter, *Nepokojná léta: Historie třicetileté války*, Přel. Dagmar Hartlová a Luděk Mandaus, Praha, Lidové noviny, 2000.

Evans, R.J.W., *The Making of the Habsburg Monarchy 1550-1700: An Interpretation*, Oxford, Clarendon Press, 1979.

Forster, Marc R., "With and Without Confessionalization. Varieties of Early Modern German Catholicism", *Journal of Early Modern History*, 1, 4 (1997), pp. 315-343.

Forster, Marc R., *Catholic Revival in the Age of the Baroque: Religious Identity in Southwest Germany, 1550-1750*, Cambridge, Cambridge University Press, 2001.

Gaži, Martin and Jarmila Hansová, *Svatyně za hradbami měst: Křížová hora u Českého Krumlova v jihočeských a středoevropských souvislostech*, České Budějovice, Národní památkový ústav, 2012.

Geltner, Guy, "William of St. Amour`s *De Periculis Novissimorum Temporum*: A False Start to Medieval Antifraternalism?", in *Defenders and Critics of Franciscan Life: Essays in Honor of John V. Fleming*, ed. by Michael F. Cusato and Guy Geltner, Leiden, Brill, 2009, pp. 105-118.

Gentilcore, David, *From Bishop to Witch: The System of the Sacred in Early Modern Terra d'Otranto*, Manchester, Manchester University Press, 1992.

Heidarzadeh, Tofigh, *A History of Physical Theories of Comets, From Aristotle to Whipple*, Dordrecht, Springer Science & Business Media, 2008.

Historia Franciscana. Katalog výstavy pořádané k 400. výročí příchodu bratří františkánů do kláštera Panny Marie Sněžné v Praze (1604-2004), Praha, Provincie bratří františkánů, 2004.

Hlaváček, Petr, *Čeští františkáni na přelomu středověku a novověku*, Praha, Academia, 2005.

Hlaváček, Petr, *Die Böhmischen Franziskaner im ausgehenden Mittelalter: Studien zur Kirchen- und Kulturgeschichte Ostmitteleuropas*, Stuttgart, F. Steiner, 2011.

Hlobil, Ivo, "Bernardinské symboly jména Ježíš v českých zemích šířené Janem Kapistránem", *Umění*, 44 (1996), pp. 223-234.

Hlobil, Ivo, "K ikonologii, symbolice a významu růžencového obrazu v kostele Neposkvrněného početí Panny Marie v Olomouci-Bělidlech", *Sborník Památkové péče Severomoravského kraje*, 1 (1971), pp. 9-16.

Hofer, Giovanni, *Giovanni da Capestrano: Una vita spesa nella lotta per la riforma della Chiesa*, L`Aquila, Provincia dei Frati Minori d`Abruzzo, 1955.

Hojda, Zdeněk, "Collegia Nordica v Olomouci a Branievě 1578-1619", *Acta Universitatis Carolinae - Historia Universitatis Carolinae Pragensis*, 30, sv. 1 (1990), pp. 49-95.

Holzapfel, Heribert, *Handbuch der Geschichte des Franziskanerordens*, Freiburg im Breisgau, Herder, 1909.

Hsia, R Po-chia, *The World of Catholic Renewal, 1540-1770*, Cambridge, Cambridge University Press, 1998.

Hsia, R. Po-chia, *Social Discipline in the Reformation: Central Europe 1550-1750*, London and New York, Routledge, 1992.

Iriarte, Lazaro, *Franciscan History: The Three Orders of St. Francis of Assisi*, Chicago, Franciscan Herald Press, 1983.

Jakubec, Ondřej, "The Divided City, 1520s-1600", in *The Transformation of Confessional Cultures in a Central European City: Olomouc, 1400-1750*, ed. by Antonín Kalous, Roma, Viella, 2015, pp. 65-94.

Johnson, Trevor, "Blood, Tears, and Xavier-Water: Jesuit Missionaries and Popular Religion in the Eighteenth-Century Upper Palatinate", in *Popular Religion in Germany and Central Europe, 1400-1800*, ed. by Robert W. Scribner and Trevor Johnson, London, Macmillan, 1996, pp. 183-202.

Johnson, Trevor, *Magistrates, Madonnas and Miracles: The Counter Reformation in the Upper Palatinate*, Farnham, Ashgate, 2009.

Kalous, Antonín, "Between Hussitism and Reformation, 1450s-1520s", in *The Transformation of Confessional Cultures in a Central European City: Olomouc, 1400-1750*, ed. by Antonín Kalous, Roma, Viella, 2015, pp. 41-64.

Kalous, Antonín, "Declaratio Brevis Corone Immaculate Virginis: A Source for the Late Medieval Popular Piety", *Umění*, 55 (2007), pp. 40-44.

Kalous, Antonín, *Matyáš Korvín (1443-1490). Uherský a český král*, České Budějovice, Veduta, 2009.

Karasek, Alfred, and Josef Lenz, *Krippenkunst in Böhmen Und Mähren Vom Frühbarock Bis Zur Gegenwart*, Marburg, N.G. Elwert Verlag, 1974.

Kašpárková, Jarmila, "Gedächtnis und Observanz: Die Chronik des Bernard Sannig für das Znaimer Klarissenkloster", in *Ordenshistoriographie in Mitteleuropa: Gestaltung und Wandlung des institutionalen und persönlichen Gedächtnisses in der frühen Neuzeit: Referate der gleichnamigen Tagung in St. Pölten von 22. bis 23. September 2014*, St. Pölten, portaro.eu, 2015, pp. 138-166.

Kašpárková, Jarmila, *Kláštery klarisek a františkánských terciářek v českých zemích v raném novověku,* Disertace, UP Olomouc, 2014.

Kašpárková, Slavomíra a Tomáš Vítek, "Klášter bernardinů s kostelem Neposkvrněného početí P. Marie", in *Od gotiky k renesanci: Výtvarná kultura Moravy a Slezska 1400-1550, III. díl, Olomoucko. Katalog výstavy*, ed. by Ivo Hlobil and Marek Perůtka, Olomouc, Muzeum umění, 1999, 208-210.

Kirschbaum, Engelbert and Wolfgang Braunfels, *Lexikon der Christlichen Ikonographie*, Rome, Freiburg, Basel, Wien, Herder, 1994.

Kohout, Štěpán, "Pobyt Jana Kapistrana v Olomouci", *Ročenka Státního okresního archívu v Olomouci (1992)*, 1995, pp. 117-140.

Kötsche, Lieselotte, "Das Heilige Grab in Jerusalem und seine Nachfolge", in *Die Reise nach Jerusalem*, ed. by Hendrik Budde and Andreas Nachama, Berlin, Argon, 1996, pp. 64-75.

Koudela, Miroslav and Zdeněk Kašpar, *Švédové v Olomouci (1642-1650)*, Praha, Danal, 1993.

Krailsheimer, Alban John, *Rabelais and the Franciscans*, Oxford, Clarendon Press, 1963.

Kšír, Josef, "Stavební historie budov Moravské filharmonie v Olomouci", *Zprávy Krajského vlastivědnéhom Muzea v Olomouci,* 58 (1958), pp. 88-92.

Kupka, Vladimír, "Olomoucké fortifikace na plánech a ve skutečnosti", in *Olomoucké baroko: Proměny ambicí jednoho města (1. Úvodní svazek)*, ed. by Martin Elbel and Ondřej Jakubec, Olomouc, Muzeum umění Olomouc, 2010, pp. 293-300.

Lambert, Malcolm, *Franciscan Poverty: The Doctrine of the Absolute Poverty of Christ and the Apostles in the Franciscan Order, 1210-1323*, revised and expanded edition, St Bonaventure, NY, Franciscan Institute, St Bonaventure University, 1998.

Laqua-O'Donnell, Simone, "Catholic Piety and Community", in *The Ashgate Research Companion to the Counter-Reformation*, ed. by Alexandra Bamji, Geert H. Janssen, and Mary Laven, Farnham, Ashgate, 2013, pp. 281-297.

Layered Landscapes, ed. by Eric Nelson and Jonathan Wright, London, Routledge, 2017.

Lemmens, Leonhard, *Geschichte der Franziskanermissionen*, Münster, Verlag der Aschendorffschen Verlagsbuchhandlung, 1929.

Locus pietatis et vitae: Sborník příspěvků z konference konané v Hejnicích ve dnech 13.-15. září 2007, ed. by Ivana Čornejová, Hedvika Kuchařová, and Kateřina Valentová, Praha, Univerzita Karlova v Praze, Scriptorium, 2008.

Louthan, Howard, "Breaking Images and Building Bridges: The Making of Sacred Space in Early Modern Bohemia", in *Sacred Space in Early Modern Europe*, ed. by Will Coster and Andrew Spicer, Cambridge, Cambridge University Press, 2005, pp. 282-301.

Louthan, Howard, *Converting Bohemia: Force and Persuasion in the Catholic Reformation*, Cambridge, Cambridge University Press, 2009.

MacCulloch, Diarmaid, *Reformation: Europe's House Divided, 1490-1700*, London, Penguin, 2004.

Mäkinen, Virp, *Property Rights in the Late Medieval Discussion on Franciscan Poverty*, Leuven, Peeters, 2001.

Malý, Tomáš, *Smrt a spása mezi Tridentinem a sekularizací: Brněnští měšťané a proměny laické zbožnosti v 17. a 18. století*, Brno, Matice moravská, 2009.

Maňas, Vladimír, Tomáš Malý, and Zdeněk Orlita, *Vnitřní krajina zmizelého města: Náboženská bratrstva barokního Brna*, Brno, Statutární město Brno a Archív města Brna, 2010.

Maňas, Vladimír, "Náboženská bratrstva na Moravě do josefínských reforem." In *Bratrstva. Světská a církevní sdružení a jejich role v kulturních a společenských strukturách od středověku do moderní doby (III. Pardubické bienále, 29.-30. dubna 2004)*, ed. by Tomáš Jiránek and Jiří Kubeš, Pardubic, Univerzita Pardubice, 2005, pp. 37-78.

Mecham, June L., "A Northern Jerusalem: The Transformation of Space at the Convent of Wienhausen", in *Defining the Holy: Sacred Space in Medieval and Early Modern Europe*, ed. by Sarah Hamilton and Andrew Spicer, Aldershot, Ashgate, 2005, pp. 139-160.

Mikulec, Jiří, *Barokní náboženská bratrstva v Čechách*, Praha, Nakladatelství Lidové noviny, 2000.

Mikulec, Jiří, "Náboženská bratrstva a třetí řády při františkánských klášterech v barokních Čechách", in *Historia Franciscana II.: Sborník textů: Kapitoly z dějin České františkánské provincie Sv. Václava u příležitosti 300. výročí úmrtí provinčního ministra a významného učence Bernarda Sanniga (1704) a 400. výročí příchodu františkánů k Panně Marii Sněžné v Praze (1604)*, ed. by Petr Regalát Beneš and Petr Hlaváček, Kostelní Vydří, Karmelitánské nakladatelství, 2005, pp. 188-203.

Mikulec, Jiří, "Proměny náboženských bratrstev v Čechách v raném novověku", in *Bratrstva. Světská a církevní sdružení a jejich role v kulturních a společenských strukturách od středověku do moderní doby (III. Pardubické bienále, 29.–30. dubna 2004)*, ed. by Tomáš Jiránek and Jiří Kubeš, Pardubic, Univerzita Pardubice, 2005, pp.19-35.

Mikulec, Jiří, "Poznámky ke vnímání řeholního života mezi barokem a osvícenstvím", *Theatrum historiae*, 3 (2008), pp. 275-287.

Mikulec, Jiří, "Klášter a barokní společnost: K vlivu řeholního prostředí na spiritualitu laiků", in *Locus pietatis et vitae: Sborník příspěvků z konference konané v Hejnicích ve dnech 13.-15. září 2007*, ed. by Ivana Čornejová, Hedvika Kuchařová, and Kateřina Valentová, Praha, Univerzita Karlova v Praze, Scriptorium, 2008, pp. 281-300.

Mikulec, Jiří et al., *Církev a společnost raného novověku v Čechách a na Moravě*, Praha, Historický ústav, 2013.

Mikulec, Jiří, *Náboženský život a barokní zbožnost v českých zemích*, Praha, Grada Publishing, 2013.

Miller, Jaroslav, *Uzavřená společnost a její nepřátelé: Město střednovýchodní Evropy (1500-1700)*, Praha, Nakladatelství Lidové noviny, 2006.

Miller, Jaroslav, "Zchudlé město bohatých měšťanů?", in *Olomoucké baroko: Proměny ambicí jednoho města (1. Úvodní svazek)*, ed. by Martin Elbel and Ondřej Jakubec, Olomouc, Muzeum umění Olomouc, 2010, pp. 71-77.

Minařík, Klemens and Bonaventura Wilhelm, *Dějiny klášterů františkánských v Čechách a na Moravě*, Třebíč, Františkánská provincie česko-moravská, 1909.

Minařík, Klemens, "Provinciál P. Bernard Sannig, učenec, spisovatel a organisátor františkánské provincie (1637-1704)", *Časopis katolického duchovenstva*, 61 (1920), passim.

Minařík, Klemens, "Provinciálové františkánské české provincie v letech 1517-1600", *Sborník Historického kroužku*, 17 (1916), passim.

Minařík, Klemens, "Provinciálové františkánské české provincie v letech 1600-1750", *Sborník Historického kroužku*, 18 (1917), passim.

Minařík, Klemens "Vikáři české františkánské provincie od r. 1451 do r. 1517", *Sborník Historického kroužku*, 16 (1915), passim.

Minty, J. M., "Judengasse to Christian Quarter: The Phenomenon of the Converted Synagogue in the Late Medieval and Early Modern Holy Roman Empire", in *Popular Religion in Germany and Central Europe, 1400-1800*, ed. by Robert W. Scribner and Trevor Johnson, London, Macmillan, 1996, pp. 58-86.

Mlčák, Leoš "K ikonografii, autorství a restaurování malířské a sochařské výzdoby kaple sv. Antonína Paduánského v Olomouci", *Vlastivědný věstník moravský*, 44 (1992), pp. 58-64.

Morris, Colin, *The Sepulchre of Christ and the Medieval West: From the Beginning to 1600*, Oxford, Oxford University Press, 2005.

Muir, Edward, *Ritual in Early Modern Europe*, Cambridge, Cambridge University Press, 1997.

Nešpor, Václav, "Svaté schody v Olomouci", *Časopis Vlastivědné společnosti musejní v Olomouci*, 37 (1926), pp. 101-103.

Nešpor, Václav, *Dějiny Olomouce*, Olomouc, Votobia, 1998.

Nešpor, Zdeněk R., *Náboženství na prahu nové doby: Česká lidová zbožnost 18. a 19. století*, Ústí nad Labem, Albis International, 2006.

Nimmo, Duncan, *Reform and Division in the Medieval Franciscan Order: From Saint Francis to the Foundations of the Capuchins*, Rome, Capuchin Historical Institute, 1987.

O`Malley, John W., *The First Jesuits*, Cambridge, Massachusetts, Harvard University Press, 1993.

od Ježíše, Terezie, *Cesta k dokonalosti*, Přel. Josef Koláček. Kostelní Vydří, Karmelitánské nakladatelství, 1991.

Oppeltová, Jana, "Premonstrátská kanonie Hradisko u Olomouce a její kulturní prostředí", in *Olomoucké baroko: Výtvarná kultura let 1620-1780 (3. Historie a kultura)*, ed. by Ondřej Jakubec and Marek Perůtka, Olomouc, Muzeum umění Olomouc, 2010, pp. 53-65.

Orlita, Zdeněk, "Pohřební průvod mezi pietou a reprezentací", in *Církev a smrt. Institucionalizace smrti v raném novověku*, ed. by Martin Holý and Jiří Mikulec, Praha, Historický ústav, 2007, pp. 187-208.

Parma, Tomáš, "The Stormy Path to a Single Religion, 1600-1650", in *The Transformation of Confessional Cultures in a Central European City: Olomouc, 1400-1750*, ed. by Antonín Kalous, Roma, Viella, 2015, pp. 95-120.

Pařez, Jan a Hedvika Kuchařová, *Hyberni v Praze: Éireannaigh I bPrág: Dějiny Františkánské Koleje Neposkvrněného Početí Panny Marie v Praze (1629-1786)*, Praha, Oswald, 2001.

Peterson, Ingrid, "The Third Order", in *The Cambridge Companion to Francis of Assisi*, ed. by Michael J.P. Robson, Cambridge, Cambridge University Press, 2012, pp. 193-207.

Pollmann, Judith, "Being a Catholic in Early Modern Europe", in *The Ashgate Research Companion to the Counter-Reformation*, ed. by Alexandra Bamji, Geert H. Janssen, and Mary Laven, Farnham, Ashgate, 2013, pp. 165-182.

Pollmann, Judith, "How to Flatter the Laity? Rethinking Catholic Responses to the Reformation", *BMGN - Low Countries Historical Review*, 126, 4 (January 2011), pp. 97-106.

Pollmann, Judith, *Memory in Early Modern Europe, 1500-1800*, Oxford, Oxford University Press, 2017.

Prchal Pavlíčková, Radmila, "The Evolution of Catholic Identity, 1650-1700", in *The Transformation of Confessional Cultures in a Central European City: Olomouc, 1400-1750*, ed. by Antonín Kalous, Roma, Viella, 2015, pp. 121-139.

Prchal, Vítězslav, "Války s Pruskem a přeměna Olomouce v pevnost", in *Olomoucké baroko: Proměny ambicí jednoho města (1. Úvodní svazek)*, ed. by Martin Elbel and Ondřej Jakubec, Olomouc, Muzeum umění Olomouc, 2010, pp. 285-292.

Procházka, Matěj, *Žiwot Bl. Jana Sarkandra mučeníka*, W Brně, Dědictwí sw. Cyrilla a Methodia, 1861.

Prosperi Valenti Rodinò, Simonetta, "La diffusione dell'iconografia francescana attraverso l'incisione", in *L'immagine di San Francesco nella Controriforma: Roma calcografia, 9 Dicembre 1982-13 Febbraio 1983*, ed. by Claudio M. Strinati e Simonetta Prosperi Valenti Rodinò, Roma, Quasar, 1982, pp. 163-164.

Prucek, Josef, "K renovaci barokní, tzv. růžencové kaple v kostele Neposkvrněného početí Panny Marie v Olomouci", *Zprávy Vlastivědného muzea v Olomouci* 28: 266 (1991), pp. 29-34.

Prucek, Josef, "Olomoucká souhrnná kronika z let 1432-1656 sestavená B. Dudíkem", *Ročenka Okresního archívu v Olomouci*, 1980-1983, passim.

Reeves, Marjorie, *The Influence of Prophecy in the Later Middle Ages: A Study in Joachimism*, Oxford, Clarendon Press, 1969.

Religion and Cultural Exchange in Europe, 1400-1700, ed. by Heinz Schilling and István György Tóth, Cambridge, Cambridge University Press, 2006.

Roest, Bert, "Observant Reform in Religious Orders", in *Cambridge History of Christianity, Volume 4: Christianity in Western Europe c. 1100-c. 1500*, ed. by Miri Rubin and Walter Simons, Cambridge, Cambridge University Press, 2011, pp. 446-457.

Ron, Vojtěch, *Lidové pašijové divadlo v českých zemích*, Praha, Vyšehrad, 2009.

Rosa, Mario, "The Catholic Clergy in Europe", in *Cambridge History of Christianity, Volume 7: Enlightenment, Reawakening and Revolution, 1660-1815*, ed. by Stewart J. Brown and Timothy Tackett, Cambridge, Cambridge University Press, 2006, pp. 89-108.

Řepa, Tomáš, *Kaple Božího hrobu v Čechách a na Moravě v období baroka*, Diplomová práce, UP Olomouc, 2010.

Scribner, Robert W., *For the Sake of Simple Folk: Popular Propaganda for the German Reformation*, Oxford, Oxford University Press, 1994.

Scribner, Robert W., *Popular Culture and Popular Movements in Reformation Germany*, London, The Hambledon Press, 1987.

Schilling, Heinz, "Urban Architecture and Ritual in Confessional Europe", in *Religion and Cultural Exchange in Europe, 1400-1700*, ed. by Heinz Schilling and István György Tóth, Cambridge, Cambridge University Press, 2006, pp. 116-137.

Signorotto, Gianvittorio, "Lo spazio delle devozioni nell`età della Controriforma", in *Luoghi sacri e spazi della santità*, ed. by Sofia Boesch Gajano and Lucetta Scaraffia, Torino, Rosenberg & Sellier, 1990, pp. 315-326

Sluhovsky, Moshe, *Believe Not Every Spirit: Possession, Mysticism, & Discernment in Early Modern Catholicism*, Chicago, University of Chicago Press, 2007.

Soukup, Daniel, "Co medle jiného od chudého františkána k očekávání? Postila *Trojí chléb nebeský* františkána Damascena Marka", in *Františkánský kontext teologického a filozofického myšlení*, ed. by Petr Hlaváček, Praha, Univerzita Karlova, 2012, pp. 146-178.

Spurný, František, Vojtěch Cekota, and Miloš Kouřil, *Šumperský farář a děkan Kryštof Alois Lautner, oběť čarodějnických inkvizičních procesů*, Šumperk, Městský úřad Šumperk, 2000.

Stejskal, Jan, "A Catholic City in the Hussite Era, 1400-1450s", in *The Transformation of Confessional Cultures in a Central European City: Olomouc, 1400-1750*, ed. by Antonín Kalous, Roma, Viella, 2015, pp. 23-39.

Stewart, Robert M., *"De Illis Qui Faciunt Penitentiam": The Rule of the Secular Franciscan Order; Origins, Development, Interpretation*, Roma, Istituto Storico dei Capuccini, 1991.

Svátek, Josef, "Organizace řeholních institucí v českých zemích a péče o jejich archívy", *Sborník archivních prací*, 20 (1970), pp. 505-624.

Szittya, Penn R., *The Antifraternal Tradition in Medieval Literature*, Princeton, Princeton University Press, 1986.

Šmahel, František, "*Spectaculum Fidei* českomoravské mise Jana Kapistrána", *Z Kralické tvrze*, 14 (1987), pp. 15-19.

The Ashgate Research Companion to the Counter-Reformation, ed. by Alexandra Bamji, Geert H. Janssen, and Mary Laven, Farnham, Ashgate, 2013.

The Origin, Development, and Refinement of Medieval Religious Mendicancies, ed. by Donald Prudlo, Leiden, Brill, 2011.

Togner, Milan and František Sysel, "Restaurátorský a uměleckohistorický průzkum interiérových stěn kostela Neposkvrněného početí P. Marie v Olomouci", *Ročenka Okresního archívu v Olomouci*, 1984, pp. 78-83.

Úloha církevních řádů při pobělohorské rekatolizaci: Sborník příspěvků z pracovního semináře konaného ve Vranově u Brna ve dnech 4.-5. 6. 2003, ed. by Ivana Čornejová, Praha, Univerzita Karlova, 2003.

Vaclík, Vladimír, *Chrámové betlémy v Čechách a na Moravě*, Praha, Vyšehrad, 1990.

Vašica, Josef, *České literární baroko: Příspěvky k jeho studiu*, Praha, Atlantis, 1995.
Vauchez, André, *Francis of Assisi: The Life and Afterlife of a Medieval Saint*, trans. by Michael F. Cusato, New Haven, Yale University Press, 2012.
Viallet, Ludovic, *Les sens de l'observance: Enquete sur les reformes franciscaines entre l'Elbe et l'Oder, de Capistran a Luther (vers 1450–vers 1520)*, Berlin, LIT Verlag, 2014.
Vlnas, Vít, *Jan Nepomucký. Česká Legenda*, Praha, Mladá fronta, 1993.
von Thiessen, Hillard, *Die Kapuziner zwischen Konfessionalisierung und Alltagskultur: Vergleichende Fallstudie am Beispiel Freiburgs und Hildesheims 1599-1750*, Freiburg im Breisgau, Rombach, 2002.
Vybíral, Bohuš, "Ještě jednou o olomouckých Svatých schodech", *Časopis Vlastivědné společnosti musejní v Olomouci*, 39 (1927), pp. 109-117.

Wandel, Lee Palmer, "The Poverty of Christ", in *The Reformation of Charity: The Secular and the Religious in Early Modern Poor Relief*, ed. by Thomas Max Saffley, London and Boston, Brill, 2003, pp. 15-25.
Winter, Eduard, *Josefinismus a jeho dějiny*, Praha, Jelínek, 1945.
Wodziński, Marcin, "Středověké židovské náhrobky na Moravě", in *Židé a Morava: Sborník příspěvků přednesených na konferenci konané 10. listopadu 1999 v Muzeu Kroměřížska*, Kroměříž, Muzeum Koroměřížska, 1999, pp. 8-17.
Wondrák, Eduard, "Otazníky kolem 'záhadných' rýh na některých olomouckých stavbách", in *Okresní archiv v Olomouci. Zpráva o činnosti Okresního archívu v Olomouci za rok 1979*, Olomouc, 1980, pp. 62-69.

Zbožných duší úl: Náboženská bratrstva v kultuře raněnovověké Moravy [Muzeum Umění Olomouc - Arcidiecézní Muzeum Olomouc: Galerie, 29. Ledna - 25. Dubna 2010: Katalog], ed. by Vladimír Maňas, Zdeněk Orlita, and Martina Potůčková, Olomouc, Muzeum umění Olomouc, 2010.
Zdichynec, Jan, "Monasteriologie a klášterní problematika v raném novověku", in *Základní problémy studia raného novověku*, ed. by Marie Šedivá Koldinská and Ivo Cerman, Praha, Lidové noviny, 2013, pp. 230-267.
da Zedelgem, Amédée (Teetaert), *Saggio storico sulla devozione alla Via Crucis*, trans. by Paolo Pellizzari, Ponzano Monferrato, Centro di Documentazione dei Sacri Monti, Calvari e Complessi devozionali europei, 2003.
Zemek, Petr, *Reformace, protireformace a rozvinutí poreformačního katolictví v Uherském Brodě - Křesťanská víra v proměnách času*, Uherský Brod, Muzeum J.A. Komenského v Uherském Brodě v nakl. Albert, 2006.
Zuber, Rudolf, "Poslední exkomunikace laiků v olomoucké diecézi". *Ročenka Státního okresního archívu v Olomouci (1992)*, 20 (1993), pp. 162-169.
Zuber, Rudolf, *Osudy moravské církve v 18. století.* Olomouc, Matice cyrilometodějská, 2003.

Index of names and places

Finito di stampare
nel mese di ottobre 2019
da The Factory srl
Roma